THE KILLER TRAIL

THE KILLER TRAIL

A COLONIAL SCANDAL IN THE HEART OF AFRICA

BERTRAND TAITHE

OXFORD
UNIVERSITY PRESS

OXFORD
UNIVERSITY PRESS

Great Clarendon Street, Oxford OX2 6DP

Oxford University Press is a department of the University of Oxford.
It furthers the University's objective of excellence in research, scholarship,
and education by publishing worldwide in

Oxford New York

Auckland Cape Town Dar es Salaam Hong Kong Karachi
Kuala Lumpur Madrid Melbourne Mexico City Nairobi
New Delhi Shanghai Taipei Toronto

With offices in

Argentina Austria Brazil Chile Czech Republic France Greece
Guatemala Hungary Italy Japan Poland Portugal Singapore
South Korea Switzerland Thailand Turkey Ukraine Vietnam

Published in the United States
by Oxford University Press Inc., New York

First published 2009

British Library Cataloguing in Publication Data
Data available

Library of Congress Cataloging in Publication Data

Data available

Typeset by SPI Publisher Services, Pondicherry, India
Printed in Great Britain
on acid-free paper by
Clays Ltd., St Ives Plc

ISBN 978–0–19–923121–8

1 3 5 7 9 10 8 6 4 2

ACKNOWLEDGEMENTS

A project such as this one takes considerable time and resources. Unusually perhaps this is a book that owes much to its publisher since it is unlikely that I would have followed this particular trail without the encouragement of my editors at Oxford University Press, Luciana O'Flaherty and Matthew Cotton. The resources for the research itself were predominantly funded by the British Academy over two separate grants over the past four years which have enabled me to conduct the necessary research in Europe and Africa. L'École des Hautes Études en Sciences Sociales (EHESS) in Paris and Amiens University also hosted me in France while I was conducting research. I am grateful for their stimulating hospitality, in particular my colleagues and friends Patrice Bourdelais and François and Sophie Delaporte.

In the archives I was immensely helped by the great archivists in post. In particular I thank Papa Mumar Diop and Atoumane M'Baye in the national archives of Senegal and AOF; Father Ivan Page at the Archives des Missionnaires d'Afrique in Rome; and the staff at the Bibliothèque Nationale de France, the John Rylands University Library, and the Bibliothèque Africaniste of the EHESS. Among my colleagues I am blessed with a considerable network of supporting and innovative scholars with whom I could discuss ideas and get precious tips. To name but a few I thank Jean-Marc Dreyfus, Peter Gatrell, Max Jones, Ana Carden-Coyne, and Steven Pierce. Steven in particular gave me many precious leads from his Africanist perspective. In France the Guerre et Médecine association helped me think through some of the important issues relating to this book, as did the Conficts Study workshops hosted by the University of Manchester. I have been influenced by the work of colleagues, in particular that of Stéphane Audoin-Rouzeau. I am also grateful to Rony Brauman, Jean-Marc Dreyfus, and Jacques Sémelin for their very different yet equally enriching views on the central subject of this book.

Finally as befits any book undertaken over a number of years it is to family that thanks and apologies are most overdue. Vicky, Louis, and Emily have had to contend with an absentee partner and father and not only when I was physically away. They bear this burden with a great deal of fortitude and I dedicate this book to all three of them.

CONTENTS

LIST OF ILLUSTRATIONS

NOTE

This story takes place in a land which was once called Soudan. The Arabs of North Africa and in particular the Moroccans who regularly interacted with the kingdoms and traders of this region called it Beled es-Sudan, the land of the blacks. Later observers, travellers, conquerors, and colonial authorities continued to refer to it as Sudan, Soudan in French. To distinguish western Sudan from eastern Sudan, I have chosen to call the French colony Soudan and the conquest of the Anglo-Egyptians, Sudan, since it still bears the name. The region itself belongs to the Sahel from a geographical point of view and most of the action of this book took place in this arid, immediate vicinity of the Sahara, which has two seasons, rainy (wintering) and dry. The countries that constituted Soudan are amongst the poorest in the world today; they are also amongst the hottest.

The spelling of African names will follow current conventions in force in the states of Senegal, Mali, Burkina Faso, and Niger or, for institutions or places that no longer exist, those used by the colonizers. It is the language of the archives even if it is often quite distant from the correct native pronunciation. The Arabic terms occasionally used follow accepted Oxford University Press rules.

PREFACE

What follows is a book devoted to a singular story which took place in Africa in 1898–9. As a public scandal of the West it made headlines in the summer of 1899 in a period rich in scandals. What makes scandals good material for historians is not so much their lurid wealth of gory details than what they reveal, which is usually ignored, glossed over, or hidden. Yet rather than any truth, what they reveal tends to be complex and difficult to decipher and says more about how the media, the state, and the public perceive reality.

Yet some scandals recur so frequently that they cannot be dismissed as the product of changing whims and erratic public taste. The scandal of violence abroad at the heart of the imperial dream of the late nineteenth century was troubling because it revealed the flaws of common assumptions about civilization and morality. The Voulet–Chanoine scandal is a story still running its course today. It has obvious echoes in the fiction of Joseph Conrad, in particular his novella, the *Heart of Darkness*, but the moral issues it raised are resonant with contemporary drama borne out of the banality of evil. The eight chapters of this book seek to uncover how a scandal comes into being and how the acts it reveals took place. The first chapter tells the story of the two officers who led a small army, a mission, towards Lake Chad and the crimes they committed. The following chapters seek to place this anecdote into a wider context. Chapters 2 and 3 reflect on what the mission tells us about European understanding of colonial encounters in Africa. Chapters 4 and 5 examine the nature of colonial warfare in an era when humanitarian campaigners portrayed the conquest of Africa as the last crusade against slavery, as the furthering of their ideals and the exporting of a liberal civilization.

Chapter 6 relates this scandal to a larger one which convulsed France at the time and aroused passions worldwide: the Dreyfus affair. Both Voulet and Chanoine had direct connections with the Parisian elites and their fate in Africa was directly linked to that of a Jewish captain wrongly accused of betraying France. Their story was the story of an army left to its own devices and which had lost its moral bearings in France and in the colonies. The final chapters, 7 and 8, seek to understand both the fuller meanings of the Voulet–Chanoine episode and map out the traces that this bloody conquest has left. In the final section of the final chapter, this book asks what can be learnt, if anything, from such traumatic stories.

I

DYING FOR FRENCH SOUDAN[1]

In the end, their tracks became clearer. Burnt villages signalled the progress of their journey. Occasionally, hanging bodies marked the entrances of villages while corpses littered the places they had visited. In the first few settlements beyond the uncertain borders of French Soudan the corpses had been arranged in shallow mass graves, a long dark blood stain hinting how the bodies had been dragged to their burial ground. Later on the corpses lay where they fell. To Colonel Klobb and his small squad of native troops of the French in West Africa, the so-called tirailleurs, it became obvious that the men they were looking for had lost their ways in every conceivable manner.

On 25 April 1899, Arsène Klobb had been sent after a much larger military 'mission' or 'colonne' led by two men: Captains Voulet and Chanoine, whose fates were so entwined that they have become almost a twin entity sharing a common tragedy: Voulet–Chanoine.[2] These men were the kind of colonial figures known for their daring and initiative, the nationalists lionized. Indeed only a few years earlier they had been welcomed back in Paris as heroes. From heroes these men became villains, worse still, a national embarrassment. There had been early signs that the mission they led would encounter 'difficulties'.

When Klobb had received Voulet in Timbuktu, in November 1898 he had confided to his diaries: 'Voulet is coming to me tomorrow. I am anxious, it seems to me that he is venturing into something he does not know. A conversation with him should tell me if that is the case.'[3] While driving his small group hard on Voulet's track, Klobb noted in increasingly telegraphic style the evidence of destruction he encountered. On 5 July he wrote:

I am starting to be exhausted—I am still running. I am on the 5th longitude East and I still have not reached anything. It's true that the expedition is a year ahead of me. I am in a village where I eat what has not been torched. Voulet burns everything—exactly. I do not encounter many difficulties: the inhabitants are terrorised by Voulet's passing through, they run away when they see me coming; when they see the tirailleurs the bows and arrows fall from their hands.[4]

On the 6th of the same month, on reaching Tibiri, 'huge village with many gaps; entirely burnt. The dry moat is 4.5 metres deep to the tip of the wall. Women hanged.'

Klobb had received orders from the governor of the military colony of French Soudan, Colonel de Trentinian, who led from the city of Kayes a huge and ill-controlled territory which would cover most of today's Burkina Faso, Mali, and (as Voulet's advance furthered its borders to the east) the south of Niger. De Trentinian was acting on orders received through two telegrams sent from Paris. The first stated that a mission should be sent to catch up with the army of Captains Voulet and Chanoine to investigate the news leaked in the daily newspaper *Le Matin*. The second, sent three days later, ordered that both Voulet and Chanoine should be arrested and held accountable for their crimes:

Recent massacre Sansané Haoussa, 15 women and children—execution tirailleur—number of exhausted porters refusing march would have been beheaded then six massacres to obtain new porters—Tirailleurs alleged to have to bring hands to captains to show orders were executed—Captain Chanoine alleged to have put on sticks heads of inhabitants found in villages which would have been burnt twelve kilometres around—I hope the allegations are unfounded—if against all probability these abominable crimes are proven Voulet and Chanoine cannot continue to lead mission without a great shame for France . . . send from Say superior and subaltern officers join mission.[5]

The minister of colonies' telegram contained a summary of the allegations published in the Parisian press. These were leaked from the correspondence of a Lieutenant Péteau, dismissed a few weeks earlier by Voulet.

Some of the accusations seemed so extreme that officers on the ground such as Klobb were originally unconvinced. It is only gradually, the official version reveals, that he came to accept that something might be grievously wrong. According to his second in command, Lt. Octave Meynier, Arsène Klobb was convinced, when, upon entering Birnin Konni, he saw little girls hanging from the low branches of the trees and over a thousand corpses rotting in the sun.[6] For Klobb the decision to arrest Voulet seemed justified and in a letter to the rear, he noted, 'I confess I find it hard to believe that French officers could have ordered such horror. I will do what I can to prevent a scandal but I will send Voulet and Chanoine back if I can.'[7] The mission had to continue but it had to change. Something had gone wrong east of the colonial border of French Soudan.

A year earlier things seemed so promising in Paris. When in January 1898 Captain Voulet, a young officer recently promoted for his heroic deeds, presented to the ministry of colonies the ambitious plan of an expedition, he carried with him considerable hopes and reputation. The project was even supported in the highest sphere of state. A few months earlier the colourful President Félix Faure had welcomed Voulet warmly in the Élysée Palace. Faure was the last dominant figure to occupy the seat of French president until de Gaulle in 1958,[8] and had proven to be a man of political renewal of French prestige. The most notable success under his presidency had been the Russian alliance which ended nearly thirty years of military and diplomatic isolation. His other aim, encouraged by vigorous foreign policy ministers, was to increase the importance of the French colonial empire. Despite the notorious instability of French governments during the *fin-de-siècle* period, some political figures nevertheless managed to steer the country in an aggressively expansionist direction. The empire the republic created was then predominantly a matter of prestige and alleged renewal for a divided nation still undermined by the catastrophic defeat in the 1870 war and twenty-eight years of bitter political conflicts. In the 1890s religious questions and political and financial scandals divided the French deeply.

The French military were not sheltered from scandal: the trial of an alleged traitor, Captain Dreyfus, had combined all the issues that split French politics: honour, race, religion, and human rights. Dreyfus was Jewish and the victim of a blatant conspiracy to make him a scapegoat for acts of treason taking place at the heart of the French high command. While his case divided France, some politicians and a very proactive 'colonial lobby' sought political diversion, new wealth and 'grandeur' in acquiring immense territories in Africa.[9]

In 1898, Voulet had only been back a few months from his previous mission in Western Africa. As was customary for expatriate officers returning from the strain of life in the tropics, he was about to be sent to a provincial post in Toulon in the south of France to recover from the African climate. While many looked forward to a well-deserved rest, Voulet had other plans. Taking leave from his obscure post, he networked his way into the pro-colonialist lobby and in particular found support in the 'French Africa Committee', which was actively raising funds for the conquest of African territories as yet unclaimed by the great powers. There he found out other missions were in the making and, from disparate corners of French society, different lobbies proposed converging adventures which might become a grand plan for the colonization of the heart of sub-Saharan (Sahel) Africa. On paper the aims of the new Voulet mission were fairly simple: he would progress from the heartland of French colonies in West Africa, Senegal, towards the territories of an African slave-trading kingdom near Lake Chad. The project was accepted as part of three converging missions sent by the French in 1898. The three missions started from the corners of their African empire: Algeria in the North, Dakar in the West, and Congo in the South.[10] On paper it might even be conceivable that from across the continent, another mission starting from Djibouti near Somalia joining with a central African one led by Commandant Marchand would establish French domination south of Egyptian Sudan. Ultimately through what is now modern Chad and Darfur, the most adventurous French colonialists hoped to establish a continuous landmass uniting Western and Eastern Sudan.

If the paper dream turned into reality the empire would cross the whole of Africa with a strip of French colonies thwarting both British and German ambitions. This grand plan was a closely kept secret and was a best case scenario. The fallback was to constitute a landmass uniting central and West African colonies through what is now Chad (Map 1).

The avowed aim of the Voulet mission was more modest than the secret plan. Voulet was to ensure the effective conquest

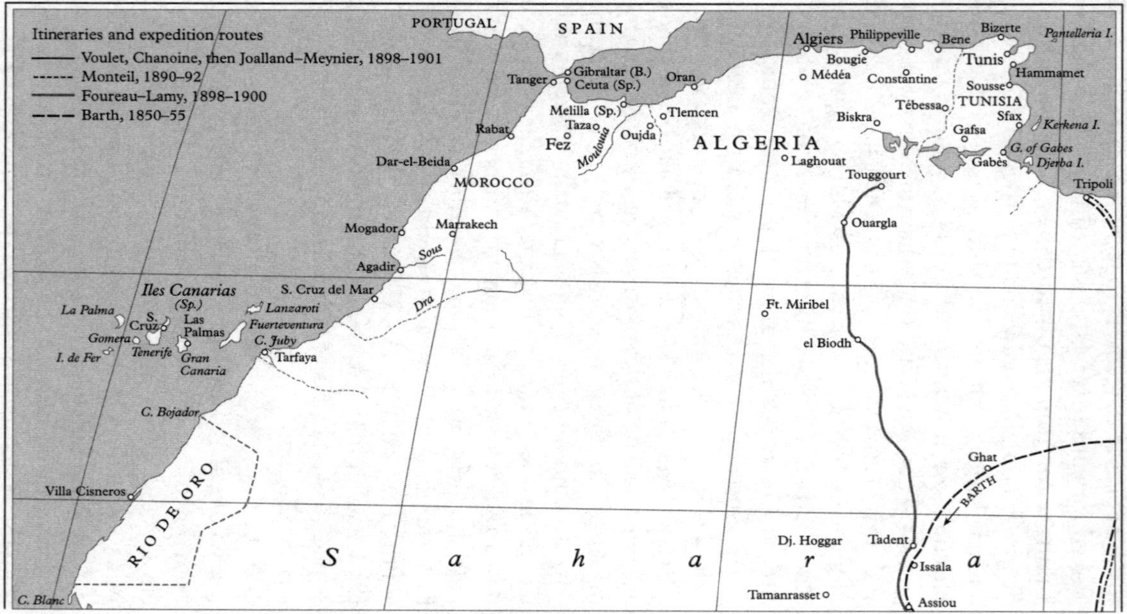

Itineraries and expedition routes
Voulet, Chanoine, then Joalland–Meynier, 1898–1901
Monteil, 1890–92
Foureau–Lamy, 1898–1900
Barth, 1850–55
PORTUGAL
SPAIN
MOROCCO
ALGERIA
TUNISIA
RIO DE ORO
S a h a r a
Algiers
Philippeville
Bene
Bizerte
Pantelleria I.
Bougie
Médéa
Constantine
Tunis
Hammamet
Sousse
Tébessa
Biskra
Gafsa
Sfax
Kerkena I.
G. of Gabes
Gabès
Djerba I.
Tripoli
Laghouat
Touggourt
Ouargla
Ft. Miribel
el Biodh
Ghat
BARTH
Tadent
Issala
Assiou
Dj. Hoggar
Tamanrasset
Tanger
Gibraltar (B.)
Ceuta (Sp.)
Oran
Melilla (Sp.)
Tlemcen
Taza
Fez
Oujda
Moulouia
Rabat
Dar-el-Beida
Mogador
Marrakech
Sous
Agadir
S. Cruz del Mar
Dra
Iles Canarias
(Sp.)
La Palma
S. Cruz
Las Palmas
Lanzaroti
Fuerteventura
Gomera
Tenerife
Gran Canaria
I. de Fer
C. Juby
Tarfaya
C. Bojador
Villa Cisneros
C. Blanc

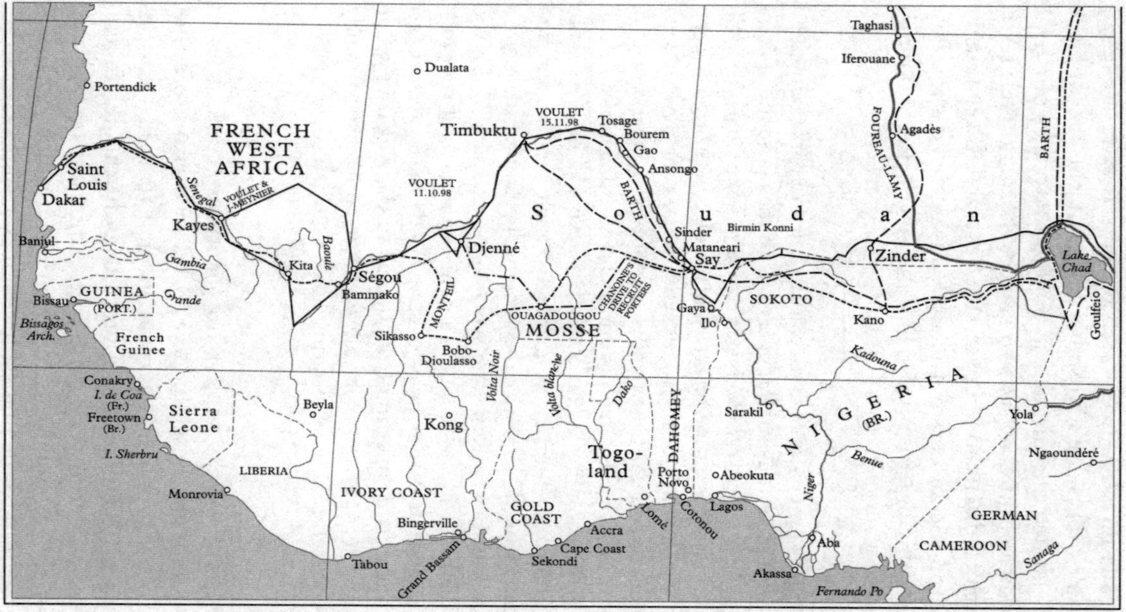

Map 1. The Voulet mission itinerary

of territories France had negotiated for herself after an agreement with Britain signed in June 1898. In this accord the British had claimed the sultanate of Sokoto (in today's northern Nigeria) and the boundary was to respect the sultanate's territory. After much discussion between the Foreign Office minister Hanotaux and his successor Delcassé, his secret instructions stated clearly this pragmatic aim but also developed its hidden agenda:

> The first part of your task is to appreciate in situ and make it intelligible to the government the exact implications of the conventions of 14 June 1898 on the line between the Niger river and Lake Chad. You will have to collect full information on the local people, on their groups, on their mutual dependency or their independence, on the development of these lands, their wealth or relative importance... you will have to respect everywhere the religious and political influences you will find avoiding thus any imprudent conflicts... you will be careful not to trespass on British territory by keeping yourself north of the new frontier. Finally you will deal with the various chieftains of the regions apportioned to us by the 14th June everywhere necessary. When you have reached lake Chad... you will begin the second half of your mission... the arrangement of 14 June does not specify the Eastern border of our sovereignty, this question being linked to the Anglo-Egyptian sphere of influence over the Nile valley cannot be defined currently. You will reconnoitre the neighbouring lands of Chad, Baghirmi..., Kanem and Ouadai.[11]

Voulet then received the support of the minister and a secret cipher unique to the mission. Beyond his own rising prestige, Voulet had other support. His friend and acolyte in his previous mission, Julien Chanoine, was a precious political ally. Julien's father, Jules, was then very close to the minister of war, and through him the mission benefited from extraordinary channels of communication to the highest levels of government.

In a letter of 6 August 1898, the son could thus request that his father should see the minister of colonies, Georges Trouillot, to complain about the governor of West Africa, Chaudié, and various colleagues in Soudan.[12]

The mission had thus begun under remarkable auspices for its success. Rarely were such young officers so finely attuned to Parisian politics. The orders Voulet had received appear, at first glance, quite directive; yet previous African experience and the scale of the operations implied that they would allow considerable freedom. Moreover, in the feverish climate of the conquest of Africa, officers received implicit encouragements to disobey the letter of their orders provided they succeeded in bringing more land under control.[13] The orders were only restrictive in order to protect the minister and there was no more than a nod and a wink towards legal niceties. The ministry fully anticipated the mission to deliver above and beyond its original demands. In the document itself, it allowed the mission to go a long way east of Lake Chad.

With financing from a private imperialist lobby, favourable editors promising articles in the press, and some additional support from the Ministry of Colonies, Voulet was effectively receiving orders directly from the government rather than from the army itself. With responsibility for the mission's budget, Voulet was establishing his own colonial enterprise. He recruited his officers, bought his supplies, and personally set up most of the logistics of his mission. The incredible burden and responsibility cast on one man also meant that the mission leader had unique authority. With full power to choose whomever he wanted, Voulet selected a team of experienced officers and friends. He started from the staff of his expedition of 1896 with Chanoine (Figure 1), the medical officer Dr Henric, Sergeant-Major Laury, and Maréchal des logis Tourot. He added Lieutenant Pallier, a close friend of his who had also served with him in Africa. Only three other young officers with promising careers were new: Lieutenants Joalland and Péteau and Sergeant Bouthel. All three knew Voulet from reputation. Joalland had seen him give a prestigious lecture attended by the then minister Lebon at the École Coloniale. Voulet was then a rising star in colonial circles. According to Joalland, Voulet then met him in the street and invited him to his home where

> without any warning he opened Shroder's map of Africa, he told me: 'Here, the aim is to go from here to here. Are you with us?' With his finger he showed me Dakar and Djibouti, that is to say Africa at its widest . . . I shook hands with him with gratitude, from that time I gave myself to him body and soul.[14]

Even with the romantic exaggerations associated with this sort of storytelling, one is struck by the emotion arising from these bold plans. If the instructions were absolutely clear up to Lake Chad, there was a possibility that the mission might go into uncharted territory and become the boldest colonial venture ever attempted. The dream would be to join up with the Marchand mission on the Nile having conquered everything along the way.[15] Of course, unbeknownst to Voulet or Joalland, the British were following master plans of their own and Kitchener's army was already travelling from Egypt to the Southern Nile. The colonial dreams of the French and British were not compatible, and literally in a race to carve up Africa, they collided in Fashoda, on the Nile, in September 1898.[16] By November, the French had to withdraw; even before Voulet could cross the French colonial borders the dream of a continuous east–west landmass was over.

Yet even the explicit side of the mission, to reconnoitre the borders between what are today Nigeria and Niger, was likely to leave plenty of space for the use of bold initiatives on the ground. Making treatises with local chiefs was a euphemism for annexing by force new territories. For a while at least the officers would be the masters of their destiny, shapers of some of their own country's.

Following the signing of the agreement between the French and British in June 1898, the lines traced in diplomatic circles needed to become 'real'. Borders needed to appear in the shape of actual occupation to satisfy their new landowners.[17] Even though the great powers were reluctant to come to blows over African land, they nevertheless postured menacingly on the ground. A ragged flag was not enough; one needed some soldiers to claim a tribe, a kingdom, a river, or a forest. Rarely were so many countries involved in such unabashed greed for land and resources as in the crucial two decades known as the Scramble for Africa. The real reason for the French haste in conquest was the race against competing powers, principally the British, but also the Germans installed in the southern Cameroons and Togoland.

A nobler excuse was the urgency of the Western civilizing mission, as claimed in a famous speech of 28 July 1885 by the French republican Jules Ferry: 'superior races have a right towards inferior races . . . because they have a duty. They have the duty to civilise the inferior races.'[18] In 1898, the main motive for a 'humanitarian war' was the struggle against the African slave trade which prospered in central Africa. This struggle was highly ambiguous as Chapter 5 will show, but, as it happened, one of the last remaining local slave-driving potentates named Rabah Zubayr (also known as Rabih Fold Allah (1840–1900)) ruled over the central region of Burnu to the south-west of Lake Chad.[19] Rabah had been dubbed the 'Arab Napoleon' and was established in the Western press as a prime target for a liberating war.[20]

To the west of Chad, the French had long waged wars against major Muslim kingdoms. For a generation the states of the jihadist leader Umar Tall and of his son Ahmadu Seku and his nephew Tidjani Tall had blocked French advances into the hinterland of Senegal.[21] But, one by one, all the great Western African states had collapsed eventually under French pressure and often as a result of their own fragility. By 1898 Rabah remained the last major opponent the French empire faced. The same year the French had closed in on the independent West African regime of Samory Touré.[22] Pushed to the limits of his resources, a young captain, Henri Gouraud, managed to capture Samory and a crowd of his warriors, slaves, and family estimated at 40,000 people.[23] The war against Rabah was to conclude this work and perhaps even close the era of imperial conquests in the region. Each part of the conquest presented different challenges and the societies the French sought to dominate had very variable levels of armament and organization. Some relied on ancient muskets; others benefited from trans-Saharan trade for the import of powder and armament; others imported contraband modern weaponry[24] and, like Samory's army, even manufactured modern breech loaded rifles; others relied on hunting clubs, bows, and arrows.[25]

According to his orders, Voulet and his officers were to board a ship in Bordeaux, and land in the harbour of Saint-Louis in Senegal. From there Voulet had to recruit local soldiers in Senegal and in the new colony of Soudan; Chanoine would then have to find some porters in the Mosse territory near Ouagadougou. Both Voulet and Chanoine would separately cross the new colony of French Soudan (today's Mali and Burkina-Faso) until its most extreme outpost, some 2000 km from Dakar, in the small town of Say. From there, they were to move 945 km east towards the small independent Sultanate of Zinder (also known as Damagaram).[26] (See Map 2) The mission was meant to take

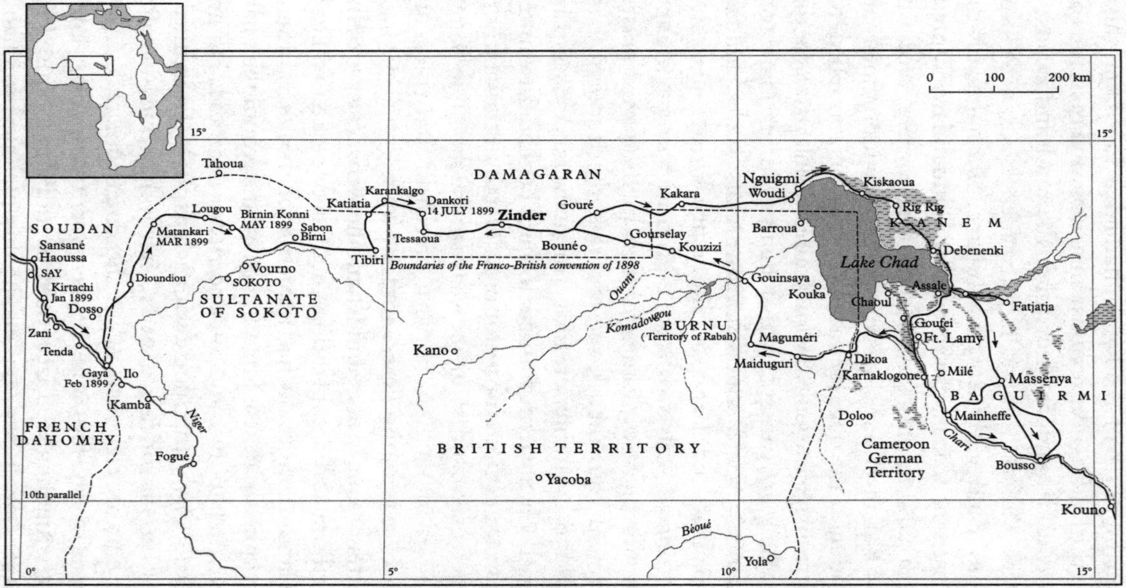

Map 2. French missions in Africa

revenge on the Sultan of Zinder, Ahmadu dan Taminun, who had murdered the leader of a previous French mission in May 1898.[27] Voulet was under orders to conquer the land and depose the Sultan.

While in Zinder Voulet could either await the arrival of the mission sent from Algeria led by Commandant Lamy and Foureau or advance east towards the territories recently conquered by Rabah of Burnu.[28] Apart from the unfortunate murdered leader, only one Frenchman had ever travelled these lands previously: Lt.-Col. Parfait-Louis Monteil (1855–1925), a mere eight years earlier.[29] His account was the main source of information Voulet and Chanoine had on the difficulties of their plan to travel east of the French border. Yet the circumstances were widely different: Monteil had travelled with about ten men on an exploratory journey. His avowed intention was not to gain territory but to find out what successive expeditions would encounter in terms of politics, landscape, and resources.[30] A few earlier European travellers had made similar journeys in the region, for instance Dr Barth in the earlier part of the nineteenth century or the German Nachtigal in the early 1870s.

Unlike these two travellers, Monteil's journey was paving the way for later action. Voulet and Chanoine were direct successors of Monteil's peaceful expeditions. Unlike Monteil, Voulet had obtained and intended to use a variety of means of war. His mission explicitly asked for all the latest technologies which would be used to awe and subdue African people. He asked his patrons for two machine guns such as the Maxim machine guns used in the British expeditions he had met in 1897;[31] he dreamt of an electrical device he could use to illuminate the sides of the camps and begged for 270 regular soldiers and their equipment.[32] In the end he did not obtain all the resources he had hoped for and he compensated for his lack of modern equipment with a larger contingent of irregular soldiers gathered along the road in the settlements he travelled through.[33]

Coming from Senegal, the Voulet–Chanoine mission as it became known split into two separate groups following different trajectories. Voulet travelled down the Niger River with much of the heavy equipment while Chanoine travelled inland to recruit soldiers, regular tirailleurs, and irregular soldiers from the Mosse and Bambara tribes. The mission hired some irregular cavalry men (so-called Spahis) from the Hausa ethnic group, Mosse porters who would carry the luggage when the river barges could no longer be used, cattle drivers, women, and perhaps, even when still in French-controlled territory, captives or slaves.

Voulet and Chanoine travelled their equally arduous routes across the new colony. Voulet on the river Niger used flat iron barges or *chalands* (see Figure 4). The river was one of the main modes of travel but it had its dangers and the journey Voulet anticipated making had never been undertaken by such a large party.

Leaving on 25 September 1898 the bulk of the mission embarked on a long and tedious journey downstream. The Europeans were on the main boats and the Africans and much of the equipment travelled on eight iron barges dragged behind. From Bamako, the Sotuba 'rapids' presented the first obstacle and one boat sunk with its load of seven soldiers and an unspecified number of women (including a native veteran non-commanding officer (NCO), Sergeant Ahmadi Diallo). A little after a week, both Voulet and Chanoine reached Ségou where they heard of the double promotion of Jules and Julien Chanoine. Julien had been made captain and his father minister of war. This promotion put Julien on a more equal footing with Voulet even if he remained second in command.

Throughout this first part of the campaign the officers and NCOs trained their soldiers who had for the best part never served in a Western armed force. The drill was relentless and the soldiers were 'broken' into an obedient war machine. The officers were confident that discipline and a rule of iron would turn their recruits into a redoubtable army. From the ancient city of Ségou to Djenné another week went by and in Djenné, Voulet obtained another 80 soldiers trained by the administrator William Ponty. Chanoine then left Voulet again to travel across the Mosse territory and Ouagadougou to gather more porters and more soldiers. He was due to move to Say and, moving along the Niger, go up as far as the large village of Sansané Haoussa on the far shore of the river.

Meanwhile Voulet followed the river Niger itself. On 4th November his group reached Timbuktu, then ruled by Lieutenant-Colonel Klobb. For fifteen days the Voulet mission stayed in Timbuktu, spending most of its time sorting and drying its wet equipment. Each bullet had to be dried by hand. Klobb contributed fifty regular soldiers of the permanent regiment of Soudanese tirailleurs and twenty Spahis cavalrymen to the expedition. Among this elite troop were two NCOs who later had a crucial role: Sgts. Demba Sar and Souley Taraore.

Klobb had decided to use Voulet's forces to make an expedition of his own and to travel with Voulet to scare and attack nomadic Tuareg. Klobb and Voulet walked for an entire month eastwards. Conflicting sources describe the relationship between the two men as tense or amicable. The confidential document sent by Voulet in January 1899 seems to show a businesslike but tense bargaining between the two men.[34] The Voulet column then split into two groups: the boats on the river and the soldiers walking beside it. On the river they had to face navigation obstacles which they managed to overcome.

On 31 December they reached the small outpost of Sinder. On 3 January 1899, Voulet heard that Chanoine was at the meeting point across the river. At last the entire force was gathered. By this stage Chanoine claimed to have enlisted about 800 porters and 360 soldiers.[35] The mission had grown into the largest military column the French had ever utilized in Soudan. Most of these forces were not on the official payroll but they would, eventually, need payment in kind.

Among the narrow circles of officers with an experience of long missions, Voulet and Chanoine were well-known organizers. Their camp was regarded as a model by their subordinates but even their organization could not solve the problems such a large group would face. Joalland wrote in his journal:

> All the squads were set on three sides of the camp with the fourth near the river; but inside the camp one could see the most extraordinary medley: first of all a huge square surrounded by a thorny hedge where they had enclosed the 800 Mosse porters. I say 800 but wrongly since when Chanoine went across Say an epidemic of dysentery had already claimed many victims. Never until then had I seen such a desolate spectacle. Most of the victims were naked; yet at this time of year the temperatures in the night and morning were low. In another enclosure were the prisoners taken between Say and Sansané Haoussa or in raids made since then.[36]

According to Joalland there were then 600 soldiers, 800 porters (possibly fewer than 600 after the epidemic of dysentery), 200 women, and 100 slaves; 150 horses, 500 cattle, 100 donkeys and mules, and 20 camels. 'Instead of decreasing,' he noted, 'this figure would only grow by the seizing of a considerable number of horses and also, I must say, by an innumerable quantity of women and prisoners. Instead of 200 women we would soon get to 800!'

This group of over 1,700 men, women, and children, cattle, and slaves represented a very large military force by the standards of West Africa of the 1890s. Its demands on resources and water in a land ravaged by thirty years of war and cyclical droughts and lacking natural wealth at the best of times were going to be overwhelming.[37] Klobb, who had been active in West Africa for ten years, an exceptionally long period in a land where most stayed a couple of years, knew this and advised Voulet to travel more lightly. But Voulet would not change his mind. He was concerned that the territories he faced were largely unknown and that he would require these resources to make his way against armed resistance. Monteil himself had argued that one would need a large armed force to beat the established kingdoms of Zinder, subjects of Sokoto, and the armies of Burnu.[38] From his experience as the conqueror of the Mosse Empire, Voulet built a generous estimate of his military needs.

Soon after Klobb left Voulet to return to Timbuktu, the large force led by Voulet and Chanoine lost its moral bearings. Even though Joalland does not mention it, the first recorded massacre took place on the site of the base camp itself, at Sansané Haoussa, a village allegedly pacified and under the 'protection' of the French resident in Say. The rationale for the massacre is unknown but the refusal to provide the huge food supplies needed was probably a factor. While allegedly dependent on Say, Sansané Haoussa was on the other side of the river and remained largely oblivious of the French. In their reports the two officers stressed that these lands were hostile and that one needed to impress on the region ahead that they meant business. This massacre, more than any other along their bloody journey, was going to be significant in their downfall. Being so close to Say it was better documented and understood; furthermore it was also an insult to their fellow officers in Say.

On Friday 13 January 1899 the column left Sansané Haoussa and began its march south-eastwards. The first village encountered, Karma, was the site of the first skirmish and inflicted the first casualties. It also witnessed the execution of two irregular soldiers who had fled the incident. According to Joalland the first head of a native resisting the mission was cut off in that village.

Within a few miles of Say and Sansané Haoussa, the column began pillaging in a systematic manner and soldiers were rewarded and praised for the loot they collected. In these early days, the French Lieutenant Péteau singled himself out by bringing back much loot and many captives. Violence and hardship grew commensurately.

Water soon ran out when the huge mission left the shores of Niger and, following its original orders, attempted to march across the arid land apportioned to France in the Franco-British treaty of June 1898. After three days without water the column had to trek back to the Niger in disarray.

In their account of August 1899 written with an eye on a likely court martial, Joalland and Pallier narrated a disastrous march in overwhelming heat moving into increasingly arid territories. At its height, the mission needed 40 tons of water per day. Walking along the Niger, Voulet expected to rely on the villages listed in previous travelogues. In fact the region had already been ransacked thoroughly, many wells being filled in, and the mission began to starve. By late January 1899, when Lieutenant Péteau was dismissed after an altercation with Chanoine, the mission was experiencing food shortages and considerable hardship a stone's throw from their base. By the end of January, they were in Kirtachi, a mere 40 km from the French outpost of Say. From Kirtachi to Zanafira they claimed to have encountered no less than thirty villages destroyed between 1895 and 1897 by raiders of a local chieftain, Ali Bouzi, taking cover in Sokoto from the French, and, Voulet alleged, French subjects from Say. Voulet estimated that his predecessors had killed at least 50,000 people.[39]

By early February 1899, the mission was in Tenda, another French outpost north of the new colony of Dahomey, going south instead of east, in the middle of Songhai territory. Temperatures reached 35 to 38°C during the day. The whole of February was spent waiting to move east when the mission split into three units leaving one after another. The mission was travelling through mostly hostile territory. After a mere 40-km march north, Voulet was wounded with an arrow while leading an attack on the fortified village of Dioundiou. While he recovered, the village was entirely destroyed and the ruins served as a training ground to coach the soldiers in taking fortified villages. The mission stayed put for another fifteen days while the mercury kept rising to over 40°C.

Another month went by and the mission was still a mere 80 km from Say as the crow flies. The original plan had been to follow closely a map boundary drawn in London and Paris which made a border of a perfect circle about 160 km from Sokoto without regard for the largely unknown conditions or resources of the country. The early failure of the mission under arid conditions led Voulet to realize that his mission was impossible if he obeyed his directives to the letter. He was not alone in having reached that conclusion. In Paris Lieutenant-Colonel Monteil expressed his unhappiness with the outcome of this tough bargaining with the British and noted that the borders drawn in 1898 were impossible to abide by for the French seeking to join Lake Chad. As the only Westerner to have made the journey Monteil knew the area well.[40]

Like its sick and troubled leaders, the mission stayed immobile for an entire month in a settlement called Matankari.

Subordinate officers could not understand why they had to remain static but Voulet was then exchanging furious letters with Paris and the rear. At this stage Voulet and Chanoine had become conscious that their reputation was in danger. Corresponding with the French colony and in particular Say, Voulet used increasingly violent language. He particularly chastized the caretaking resident of Say, a young Lieutenant Delaunay who had reported indignantly the atrocities of Sansané Haoussa. His superior, Captain Granderye was more in tune with Voulet's methods but reproved his 'excesses' and denounced them in a tightly argued report in March 1899.[41] Chanoine and Voulet confronted Delaunay[42] and claimed that his territory was unsafe, taking it upon themselves to 'act vigorously from the start'.[43] They also accused Granderye of leaking the aims of their mission and of being so passive that the people on the other side of the river expected to defeat them easily. Granderye for his part accused them of stealing some of 'his' subjects, as well as stealing free men and women and trading some of them for horses. A small scandal was brewing in the colony of Soudan.

The news of the massacre of 101 men, women, and children at the village of Sansané Haoussa and of its sacking and burning had reached Say in February. The investigation led by a visitor, Commandant Crave, confirmed the evidence given by the chief, Yousouf Ousaman.[44] This event deeply troubled Delaunay, who did not have the prestige or the weapons of Voulet's force. Furthermore Delaunay and his successor Granderye had to stay in Say and face the consequences of Voulet's war techniques: 'Everyday I receive complaints from Sansané Haoussa . . . I have seen for myself the result you obtained by using 500 rifles to obtain submission. The land is completely deserted and the market is ruined.'[45] The concern for the market was particularly sensitive. Among the responsibilities of the 'resident' of Say, tax collecting was crucial and a low return would be noted by the authorities against the officer. Perhaps more troubling than the killing, Voulet's methods seemed to be affecting the normal running of the new colony.

On 15 February 1899 after a bitter exchange of letters, Delaunay reported to Granderye, who was coming to take over. The latter filed his first report to his superiors. His words were damning:

From Sansané Haoussa we have had the greatest difficulties finding guides, the country has been utterly devastated [*à feu et à sang*] by the Voulet mission, the few inhabitants who survived the massacres in the few villages which were not burnt ran away as quickly as they could when they saw the tricolour, and this on both sides of the river [Niger].[46]

A conflict of personalities added to the bitterness of the exchanges between Voulet and Say. If originally the officers seemed to be unwilling to write down what they had witnessed, Voulet's aggressive letters shattered their restraint.[47] This conflict between Say and the mission was to be a crucial component of Voulet's downfall especially after Voulet lost the means to communicate with his base in Paris and the capital of the Soudan colony in Kayes. Then Granderye and his colleagues from the Soudanese border started filing a multitude of small reports condemning the Voulet mission in February and March 1899, nearly three months after the events.[48] Voulet's riposte, written on 1 March 1899, was only received in Paris on 23 May, over a month and a half after Klobb had been sent on his track.

In this letter Voulet explained the events near Say as defensive measures, explaining his taking of French subjects as the accidental result of war incidents:

Several of our isolated soldiers had been killed or wounded and we had to take preventative measures and reconnoitre some distance from the camps of the mission—during these patrols we had to brace ourselves for war in order to disperse the armed groups organized against us. Several prisoners fell in our hands and to our great stupefaction we found Fulbe people from Say.[49]

On the southern side of the colonial border, in French Dahomey and around the isolated outpost of Dosso, Voulet had friends and one finds no such condemnation of his 'policing operations'.[50] In fact the mission encountered organized resistance throughout the land. Some of it became the stuff of legend. In particular the resistance of the village of Lougou where a female 'witch' ruler, or Saranouia,[51]

claims that she will stop our march; her men have a reputation of invincible warriors; we could not do anything else than respond to her provocation. We walked throughout the night through difficult terrain and on 16th April at 6 am we began a battle which lasted until 1 and which was one of the most difficult of the campaign.[52]

Joalland led the fight which cost the mission 7,000 cartridges and six casualties. Poisoned arrows were blamed for the fatalities in this unequal battle. The Lougou casualties were not recorded but the Saranouia escaped the French to become a legendary figure of resistance.

Finally, after much hesitation, on 15 April 1899, Voulet decided to ignore his written orders to achieve the gist of his directives. He chose to move along the only available route open to his force. This new route took his army into territory allegedly dependent on the British 'protectorate' of Sokoto. Crossing the river, a few weeks earlier, Chanoine had portrayed the land ahead of them in these terms:

Our enemies are:

1. The Fulbe of Say who are furious to see us cross the Niger as this is the area of their systematic pillaging.
2. The Tuareg for whom the Niger is a base, they need the river for their herds and to see the French take both sides of the river makes them understandably angry.
3. The Djermas a sedentary but warlike people whose villages are on the left bank of the river . . .
4. The Almamy of Sokoto who does not know yet that he belongs to the English and who still thinks we are threatening him with invasion.
5. But our worse enemies were not tangible and material of the kind you can take by the throat and strangle, no our worst enemies have been the demoralization and despair that some have tried to put in our soldiers' hearts.[53]

In a climate of distrust, Voulet and Chanoine behaved as if they were in open war with every African they met. Their distrust of their colleagues and supply lines was not entirely unjustified, but it also meant that they pushed aside any intelligence passed to them by their own superiors.

Harassed by constant skirmishes, the mission seemed to sink into an overly aggressive attitude to all and a general unease within. Having failed to obey the original mission brief which forbade a venture into the land of Sokoto, Voulet decided to increase the pace and brutality of his slow moving army. In April, Chanoine calculated that they hardly walked at more than 2 miles (3.5 km) per hour even without any luggage.[54] More than once the mission nearly faced total disaster. One of the worst incidents took place when they went across a desert area of 65 km. Dehydrated, the bulk of the column had to be brought water from the vanguard led by Voulet. Twenty-five men and women died of dehydration on a single day on 19 April 1899.

They then moved into Hausa territory towards Tougana and Birnin Konni.[55] From the town of Birnin Konni Voulet requested a tribute of 12 bullocks as a token of the local Sultan's submission. The leader of Birnin Konni offered 1,000 kola nuts instead. In fact the region was already on its knees and could ill afford to supply the huge invading army and kola nuts were of course of some comfort since the kola substance had stimulant qualities which made it popular in Europe and America in various wines and soft drinks. It was not what was asked though, and Voulet responded with a full assault on the fortified city. The initial resistance led to extremely violent reprisals and pillages. According to most official accounts this battle was the turning point of the campaign. Birnin Konni was a town surrounded by a moat and high walls forming a considerable 800 m-square fort. Its population had been roughly estimated at over 10,000 but estimates of population remained wildly inaccurate until later in the colonial era and the population could have been half that size.

With the help of Joalland's artillery the town was captured, plundered, and pulled down at a cost of only four men to the assaliants. A mere 200 km from the border the Voulet mission had already destroyed most of the significant urban settlements.

Writing to the ministry on 25 May 1899, in a letter that took months to arrive, Voulet reiterated his request for more weapons and admitted that he would not be able to return the way he had come. Writing in the 'infested atmosphere reeking of corpses',[56] Voulet battled with invisible opponents in Paris to make his views accepted. While hundreds of miles from his endpoint Voulet already attempted to negotiate his independence from Governor Gentil with whom he was due to meet to fight Rabah.

He obviously did not know that both he and Chanoine had already been dismissed and that his career was in tatters.[57]

Within the mission, Chanoine had imposed the harshest possible interpretation of French army discipline. He even went further than the customs of the colonial forces already illegal in French law. Voulet and he had created an atmosphere of constant brutalization. Ruling through extreme forms of discipline Voulet and Chanoine did not hesitate to use collective punishment for their own men. At one stage, an entire section was whipped twenty-five times, each row of soldiers whipping those in front. This rampant violence crept into every human encounter. Suspicious of everyone, Voulet and Chanoine ensured that natives who did not volunteer information, guides who hesitated or got lost, or local people who hid their food were beheaded and their heads left on sticks.

This climate of fear was not entirely of Voulet and Chanoine's own making and there was the constant reminder of danger in the story of Cazemajou, who the year before had been ambushed, robbed, and murdered in Zinder. His corpse and that of his translator had then been thrown into a well. From the evidence of their letters and papers, Voulet and Chanoine seem to have lived in fear of their enemies and of their own soldiers and companions. The officers faced threats of poisoned arrows at a time when their own physical and mental health was probably damaged by heat and fever.[58] Not all the resistance was in response to aggression. The Soudan region, which sits at the border of several worlds, was a land of remarkable ethnic diversity and represented the southern frontier of Islam. Over the previous hundred years local states, some very short-lived, had embraced Islam as a mobilizing force for war. The charismatic leaders of these movements had created a sequence of relatively unstable but often highly organized military states. These kingdoms often lacked a real economic base beyond warfare and operated pillaging raids on neighbouring lands.[59] Periodically raided and pillaged the local people could only see Voulet's men as another predatory group. Indeed, their behaviour did nothing to contradict this point of view.

When the mission crossed their territories the villagers often attempted to resist and fight, to be killed at 300 m by the salves of French long-range weapons; their walled villages turned to rubble by the pounding of the French single mountain artillery gun. Any form of resistance led to enslavement and destruction but in effect reprisals took place on the faintest evidence of noncollaboration. Ultimately this violent tactic led the Africans to flee before the mission.

The expedition obeyed the letter of the rulebooks on long distance missions. It was composed of cavalry, infantry, and artillery. The cavalry was ahead and on the edges of the main column which was split into warring units and supply units.[60] The supplies were cumbersome, cattle herded by Fulbe men and porters from a diversity of ethnic groups were grouped together and treated as one, and the soldiers protecting them were also their prison wardens. The column thus walked at the pace of the slowest cohort. Women and children were already numerous as they followed their men-folk into war but the column grew steadily from its rapine. Originally the taking of slaves was primarily to replace the poorly treated porters who had died in the first few weeks of the mission. Later on the taking of slaves became a central part of the economic underpinning of the mission. Voulet sought to be obeyed by his men and regarded them as responding to rewards and harsh discipline. So while he had no regrets about executing an NCO accused of wasting his cartridges[61] (in all likelihood a euphemism for sleeping with one of the women reserved for a white officer), he saw fit to reward his soldiers with slaves and cattle raided along the way. Irregular troops had been recruited on the promise of loot. This initiated a vicious circle. The raids took time and the crowd of captives grew to 800 women at least. The mission slowed down, it used resources more extensively than before, it became harder to obtain local collaboration, more reprisals took place, and more captives were taken. When the reputation of the mission preceded it, the villagers fled, for they had much to fear as the violence took increasingly aberrant forms. Soon after the mission had left the more controlled territories of the burgeoning Soudan colony, the soldiers were set to pillage and rape.[62]

From one reprisal to another 'accidental' fire, the mission left in its wake destruction as varied in its manifestations as it was relentless. To say so is not to sensationalize the events—the secret reports of the French army did no such thing. They were looking for Voulet and Chanoine and that is how they found them.

11 July 1899

A long walk in the bush. Arrived in a small village, burnt down, full of corpses. Two little girls hanged from a branch. The smell is unbearable. The wells do not provide enough water for the men. The animals do not drink; the water is corrupted by the corpses.[63]

The 'horde' of Captains Voulet and Chanoine had left a long trail of unusual devastation even by the standards of 1899 in Western or central Africa. The smaller mission led by Klobb was the opposite of the Voulet mission. With only thirty soldiers and two white officers it made exceptionally good progress, catching up with Voulet's Mission as it travelled along a devastated route littered with corpses and burnt villages. By that stage the large villages and small towns they found had already been evacuated before Voulet's arrival. In Tibiri the mission gathered again in a deserted town. Again they had to follow the course of water supplies and instead of moving east the mission continued its erratic route. Along the way in Karankalgo for instance they destroyed a village that resisted, killing 400 inhabitants. In fact, when the rearguard of Voulet's mission left Sabon Guida, some 96 km east of Birnin Konni, on 21 June, it was ahead of Klobb by a matter of days rather than weeks.

Increasingly uncompromising; Voulet moved along his warpath. The Sultan of Zinder sent a diplomatic mission to negotiate with Voulet. With typical understatement Joalland states that 'Voulet did not receive [them] very well. He had the two guards of the envoy beheaded and he put the envoy in chains.'[64] In diplomatic terms imprisoning and later beheading an envoy tends to be regarded as a sign of hostility and it was clear by then that the mission had decided to avenge its predecessor Cazemajou.[65]

By early July, Klobb was immediately behind Voulet's mission and fresh evidence of its violence made it clear that he had to take over from Voulet and Chanoine. Sending soldiers ahead of him, Klobb intimated that he was coming to take over and investigate. Instead of slowing down to enable the colonel to catch up, Voulet hastened the pace and split his forces in order to keep his more faithful men separate from those led by other French officers. Eventually, on 14 July 1899, the two missions met and confronted each other near the village of Dankori. Joalland, although a problematic witness, provided one of the most complete versions of the events which became the account the authorities accepted:

On 10 July the fighting column, under the orders of Captain Chanoine, Pallier and Joalland was in Guidam Boultou where Voulet and Dr Henric met them, the Sergeant Bouthel camped 4 kilometres away with the cattle. The NCOs Laury and Tourot [and the cavalry] were camping in villages to the North and East.

After a joyful dinner Chanoine left at two in the morning to meet Voulet. Aware of Klobb's imminent arrival, Voulet had made preparations to flee. Klobb had sent a letter which probably reached Voulet on the 12th. In all reports it seems that many, if not all, the officers knew that Klobb was arriving soon.[66] On the 12th Voulet released some of his cattle and buried his ice-making equipment. The machine was a good symbol of some of the inefficiencies of the mission. It had been carried on a man's head since Say and had never been used even though many officers had suffered from the fever it was intended to alleviate. He then gathered his African NCOs and allegedly revealed his plan. The next day Voulet kept his European officers at arm's length, sending them some champagne to celebrate the 14th of July.

On the same day Voulet sent Klobb a letter which clearly stated that he would not hand over his mission.

In the morning of 14 July Voulet and 80 men ambushed Klobb and his force and shot him dead. Later that morning Voulet approached his officers some 8 km away. Joalland gave a convenient account that exonerated him and all his fellow French officers apart from Julien Chanoine:

'Good morning Captain,' said I as I approached him to shake hands.

'Wait, do not touch me before you have heard me.' Said Voulet. 'Colonel Klobb was coming to send us to an inquest; he was coming to rob me of my command. I have given him the order to do a U-turn. He did not listen to me and I killed him. He was shot thrice in the head and twice in the chest. Lieutenant Meynier who was with him is wounded to the leg. You are not concerned. I kept you in ignorance and I will provide you with documents to establish this.'[67]

Then he lost his calm and he started to talk with a prophetic exaltation:

'I do not regret anything of what I have done. Now I am an outlaw, I [*renie*] disavow my family, my country, I am not French anymore, I am a black leader. Africa is large; I have a gun, plenty of ammunition, 600 men who are devoted to me heart and soul. We will create an empire in Africa, a strong impregnable empire that I will surround with deserted bush; to seize me you will need 10,000 men and 20 million francs. They will never dare to attack me. When France wants to negotiate with us, it will need to pay us dear. What I have done is nothing but a coup. If I were in Paris I would be the master of France!'

Turning to Chanoine he told him that he was even more compromised than him in the accusations carried by Klobb. Chanoine chose to follow Voulet. He then went to speak to the NCOs while the local court singers, 'griots', sang songs of praise comparing Voulet to Samory and Ahmadu and beat the war drums.[68] The remaining officers realized at that moment that they were under the close scrutiny of the cavalrymen of Voulet's guard.[69]

Breaking the regular units away from his officers, Pallier and Joalland, Voulet foresaw that his troops might soon take sides and that an open conflict might begin. Chanoine took them away on the evening of 14 July, leaving behind the French officers and the units that had killed Klobb with Voulet. The French officers then retired for the night. The following day the French officers asked to be sent back to Soudan. Joalland, Pallier, and one NCO, the severely ill Laury, then left with thirty men to meet Meynier and Henric, both bed-ridden, and to return to Say.

On the 15th further internecine war seemed to have been avoided but the mission was over. It had broken ranks with the French state and Voulet's intentions were unclear. Sergeant Bouthel was kept as an officer by Voulet, allegedly against his will. The remaining French officers were either ill (Dr Henric,

Sgt. Bouthel) or having to fend for themselves in hostile territory. Expecting deserters from Voulet's column, they decided to regroup and possibly march against Voulet to take control of his mission. On the 16th events overtook them. Voulet had gathered his men and announced his intention to become the equal of Samory Touré.[70] In the process he had allegedly told them that they would never return home but instead build an empire around them. He also predicted that the other French officers would die on their way back. Under the command of a regular tirailleur, Souley Taraore, the native sergeants rebelled and planned for their men to escape from Voulet's camp.

Voulet and Chanoine's interpreters realized what was happening and warned their masters. At that stage events become confused, mostly because the witnesses agreed later on a version of events that contained inconsistencies. In the Joalland version of events the rebellion against. Voulet was led by a 'patriotic' Sergeant Souley Taraore whose pidgin words he recorded for posterity despite being miles away and which ought to belong rightfully to fantasy colonial literature:

> 'The captains has said that we were no longer French; yes we are! Soudanese tirailleurs when we leave the French are protecting our mothers and our homes in our villages. The captain said he no longer had insignias; we don't have to obey him. The ones in charge are the lieutenants over there who have refused to follow the captain.'

'What wonderfully elevated language', Joalland wrote lyrically. 'Here is a young sergeant who has a clear notion of his duties and who convinces his comrades that they belong at the side of their officers.'[71]

Even though the words are probably largely invented, a similar version was later recorded by the investigators into the events. One could read Souley Taraore's speech, if he ever used these words, in a rather less 'patriotic' but also more lucid manner. One way would be to see the reference to the French protection of villages and families as a reminder of reprisals that rebels could expect on their loved ones, while the reference to the lack of insignia as a clear understanding of Voulet's broken relations with the army. Soudanese tirailleurs understood ranks and power relations within the army. Removing their own insignias would have reminded them of what had happened to a fellow NCO just a few weeks earlier, when Joalland had led a court martial which degraded the NCO prior to his execution. Whatever was said, it remains likely that the NCOs managed to control their soldiers and take them away from Voulet.

According to Bouthel, the African soldiers regrouped on the hill outside the village and shot in the general direction of Voulet's hut. The soldiers were apparently firing high but the camp was under sustained fire. Riding towards them Chanoine came shouting, 'France, France!' Shot at by the troops, he responded with his handgun before being killed by two shots in the head, five in the body, and two sabre cuts.[72] Voulet, followed by a few cavalrymen and one Tuareg woman, had to flee from his mutinous soldiers.

The evidence is not absolutely clear on what happened next. It seems that the African soldiers were divided and Souley Taraore had to execute some of Voulet's partisans. Voulet was then alone with a handful of cavalrymen who returned to camp when they realized how weak their leader was. Chanoine's interpreter, Sidi Berete, was with Voulet for a while before he too returned to camp. Versions of events diverge here but it seems that Sidi Berete attempted to raise the troopers against their NCOs. As he left the village of Mayjirgui, he was shot in the head by a tirailleur. The last remaining follower of Voulet, another translator, Mahmadou Koulibaly, ran for his life to Tessaoua, where he was eventually arrested. Eventually Voulet was left alone, with a woman named Fatma, the Tuareg common-law wife of 'another European'. The sources are discreet on her partner or indeed her real identity; *fatma* was the generic term the French used to name Arabic women.

This strange couple travelled in silence and in despair; dehydrated and hungry they arrived in a neighbouring village where they were fed and given a roof for the night. In the early morning Fatma left Voulet to sleep. On waking alone Voulet attempted to enter the encampment, when, at 5.30 am, he was shot by the sentry. The deaths of both Chanoine and Voulet were recorded but not witnessed by any Europeans and indeed some of the key witnesses soon disappeared. The systematic destruction or loss of evidence implies that a significant rewriting of the events took place. The main witness and closest to Voulet was his translator, Koulibali. Within a few days he was executed by Captain Pallier for no other reason than obeying his masters. The accusation was 'that he had not represented to Captain Voulet who often listened to him the danger that there would be in killing the colonel'.[73] Pallier also decided to burn the private belongings and most of the papers of Klobb, including the bulk of the records of atrocities. Voulet and Chanoine's belongings and papers were also allegedly lost in the fracas, together with Voulet's camera and the pictures he had taken.

News of the events travelled fast when the survivors of Klobb's mission returned to Say on 9 August 1899.[74] Through them and other deserters, the course of events was related throughout Soudan. In Ouagadougou, the missionary community, the so-called White Fathers noted a slightly different version in their official journal. This lack of clarity later led some to believe that both Voulet and Chanoine, far from being buried side by side as documented by the survivors, had instead managed to escape among the Tuareg to lead lives as African chieftains. The myth lasted for a considerable time as will be discussed later. Joalland felt the need to emphasize that both Voulet and Chanoine had been buried, and the cover of his book featured a picture of their graves. Although he hoped to silence the rumour, the legend did not die. In the 1920s some, including the Pulitzer Prize-winning journalist Albert Londres, still referred to Chanoine as a Tuareg chief.[75] A missionary White Father, historian of the Mosse, practiced early oral history and reported to his great surprise that an African soldier who had served with Voulet in 1897 and 1898–9 declared him to be alive and living among African tribes many years later.[76]

Meanwhile another myth had to be established around Klobb (See Figure 9). Unlike his assassins, Klobb was given military honours in death through a ceremony designed to reign in the rebellious soldiers. Klobb had walked to his death, it was alleged, ignoring the salves shot over his head and his own posture was described in heroic terms by the survivors if only to establish a stark contrast with the insanity of Voulet and the guilt of Chanoine. In their memoirs Voulet's lieutenants remained loyal to him. Joalland took a view commonly shared by his comrades, blaming the second in command for much of the preparations of the crime and even for most of the atrocities along the way. Less popular than Voulet, Chanoine had a well-established reputation of brutality and his father's position led to suspicion of nepotism and accelerated promotion.

Voulet had been loved and Chanoine was unlovable. Yet one could doubt the parallels made by Joalland between Voulet the hero and Voulet the victim as we will see later. The Voulet of Mosse had committed many acts of brutality in his time and Chanoine was the real organizer of much of the logistical underpinning of their joint operations. They seem to have been complementary rather than opposites.

Joalland then advanced what he saw as the conclusive evidence of Voulet's insanity, a theme which will resurface many times:

And the proof of what I say is that Voulet who was often surprising people by his precise judgement had come [so low as to] judge like a black chief and not like a European . . . We no longer have any hatred or any repulsion for the man, only his crime horrifies us, but since he now appears to us a sick man, we pray for the public to see him as we do! He is indefensible, it is true but let his past be like a shroud under which we will bury the Voulet who has failed.[77]

This heroic portrayal of a failed hero of colonial conquest has satisfied many historians. The final scene of internecine killing has dominated all accounts since and even this has been brushed aside as evidence of insanity. Undoubtedly Klobb became the hero of the story and his death was sanctified by the survivors and Meynier, his subordinate of the rescue mission, but his murder became the tree that hid a forest. The killing of one white officer became the scandal instead of the sustained murder of thousands of Africans.

The news of Klobb's death travelled back to Paris relatively quickly in August 1899 as scattered survivors of his mission managed to return to Say where they announced the rebellion of Voulet but not his death a few days later. On 26 August 1899 the French Foreign Office noted:

It is impossible to predict what decision this rebellious officer might take and we must envisage that he might violate some foreign territory. It will not escape your notice that the government of the Republic is deeply concerned by the consequences of aggressions led by this outlawed officer.[78]

At one stage the French administration started to prepare for the possibility of a violent confrontation with Voulet's army.

Voulet's alleged analysis that with 600 rifles he would be virtually invincible was correct as witness the reports issued after Klobb's death. The mission was officially dismantled and all neighbouring colonies were warned against Voulet. The two other missions in the field, Foureau-Lamy's and Gentil's, were instructed to prepare for a violent confrontation. The supplies ordered for Voulet were kept in Libreville in Congo while every officer in Africa received the order to arrest the outlaw. Chanoine was never mentioned in the telegrams.

Nevertheless the ministry ruled out sending a third mission to destroy Voulet. Ultimately, they hoped that the Africans would manage to rid themselves of this new African chieftain.[79] 'It does not seem at this stage that the mission could last with its current resources in the region of lake Chad . . . its ammunition supplies are not unlimited . . . the model 1886 cartridges are not available in the native countries of Central Africa'.[80] This panic lasted until proof of Voulet and Chanoine's deaths, rumoured since the end of August, reached Paris in October 1899.

Good news came, and the renewal of the mission under Pallier's orders was soon announced. Following the death of its original leaders, the ex-Voulet mission had seized the city of Zinder. After a short battle the mission entered the deserted city and pillaged it, possibly rewarding the soldiers for their 'patriotism'. Following this heroic feat the mission settled in the area and set about hunting the Sultan of Zinder. Joalland explained that he had to settle a score with the murderer of Cazemajou—in an environment where murder had become the norm. Joalland was keen to establish some form of order and justice. His execution of Sergeant Manga Sankare for mutiny thus followed all the established rules of military justice in wartime. Commandant Lamy, who arrived in November 1899 from his arduous crossing of the Sahara, was less impressed with Pallier's and Joalland's techniques:

'The surrounding countryside seems still terrorized by the memory of the Soudanese infernal columns that have criss-crossed it looking for the Sultan Ahmadu.'[81] Lamy used the phrase 'colonne infernale' which had peculiar resonances in France since it referred to the bloody, to some almost genocidal, reprisals of the Vendée insurrection during the French Revolution. Far from the 'police operation' Joalland was later keen to represent, the remains of the Voulet mission continued its violent practices unabashed by the death of its former leaders. Joalland waged a bloody campaign to 'pacify' a region still devoted to its sultan. Eventually Ahmadu was betrayed and killed, only to be replaced by one of his brothers, in the long-established French tradition of using feeble local chieftains as proxies. The next sultan was himself deposed five years later.[82] It was Sergeant Taraore, instrumental in suppressing the Voulet coup, who beheaded the sultan and brought his head back to Zinder. Pallier and Joalland had it put on a stick.

By the end of August the French faced another, peaceful but decided, mutiny among their soldiers.[83] By that stage, the mission leader, Pallier, had decided to split it into three groups: one composed of a few French officers leading three hundred men and among them sixty mutinous soldiers which returned on its tracks back home to Senegal with its women and slaves; the second a French sergeant and a garrison of 100 men to remain in Zinder, now baptized Fort Cazemajou; and the third, composed mostly of a small core of about two hundred regular Senegalese soldiers, to move towards Lake Chad under the command of two officers. This continuation of the Voulet–Chanoine mission was led by one officer from each mission, Joalland, who had followed Voulet, and Meynier, who had served under Klobb.

Their orders were vague and one interpretation was to await the Algerian mission in Zinder. They chose to do the reverse and sought the most efficient way of making distance between themselves and Zinder. They equipped their soldiers with stolen camels, and replaced the porters with horses and mules. From a logistical point of view the new mission was the exact opposite of the cumbersome Voulet 'horde'. It was fast and highly mobile. Its discipline followed textbook rules and if there were still instances of death sentences handed out, the ritual forms of a tribunal were now respected. If its warring practices changed, it was mostly because Joalland did not want to accumulate 'impedimenta', captives and cattle, which might slow his progress. The violence exerted against uncooperative villages remained much the same.

It is difficult not to see in this flight a deliberate desire to salvage whatever honour and reputation the officers had. Joalland knew full well that their future was in danger and that they were all likely to face the twin disgrace of a court martial and unfavourable newspaper reports. Instead they headed east as fast as they could in the hope of meeting the Gentil mission coming from the south which might not yet be aware of the events of Dankori. Lamy fully understood this manoeuvre for what it was and complained to his friend Captain Giraud:

> Think of our painful stupefaction of good folks like us who had only one thought in mind, to shake hands over the Sahara with our brothers coming from Soudan and continue to sail with them towards a useful aim for France, when we found out that our so-called brothers, whose meeting I recalled to my soldiers to strengthen their resolve, only had one thought: flee from us and avoid us as far as possible. The same, when they knew that a new commander was sent to them from Soudan had ambushed him after insulting him when he was coming to them under the protection of the French flag.[84]

This gamble paid off in the end. Lamy was furious at Joalland's conduct but had to accept him when Joalland came to meet him near Lake Chad. Facing the most important warlord remaining in Africa, Lamy had no choice but to allow him to join in his combined forces against Rabah. In the battles against the African leader, Joalland and Meynier found a new legitimacy as young heroes of the colonial enterprise. The newspapers relayed their daring and rehabilitated them as the 'healthy' part of the Voulet–Chanoine mission. There was so little to rehabilitate that the press and right-wing politicians seized upon these men as the symbols of French military values. In 1901 Auguste Terrier, the leading journalist of the colonial cause and the propagandist of the conquest of Chad, glossed over the portraits of the two officers who left Zinder in October 1899 to reach Lake Chad in twenty-one days. Lobbied by Joalland, Terrier swiftly forgot Joalland's friendship with Voulet and Chanoine and promoted the latest adventures as if nothing untoward had preceded them.

Yet both Chanoine and Voulet had been keen correspondents. As late as April 1899, Chanoine had asked for new supplies, for 200 new Lumière plates for his Verascope camera, asking Terrier to 'check especially the packaging if you want us to bring you back some nice pictures. Do you remember "An enormous lion devouring some corpses"?'[85]

Terrier had wanted sensational news from Voulet and Chanoine, but not the sort of scandalous reports coming in their wake. Joalland did not make the same mistakes and he ensured that any news of his own expedition in Chad came only from him or his closest associates.

Yet when one reads between the lines the break with Voulet's methods was less complete than Joalland liked to pretend. As soon as he reached the lakeside village of Nguigmi Joalland's men resumed some of their marauding customs, assaulting a convoy for its millet and stealing camels. The local warring that Voulet had encouraged by supporting one local chieftain over another on the basis of hastily made political decisions—primarily taken on a first come, first served basis—remained. In order to establish the new authority of the Republic, Joalland immediately launched a 'police operation' which supported the interests of the chieftain of Nguigmi at the expense of the neighbouring village. Even glossed over as mere policing, it seems that business was back to normal. Sergeant Taraore 'fulfilled his mission well and returned with a full load of millet'.[86] The story does not say what had taken place in the village where the millet was found. Even though a close accounting of all of Voulet's exactions took place, none was undertaken for the other missions. The reporting of Voulet's crimes appear to be very singular indeed. As I shall explore later, however, it is difficult to assess just how exceptional Voulet's behaviour was or indeed if the scandal provided a glimpse of the customary brutality of colonial conquest.

The year 1899 was not lacking in scandals in France. Apart from the concluding moments of the Dreyfus affair, a failed nationalist uprising, and anarchist violence, the Voulet–Chanoine affair had been fed in instalments to readers in France and abroad. In the first instance, the French public was horrified by what crimes were reported to have been committed in its name and all the observers were disturbed by the descriptions of grotesque violence and instances of sadistic savagery. The public was divided along Dreyfusard–anti-Dreyfusard lines on the veracity of the early news. Ultimately the news of the killing of Klobb was received with even greater disbelief and consternation. This mutinous violence revived the ghost of past civil wars, last seen in the bloodbath of the Paris Commune in May 1871. The rationale of colonialism and imperialism itself were under scrutiny. There had long been doubts on the 'civilizing mission' of the empire but the accounts of colonial violence in Soudan and also in Congo were now recurring more frequently. The humanitarian war against slavery in Africa was discredited just at the time when it seemed most successful as Rabah's rule ended. Many excuses were evoked to explain the two captains' numerous crimes and their rebellion: the one that dominated was the deleterious effect of tropical sun and climate; another was that ambition allied to absolute power and independence resulted in a reign of terror and a return to savagery.

Even while it was unfolding, this story met its fictional match in the plot of Joseph Conrad's *Heart of Darkness*, published in the spring of 1899. The novella, based on Conrad's own experiences ten years earlier, narrates a similar story of two missions, one seeking another one, a civilized man attempting to rescue his peer who has sunk into barbarity. As in the Voulet–Chanoine story, white men seemed both fragile and ruthlessly violent in an uncompromisingly alien environment. In his remarkable if contentious book, *Exterminate all the Brutes*, Sven Lindqvist refers directly to the Mission Afrique Centrale and its excesses and notes allusively its troubling parallels with Conrad's novella.[87] In the collective memory of the French empire it took a very long time for these deaths to find their way back. As explorers go these men were lost and remained so for a very long time. Voulet and Chanoine were no Livingstone or Gordon. They have no statue and few memorials of any kind; they are not remembered fondly by anyone. Yet Voulet had brought the Mosse land and Ouagadougou into the empire. Had he died of fever or in battle, his name would have featured on the walls of the 'musée permanent des colonies' built for the great celebration of the empire in 1931 at the Porte Dorée in Paris.[88] Instead he died an ignominious death, narrated second or third hand by survivors treading an uncomfortable path of their own between collective responsibility and guilt, and pleading that they had only obeyed orders.[89] They had left France behind, and France has reciprocated. They may have wanted to be African kings, albeit for a few hours but that madness has coloured their entire story.

The rest of this book is an attempt to see that 'insanity' in its true light, in the midst of many such 'incidents' and as a reflection of what power and weaponry do to men far away from home. Theirs is the story of imperialism in its naked arrogance: its overpowering military strength combined with ethical relativism. Of course, in the age of the Geneva Convention and budding international law, when humanitarian ideals were in full bloom, it happened under the tropical sun—it had to happen under such a sky—the sky itself was to be blamed. It was the sun, it was the fever, the malarial influences, the hunger, perhaps the alcohol, the land itself—it was madness, it was the madness of being there—the insanity of Soudan—*Soudanitis*.

Yet their story is confusing on several accounts: First it is relatively unclear why the original mission was perceived to be abnormally violent when similar methods had been used in a neighbouring region to general approval. Only two years earlier, in 1897 the same Voulet had set Ouagadougou on fire for daring to resist him for one afternoon and had 'pacified' the territory by means of arbitrary executions.[90] All surviving accounts recorded in the early 1960s described his acts as that of a demonic force.[91] Had warfare changed in the late 1890s? Had humanitarian consciousness made some practices unacceptable?

Furthermore, this story played out in European and American media. What role did the media play in this tragedy? On the one hand the investigation launched by the government signalled the shortening of distances in the Empire and the loss of local autonomy for the empire builders, but, on the other, news seems to have travelled both ways as Voulet and

Chanoine attempted to manage their image from the bush. Writing to Terrier in April 1899 Chanoine often gave his opinion on whatever news he had received and on the action of some Parisian politicians. Throughout their slow advance Voulet and Chanoine managed to send letters home in order to shape public awareness of their work. Yet they also seemed to have become aware of the growing unease with their methods, which they began to interpret as a betrayal. While anxieties grew in Soudan and Paris, especially in April 1899 and afterwards, Voulet and Chanoine's mail ceased to arrive regularly in Paris. Letters sent in April did not arrive until after their deaths in July. The breakdown of communication was almost complete by the end of the mission. Bundles of letters were found stuck in various parts of northern Niger by the Foureau-Lamy mission. The two men had, it seems, neglected to maintain these crucial links between their enterprise and their backers in Paris. If Napoleon had experienced the breakdown of supply lines in Russia, Voulet and Chanoine suffered from a new military logistical problem, the collapse of positive news coverage.

The response of Voulet and Chanoine to the arrival of Colonel Klobb's rescue mission presents a key psychological mystery. What drove these 'men of honour' to challenge their superior and shoot him? In the small community of colonial soldiers, they knew and had socialized with Klobb. The roll of the French army in Soudan in the 1890s reads like a who's who of future military leaders, many of whom played crucial roles during the Great War, such as Joffre, Gallieni, and Mangin. This small, largely self-selected, group of officers had strong bonds of comradeship. However, Voulet and Chanoine's violence became so troubling that it was ignored in later writings such as Colonel Baratier's *Épopées Africaines* and Gatelet's *Histoire de la conquête du Soudan Français*.[92] Voulet and Chanoine, who figured prominently in the history of the conquest, seem to vanish entirely from official military accounts. What remains of them is a troublesome memory—a haunting, recurring one that made its way into the writings of Jules Verne and numerous others, and perhaps even into the political culture of that part of Africa—to use the psychiatric term that is so conveniently used in such uncomfortable circumstances—a trauma.

2

CIVILIZATION AND AFRICA

In his answer to Jules Ferry's speech of 28 July 1885 which had defined explicitly the rights of civilized people to rule the world, the Radical leader Georges Clemenceau outlined equally clearly the anticolonial position:[1]

Superior races! Inferior races! That's easily said! As for myself I am not so proud since I have seen German scholars demonstrate scientifically that France had to be defeated in the Franco-German war because the French are a race inferior to the Germans. Ever since then, I think twice before looking at someone and at a civilization and state: inferior man or civilization . . . Consider the history of the conquest of these people you call barbaric, and you will see violence, all the crimes unleashed, oppression, and rivers of blood, and the weak oppressed and under the yoke of the victors. Here is the history of our civilization . . . I say nothing of the vices Europeans bring with them: of the alcohol, the opium they spread around . . . No there is no right for so-called superior nations against that of inferior races; there is a struggle for life which is a fatal necessity that we must constrain within the boundaries of justice and laws, as we rise in civilization; but let us not dress up violence in the hypocritical guise of civilization; do not talk of rights and duties![2]

He also touched on deep anxieties as to the meanings of the word 'civilization' which was so crucial in the justifying of the colonial enterprise.

By the end of the nineteenth century, amongst much gloating about unprecedented technological progress, there was a concern about what being civilized meant. The central justification of French imperialism and the least contested part of it was 'the civilizing mission', akin to the 'White Man's Burden' versified by Kipling on the occasion of the American invasion of the Philippines.[3] The central ideal of the civilizing mission was that a duty to elevate morally, and to educate, befell on the superior civilization of Europe. More than any other country in the world, the French believed themselves to be the guardians and promoters of a civilizing process. Their civilization was, in their own eyes at least, 'the' civilization. Yet for pessimists like Clemenceau, civilization was but a veneer, an insubstantial layer glued onto the surface, easily scratched, dented, or peeled. As the historian Christopher Forth has argued, few countries have justified themselves as the land of civilization in the manner the French have.[4] If the Voulet–Chanoine story stood for one thing in 1899, it was to show how fragile these ideas were and how weak men could be in an environment where the social bind could loosen.

Prior to any structured notion of the unconscious, such as Sigmund Freud's, ideas of unconscious forces abounded in France. When in the 1880s the psychiatrist Jean-Martin Charcot attributed hysteria to the obscure workings of the unknowable mind responding to forgotten trauma,[5] the dark recesses of the psyche became a more alien land than Africa could ever be. Another Frenchman, the sociologist and amateur psychologist Gustave Le Bon who later published the works of the survivor of the Klobb mission, Octave Meynier, had written extensively on the psychology of the crowd. Some of this was less science than political commentary. It notably reflected on the recent political turmoil of the young republic. In the 1880s France had been shaken by the threat of a populist coup led by the gallant but inept General Boulanger.[6] This rise of apparently irrational politics had motivated this reflection on how strong leaders could use irrational forces in a group. In LeBon's analysis, a chief appeared as troubled and deluded as the crowd behind him:

The chief is often nothing more than a ringleader or agitator, but as such he plays a considerable part. His will is the nucleus around which the opinions of the crowd are grouped and attain to identity. He constitutes the first element towards the organization of heterogeneous crowds, and paves the way for their organization in sects; in the meantime he directs them. A crowd is a servile flock that is incapable of ever doing without a master. The leader has most often started as one of the led. He has himself been hypnotized by the idea, whose apostle he has since become. It has taken possession of him to such a degree that everything outside it vanishes, and that every contrary opinion appears to him an error or a superstition.[7]

The idea that a chief might not be in control would be deeply disturbing to the military whose entire ethos rested on the idealization of what a chief should be. The fear of the crowd and the fear of losing oneself in such a mass were two sides of the same coin. In 1898 the fear of a military coup had dissipated and a fresh attempt in March 1899 led by an ultranationalist, Paul Déroulède, ended in farce. But other anxieties had replaced that fear. The 1890s had been the decade of terrorist acts, of the so-called 'propaganda by the deed', namely anarchist murders and bombs. In the factories and in the workplace, radicalized trade unionism and socialist movements raised their heads again after nearly twenty years of relative silence. The Commune of Paris, allegedly one the most significant 'socialist' revolutions ever, had been crushed in May 1871. The generals who had led the conquest of Paris had become the political leaders of the new republican army and its ministers of war. General Gallifet who succeeded Jules Chanoine had been, like him, in the armies that had massacred up to twenty thousand Parisians in one week of May 1871.[8] For the men of 1871 and their sons (Julien Chanoine was born in 1870), the meaning of civilization was not fixed. It was a struggle against the enemies within—the forces of the vulgar masses—as well as the enemies without—the undistinguishable others encountered in the colonial world.

The main fact was that if France was a civilization or even the civilizing model, that model was threatened and seemed difficult to defend against rising tides of foes. Furthermore French racial attributes seemed to be waning. Pessimists attributed the defeat of 1870 to the lack of education of the French masses against their German counterparts. Alarming signs abounded, and the period following 1870 witnessed the smallest increase of population in Europe.[9] Barren and weak, the nation seemed divided and going through a genuine crisis of confidence.

Only the colonial empire seemed to open new avenues and the possibility of renewal. Yet that empire was also fundamentally as threatening to the colonist as it was potentially enriching to the nation. The gap between individual experiences and the national expectation jarred most blatantly when the colonists eventually landed in the bleak outposts of empire. Their individual reputation was also at stake. Colonists were famed for sloppiness and an indecorous attitude. Colonial service had long been the reserve of adventurous men who had left behind a misspent youth, and the Parisian imperialists found it difficult to find volunteers of the right calibre whose aspirations might be as lofty as theirs. Voulet and Chanoine seemed to fit this demanding role. Yet by 1899, the two men were vilified, accused of barbarity, and stood as the opposite of whatever mission the French claimed to incarnate in Africa. What had gone wrong?

It was madness: the insanity of Africa or 'Africanitis' as the *Pall Mall Gazette* labelled it, which the friends, associates, colleagues, and even enemies of Voulet and Chanoine blamed for the disaster.[10] Their madness was to have a more precise name, Soudanitis. In many ways this myth has stuck to the legend of Voulet and Chanoine. Yet from a medical viewpoint Soudanitis was not a disease, but a term invented for the purpose of explaining the social tensions dividing the French colonists. As the first female French visitor to Soudan, Raymonde Bonnetain, expressed it:

> The soldiers call Soudanitis a disease which consists of avenging oneself of ennui by being malicious, impatient, quarrelsome. Every year—it is forbidden to duel on the front—comrades, divided by this so-called Soudanitis, take the boat back ready to cut each other's throat on their return to France. Sea air and the joy of coming back cure them. When they arrive in Bordeaux and have their last common meal the enemies have forgotten to meet on the field! One could think that this is specific to the officers. Not at all. Not only are civilians equally prone to it but even simple privates! The Captain commanding the cercle of Bakel[11] told me that in his fort he had seven soldiers from various arms and occupying different roles and that these seven men who were close friends to begin with had ended up living separately and not communicating except in service. 'Yes Madam, they were cooking seven separate meals eaten at seven separate tables!'...I am not far from thinking that Soudanitis reigns in Kayes, and once again, I can explain it without excusing it: 'We are bored!'[12]

In its first recorded form Soudanitis referred to social divisions and bickering, the jealousy and petty squabbles of an isolated society. For others, like the official who published his denunciation of the Soudan administration under the pseudonym Jean Rode in *La Revue Blanche*, Soudanitis was the product of a specific promotion-obsessed and hysterically violent military culture.[13] A few years later, the 'disease' reappeared, in the light of the Voulet–Chanoine affair, but in a radically worsened guise affecting men of all ranks:

> Fever, dysentery, anaemia; for them, absinth and deadly spirits, the despair of interminable isolation, agony or the disorder of the senses and brain. They are not obsessed with rank like their officers; they are not savages like their indigenous comrades; but the excess of suffering and the feeling that so much pain heroically withstood are of no use to the motherland fill them with a dark anger. They grow accustomed to slaughter. Human life loses its worth in their eyes.[14]

The maverick anarchist journalist of *L'Aurore*, Urbain Gohier, a notorious anti-militarist, anti-Semite, and somewhat oddly, also a partisan of Alfred Dreyfus, then added that this colonial disease was exploited to repress the workers, as in the massacre of striking miners in Fourmies a few years earlier.[15]

This medical explanation for the violence of working-class men employed by the army was used, in very similar form, to explain the crimes of their superiors. The *folie des galons*, a mad rush for premature promotion, was added to the other sensual and physical alterations caused by life in the colonial desolate lands. This anxiety had deep roots. Such was the fear of loss of energy and vitality in mid- to late-nineteenth-century France. It built on ideas of nostalgia, on the well-known depressive apathy of the colonial soldier, nicknamed the *Biskrite, Saharite, coup de bamboo*, and on that of deadly climate portrayed consistently by many colonial doctors.[16]

Since the early nineteenth century at least, nostalgia had been regarded as a disease that killed men in uniform away from their homes. Nostalgia had been an ailment rife during the Napoleonic wars but which increasingly lost its medical credibility, as a serious psychiatric disease. As Lisa O'Sullivan has shown, its heyday for France was in the earlier part of the nineteenth century. Then, the disease would rapidly kill men away from home. It was affecting especially the most provincial men whose home was a village or a small town. The only known cure was repatriation. Even the medical notion of nostalgia was grounded in this French provincial experience. While the disease has been described as a disease of memory, it was really one that focused on space and especially on the desire to return, to travel back, or even, in some cases to discover the real *pays*. The emphasis on *pays* (close here in meaning to a sort of domestic home) made it a disease of the motherland narrowly defined akin to what we might term extreme morbid homesickness.[17]

If the prognosis seems to have disappeared in France by the 1880s, it remained in the colonial setting. Even much later in the twentieth century, the idea that nostalgia might prove lethal remained common in medical reports coming from the empire. Powerless at healing the colonists, French doctors attempted to define who should be allowed to go. Reynaud, a retired chief medical officer of the French colonial medical corps, identified entire categories of unsuitable colonists: 'Obese, too sanguine or lymphatic with a white skin, neurotic and effeminate men are the least suitable for colonization. They are predisposed, some to heat strokes, to pernicious attacks, others to anaemia and nostalgia.'[18] Beyond the references to hot and cold humours, by then a genuinely antiquated way of thinking about the human body, the emphasis was on the general adequacy of constitution to the environment and to the holistic appraisal of the colonist's body. The emphasis of the colonial hygienic advice books was relentlessly moralistic and emphasized the need for the colonists to behave well in all aspects of their lifestyle. Reynaud built on his considerable experience to paint a bleak picture of the colonizer's body. The inability of Scandinavians, Belgians, and Spaniards to withstand the climate of Congo led him to justify the all-embracing category of European as opposed to 'coloured' and to describe the former as unsuited to any arduous task in the tropics.

In the colonial context the idea of nostalgia remained also pinned down to a village or a region and authors took great pains to distinguish patriotism from nostalgia. One was lofty and conceptual while the other remained grounded in childish experiences, tastes, and flavours, magnified by distance into a dream world of comforting images. Often blamed on emotional immaturity, the disease was deemed to be most prevalent among peasant soldiers originating from 'backward' areas of the country such as Brittany, the Basque Country, Corsica, and Savoy. Some medical authors censoriously claimed that the soldiers were unable to see the broader picture and to turn their childish love for the play things of the past into a healthier and more abstract love for the nation.[19] Doctors persistently denounced the immaturity implicit in nostalgia and emphasized that the colonist's complex relationship to the nation had to transcend the *petit pays* to emphasize the *grand pays*.[20] Both were remote yet one was a concept a patriotic Frenchman would never be without, which combined with other values such as civilization, civility, and hygiene, while the other was the petty residue of youth.

Even in 1931, while France celebrated its colonial empire at the major exhibition of Vincennes, Dr Gustave Martin still identified the colonist community as being largely composed of *débiles* and if he refused explicitly to focus on nostalgia as a simple explanation for mental illness in the colonies it was because he perceived this category as easily broken down into five new ones including lunatic (*cyclothymique*), hyperemotive, pervert, mythomaniac, and paranoiac.[21] These were not healthy climes for either mental or physical hygiene.

The irony of Soudanitis as a variant form of nostalgia, however, was that it seemed to apply to highly educated young and vigorous men, the sort of individuals apparently immune to the original ailment. Officers were not meant to be childish creatures longing for their mother or their home. Other factors were called upon to explain their vulnerability.

Diet and abuses of every kind were evoked. Observers opposed an ideal, monk-like, role model to a reality of indulgence. They also criticized the nature and forms of colonial diets. Among the main causes of Soudanitis, they identified the high consumption of meat and alcohol. Banquets and social occasions were not seen as the cure for the dreaded isolation of frontier soldiers; they were another form of danger that compounded the risks. In their often read but little observed diet and hygiene manuals, doctors advised moderation and sobriety in every aspect of life and they attempted to make the military administration responsible for the mental health of soldiers.[22]

The recommended narrow diet taken in small quantities would avoid parasite-infected meats and feverish spices, and favour wine over spirits and colonial beers such as the Dutch or English Pale Ales. Doctors always reiterated the fear that alcohol could provide solace in an alien environment and might strike equally the 'head that leads and the arms that execute'. Helplessly, they stressed the direct correlation between isolation and alcohol consumption: 'the further a man is from civilization, the more drunkenness becomes a sort of fury'.[23] Yet even when the colonist was at the heart of the liveliest community, the same medical experts denounced the alcohol-fuelled social encounters at the *cercle* and the cult of the *apéritif* taking place in these masculine environments. Thirty years after the

Voulet–Chanoine affair, when climatic ideas had become less fashionable, doctors no longer hesitated to blame all forms of Soudanitis on alcohol abuse.[24]

All the evidence shows that the advice of doctors was unheeded in the daily boredom of colonial life:

> After a few months in the colony [he] has become so apathetic and his organism has become so weak to the point that he only leaves his home with difficulty to find some exercise in and enjoy the short lived cool air of the morning or evening . . . he does not find any aim, any meeting, any distraction and he is soon back to his home to spend hours in his hammock smoking tobacco and drinking.[25]

This increased passivity fitted with contemporary ideas of neurasthenia or Beard's disease, a disease of civilization which so weakened the nervous system that its victims were left utterly despondent and demoralized. In his memoirs Joalland portrayed Voulet as a neurasthenic. The symptoms of the disease were primarily found in cities inhabited by overexposed decadents such as the hero of Joris-Karl Huysmans' 1884 novel *Against Nature*. Yet the slow-moving colonial environment and in particular sub-Saharan Africa seemed to generate similar enfeeblement.[26]

Three hundred years after the first settlement, the colonial landscape devoid of a large settler community failed to thrive and generate the entertainment or activities necessary to be a gentleman. Ultimately the blood itself would, it seemed, lose its ability to store oxygen. Asphyxiating slowly, anaemic Western men and their beasts of burden would decay at the same rate in the sub-Saharan colonies.[27] Of course these were the symptoms of malaria, known since 1880 to be caused by a parasite carried by mosquitoes, but the discovery of the cause of the disease did not alter the way people thought about it. In the same way today people still believe one can catch a cold from being cold even though they are aware of the existence of viruses. Colonial medicine presented a contradictory message mixing the latest technological research in laboratories with many archaic views on the tropical world.[28]

To talk of a tropical condition was a way of hiding away what was new or the result of colonial action itself. The scourge of colonial rule, sleeping sickness, was made a wider problem by colonial practices which created an environment in which the Tse Tse flies could thrive;[29] many of the sufferings of the colonized and the colonizers alike took place because of what men did and what they chose not to do. In essence, much of the contemporary medical advice merely highlighted how individuals and their sense of self might change in another world—away from the civilizing influences of family and home.

Some of the products most reminiscent of home proved to be pernicious. If alcohol remained the staple drink it was because it made some sense in a world where invisible leeches, not to mention the endless list of unmentionable microscopic beings, contaminated drinking water. Without a cumbersome filtering processing plant, the colonist was dependent on the supply line and could only trust sealed containers of food or liquid such as bottled alcohol.[30] Thanks to the bureaucracy and the receipts Voulet had to produce, accurate details remain of what food was packed for their journey after they had left France. Beyond what they might have bought or confiscated along the way, the soldiers could rely on standard ration packs set up for colonial expeditions by a specialized supplier. Each box, weighing 25 kg, contained an impressive range of tins of vegetables (peas, beans, carrots), confits, *choucroute*, foie gras, preserved meat, Lyons sausage, sardines, herrings, tuna, two tins of cooked tripe, 2 tins of onion soup, preserved butter, lard, jam, condensed milk, pasta, sugar, dried fruits, 2 flasks of Worcestershire sauce, mustard, spices, and curry powder. The Worcestershire sauce was extra to the normal ration boxes and was sometimes in addition to Yorkshire relish.[31] The mission also carried Maigneu asbestos water filters.

To eat a *choucroute garnie* when it was 40°C in the shade would in itself be quite a challenge, but each pack represented a condensed and tinned version of bourgeois French cuisine. All in all the food contributed substantially to the thirty tons of luggage the mission had to carry.[32] Wine was also included in the luggage. The boxes were attached to the carriage of Dr Henric and included a selection of fine wines, 40 bottles of Listrac Medoc, 40 bottles of Saint Estèphe, 40 bottles of Bordeaux superior, 60 bottles of rum, 120 bottles of champagne, 20 bottles of 60 per cent absinthe, 5 bottles of chartreuse, 5 bottles of marc, and 30 bottles of champagne brandy. We do not know whether the champagne came from Julien Chanoine's family production of Chanoine Champagne. In total there were 240 bottles of wine and 120 bottles of spirits for the nine officers and NCOs of the mission, or about 13 bottles of spirit and 26 bottles of wine each for a journey then estimated at 180 days. If the quality was good, the quantities were relatively modest in relation to average alcohol consumption in France.[33] The archival records only mention drinking (champagne) once, on 14 July 1899, the day Klobb was murdered. Alcohol abuse by itself does not explain the behaviour of the members of the Voulet–Chanoine mission.

In the colonial custom much of this wine was intended for medicinal use to help in the recovery from fever or to cure the many problems created by inadequate food. Wine might help the anaemic. Adding alcohol might clean water and prevent dysentery.[34] The receipts for homebrewing using local products ensured that ersatz wine could be produced in every colonial circumstance while local brews such as *Dolo*, a millet beer, also found their use.[35]

Yet if in mainland France the rule of hygiene for soldiers which included washing, good behaviour, good diet, and good morality remained predominantly an ideal usually undermined by complex problems and sometimes local politics, in the colonial world the punishment of the unhygienic was swift.[36] All commentators concurred on the imbalance of tropical life and its dangers. As the professor of hygiene at the medical school of Bordeaux where navy doctors often studied put it: 'White race colonists from Europe transplanted to tropical countries are set to live there in an eminently unstable physiological environment which will become precarious.'[37]

Apart from general advice, usually involving a multitude of layers of flannel, ventilated cork hats, filters, long trousers, and vests, medicine had little to offer the natives or the expatriates.[38] The flannel underwear the colonials wore was meant to absorb sweat and protect the men from colds and fevers, the red belt around the stomach was meant to end colic and poor digestion.[39] In effect these measures were seldom practical. Alphonse Daudet's *Tartarin de Tarascon*, published in 1872, pictured a provincial buffoon seeking adventures in the colonial empire and who, alone it seems, took all medical advice seriously. Tartarin ended up looking like a prototype of the Michelin man, sweating profusely before returning home with his baobab tree in a pot. The dangers that welcomed Tartarin in North Africa were not that dissimilar from those of other much closer malarial environments, such as the Camargue a mere 96 km from Tarascon. Unlike the Camargue, however, Soudan had more dangerous illnesses such as yellow fever and in particular the very dramatic bilious hematuric fever which killed most of its victims in a matter of hours. Dark blood-stained urine usually signalled its onset to victims who continued to perceive it as resulting from imprudent acts such as swimming late at night in the River Niger.[40] Soudan was statistically the worst colony of the whole French empire when it came to health.[41]

For many who had lived in sub-Saharan Africa the continent was the opposite of civilization. Worse even it was an environment corrosive of men and their moral values. Reversals of hierarchies abounded: native soldiers were allegedly immune to the fevers enfeebling the French soldiers, including nostalgia and Soudanitis. African soldiers could carry burdens that would kill the supposedly racially superior Frenchmen.

The debates on the influence of climate on the colonizers raged in colonial circles. There were real anxieties on the dangers of life in the tropics and the pernicious influence of climate on civilization. These were the lands of ancient plagues which might return to France.

Never was the colonial enterprise perceived to be one of unilateral trades or of simple acts of subordination. Some thirty years earlier, Saint-Vel had envisaged the exchanges of population involved in the colonial enterprise as a trade-off whereby the colonist and the West Indian Creole could exchange environments, at much greater risks for the former.[42] The 'purer' their race, the weaker the men in the tropics. In the colonies, notions of milieu and climate borrowed heavily from the classics and ancient wisdom and were used in new scientific ways.[43] Winds were often bearing illnesses; the mist could be the 'shroud of Europeans'.[44] The air they breathed a poisonous 'miasmatic' brew, fermenting illnesses that fed on the living; the soil itself seemed to be slowly releasing its poisons. This climate seemed to act in opposition to the 'civilizing forces' of colonization.

Some Europeans resisted better than others, some died quickly, and some lived for years. To explain these discrepancies doctors used the notion of *terrain favorable, d'élection* (predisposition). This analysis of differences in physical and moral aspects dominated all discussions of the colonists' bodies. Yet these ideas were often useless when applied to the colonized: the people of such or such a land were attributed moral and physical qualities denied to another group. Yet, this racial classification of inequality among the subordinates was constantly proven wrong when displaced African or Asian workers or soldiers failed to adapt from one site to another.[45]

Ultimately the essential question related to the unique suitability of the human body to its original environment and the difficulty of successfully transplanting temperate beings to hot climates. This climatic discourse, complete with its political associations dating from Montesquieu whereby moderate climates produced moderate nations and extreme climates made equally violent societies, was directly contradictory to any hope of racial expansion throughout the empire. In this context and until more positive medical textbooks were issued from the colonialist 'party', the medical outlook on colonization remained gloomy throughout the nineteenth century and cautious after 1918. All the more so since much of this writing, like Berenger Ferraud's key textbook, was the product of disillusioned naval surgeons, many of whom wrote of their experiences after they had been pensioned off for ill-health.[46] As the Ministère de la Marine remained in charge of the colonies until 1893, these naval surgeons shaped the discourse on hygiene in the colonies by relating how men might lose their minds and their grip on civilized mores under the tropical sun.

Jean-Baptiste Fonssagrives was such a man, whom, from being a surgeon on board a ship, became a doctor and teacher first at the École navale de médecine in Brest before moving to the chair of hygiene in Montpellier in 1864.[47] His work on colonial medicine and hygiene remained quoted until the 1890s.[48] It was his book that foresaw the dementia of isolated transplanted men. Many dreaded the influence of African people and climate on the colonists. Tales of immorality and early deaths dominated the literature devoted to these territories, some of which, like Saint-Louis du Senegal, were regarded as fully French and returned deputies to the French parliament.[49]

The man who most forcefully denounced Voulet and Chanoine was also a medical doctor, Paul Vigné d'Octon. He developed and kept alive the Voulet–Chanoine affair by bringing it to parliament and publishing a 'factual' denunciation of colonial crimes in 1899 and 1900. But his interest in the story came from his own colonial experience. Vigné d'Octon had long been one of the outspoken critics on the dangers of Africa. He had previously written a major bestseller entitled *Soudan, Dahomey, Land of Death*. His other writings were thinly veiled autobiographical accounts of sexual gratification and moral perdition in the colonies. In his notorious and commercially successful neo-realist novel *Black Flesh* (*Chair noire*) of 1889, Vigné d'Octon portrays native women as destructive, by their very nature, of civilized men's grasp over their own sanity. He denounced the common practice of taking, by force or bribe, a wife *à la mode du pays* whose children constituted a mixed race of indeterminate status.[50]

Racial Darwinism was a common thread in Vigné d'Octon's work and it linked directly to his own medical perspective.[51] Using currently available psychiatric lore, he emphasized the racial danger of colonial miscegenation and outlined the importance of sex, using dream sequences to explore the unconscious in a manner that prefigured his later readings of Sigmund Freud in the 1910s.[52] Vigné d'Octon was then a political journalist at the daily *L'Aurore*, which became one of France's leading newspapers during the Dreyfus affair. With Clemenceau and Gohier, he developed an original critique of colonialism that bridged

Social Darwinism, scientific racism, and psychiatric theory.[53] Vigné d'Octon was undoubtedly racist and anticolonialist. His Darwinism was a bleak affair which recognized sexuality as the key to understanding social interaction between the races in the colonies. Throughout his work the emphasis was on sex and death, on seductive feral sexual gratification in Africa, and on the dangers it presented to the mind of the colonists. His heroes thus die tragically while recalling the women they have left at home and betrayed in the sweaty trap of provincial African outposts. Inspired by the psychological novels of Paul Bourget and of the naturalism of his friend Émile Zola, Vigné d'Octon never shied away from finding a psychological causation and a sexual origin to crimes of violence.[54] Vigné d'Octon is now most famous for his denunciation of exploitation in colonial Tunisia, published under the title *La Sueur du Burnou* in 1911, which is still in print. His rustic peasant love stories, such as *Les Amours de Nine* (1893), are also still in print no doubt for their quaint folkloric qualities. In 2000 his name became linked with a prize awarded by the Académie des Sciences Morales et Politiques to medical writers addressing humanistic issues.

Paul Vigné d'Octon like Urbain Gohier was close to and had even briefly followed the classes of the most famous psychiatrist of the day, Charcot.[55] Like Clemenceau, Vigné d'Octon was a medical man with a political career.[56] All this influenced the way he wrote. The most topical research in psychiatric disorders fed his descriptions of colonial life.[57] The sadism he complacently described associated the excesses of power and decay with an African sojourn:

> Sitting on his reclining wicker chair, he was contemplating with a lubricous gaze the torture he had ordered for a peccadillo. Every time the whip took away a strip of skin, he juddered on his seat, his yellow

bilious eyes were shining and his lips were twisted by the sad smile of his erotic madness.[58]

Vigné d'Octon had had some experience of Africa, as a medical doctor in the navy and his experience was unequivocally negative. He blamed the army and the politicians for colluding in a compromised enterprise. In his eyes the colonial troops were sacrificed to the ambition of a handful of men, while the nobler aspirations of colonialism were contradicted by the violence of colonial rule. In his writings there is little evidence of the generous belief in the equality of all men found in Clemenceau. Vigné d'Octon believed in the inequality of races, but seriously doubted that colonialism would bring up the inferior races—in fact, he feared that the reverse might be true. Unlike most anticolonial movements that arose in the immediate aftermath of the First World War, which were more often inspired by socialist ideals, the pre-war anticolonialists were often motivated by racial ideas on degeneracy and the fear of racial mixing.[59] Furthermore they were generally suspicious of the political aims of imperialists. They saw the empire as a diversion from the real issues dividing France.[60] Thus Georges Clemenceau, who edited the newspaper *L'Aurore* which published Vigné's articles on a regular basis from 1897 onwards, denounced imperialism as a betrayal of social progress and as inhumane for the colonizers. His main object was to condemn the colonizers rather than empathize with the victims of colonization.[61] The enterprise seemed worthless, a mere diversion from the national reconstruction needed to face closer enemies and, at worse, it degraded the Frenchmen undertaking it to the ranks of the native people themselves. The anticolonialists also grounded their opposition to imperialism in their disdain for Africa. They could not see what the Africans or their land could offer civilization.[62] More moderate forces such as the small 'committee for the protection and defence of indigenous people' similarly denounced not colonialism but the abuse of power that took place in the judicial vacuum of frontier territories. Their motto, 'humanity, civilization', presupposed that French civilization owed it to itself to be magnanimous in conquest and in the way it managed its empire.[63]

At the other end of the spectrum of opinions there were many utopian voices extolling the civilizing mission of France in Africa and its ability to bring progress to a land that civilization had allegedly forgotten. Despite the alleged anticolonial feelings of the French public, the dominant political message was covered enthusiastically by a vocal press and imperialist lobby. They cited the crucial role of the French army in its struggle against feudal regimes allegedly practising cannibalism and slavery as exemplified in the kingdom of Dahomey defeated in 1898. They stressed heroic masculinity and they monopolized the booming 'adventure' narrative industry which published successful popular stories such as *Journal des voyages et des aventures*. The colonial entrepreneurs were closely connected to the hack writers on these sheets and from the depth of their missions provided detailed accounts and illustrations of their hunting, colonizing, and warring exploits.

The result was a kaleidoscopic conflation of images from all continents, a moveable feast which alternated sober travel accounts with tense hunting stories or exhilarating battle accounts. Even though historians tend to agree that the power of images and films became really crucial in a late phase of the empire, so that the empire had its largest imperialist constituency just as it was unravelling,[64] these images and stories appeared in considerable numbers well before and crucially targeted the young reading public. In these stories there were no sustained mentions of illnesses, neurosis, and self-destructive lasciviousness. The natives seemed to emerge indifferently from igloos, huts, or tents and, in their very sameness, they shared the common features of second-rate, primitive humanity. Many of the most ambitious colonial officers became authors themselves and followed the printing of their accounts with a series of conferences in various local societies across France. Some of these books became a major success and, while some authors, such as Loti, gradually established writing careers, most did not. They relied on professional writers to kick into shape their self-glorifying stories. The academician prefacing Monteil's book compared most of these books to 'the illegitimate children' of army officers in the custody of the pro-colonial lobby.[65]

The cavalier comment intimated a sort of incestuous relationship between colonial lobbies and officers which was reinforced by private friendships and patronage. These 'orphan' books were meant to inspire the next generation of colonial officers as well as provide clear information on the regions visited. Voulet and Chanoine were well versed in the colonial literature available and many books made it to Soudan in their cases. Highly censured and novelized, these books and articles conveyed a peculiarly heroic sense of war in the empire: that of the *épopée*, the epic story.[66] This fever was strongest in the final years of the nineteenth century when the empire was growing exponentially.

It was not only to be found in militaristic texts; the religious press also carried similar images. For instance the Catholic monthly devoted to missionary work offered similar visions of the world. Of course in these the emphasis was less on adventure than on 'worthy and uplifting' accounts of conversions; yet the magazine was also heavily illustrated and the French and foreign missionaries faced more than their fair share of danger. The year 1899 was the peak for French missionaries who, at the time, dominated the Catholic missionary renewal of the late nineteenth century. Between the penny dreadful and the self-righteous press of the nineteenth century, images of foreign places were constantly presented to an avid public as lands up for grabs and bereft of any enlightenment of their own. Despite this heady propaganda, historians have doubted the existence of a genuine popular imperialism until the empire had actually been made an economic and political reality for the man and woman in the street. One could query what was meant by popular imperialism.[67] Soudan was not 'popular' by any stretch of the imagination, not even among the colonialists; yet victory was popular and so was the anti-slavery cause which found so many rallies in civic halls or churches throughout the country. What the colonialists intended to deliver was, in the first instance, symbolic rather than material. Their conquests made sense on a globe or on the school maps of the world. Beyond getting school children of France another difficult spelling to master, 'Tombouctou' or 'Zinder', the Sahel part of the empire counted for little in itself.

It was nevertheless a battleground for a thorny and mythical issue which still resonates today: the 'conflict of civilizations'. In Soudan the French thought (wrongly) they faced either Muslim society or animist society, which they also called 'spiritualist', often described as heathens by the missionaries. The animists were portrayed as furthest from real civilization and were either despised or underestimated by the vast majority of French officers and administrators. The religion of the cities and that of the organized kingdoms related more closely to the North African experience and were already largely Islamic. The French had a very ambiguous attitude towards Islam. On the one hand Muslim Africa seemed less alien and some favoured the conversion of the animists to Islam. An Islamic society had features the French administrators thought themselves better equipped for. They thought they understood Islamic values, and, although generally despised, Islamic values seemed only slightly inferior to those of Western society. On the other hand many were fearful of the power of Muslim mobilization. The more knowledge was gathered about the nature of Islam in sub-Saharan Africa, the more complex a picture emerged and the scarier 'Islamism' seemed.

For Christians involved in the colonial project, such as the missionaries but also the officers close to them, 'Islamism' was the enemy. The phrase had been coined in Algeria in the 1860s. It referred to the combination of Islam and politics, and to a Western belief that in Islam social order could not be separated from fanatical dogma. To explain the divergent interpretations of Islam one must see that in Algeria as indeed in Sudan, Islam was complex and impenetrable to inexperienced Frenchmen. Susceptible to Mahdism and messianic revivalism as well as to the cult of the saints, African Islam was not one but rather a multitude of trends and movements which varied from the austere M'Zab of the oasis of the Sahara to Maleki Islam in Kabylia or to the widespread cult of saintly marabous.[68] Most worrying for French military observers such as Captain Rinn were the secret societies and Sufi revivalism which occasionally appeared in response to French colonization.[69] The greatest opponents of French colonization had also been great religious leaders like Sheikh Abd' El-Kadir's Qadiriyya Sufi religious state.[70] In sub-Saharan Africa, Islam had also been the enemy of French influence.

All the major political organizations arising in the nineteenth century were led by Islamic leaders who claimed to impose Islamic rule and used freely the language of jihad. Jihad is obviously well known to early-twenty-first-century readers since the term has become associated with the terrorist movements in North Africa and the Middle East over the past twenty years. It is a complex aspect of Muslim theology since it refers both to an armed struggle against the unbelievers and to a spiritual struggle against unbelief—one can morph into open warfare while the other invites meditation and spiritual renewal.

In Soudan the great Toucouleur regimes of El-Hajj Umar Tall and his son Ahmadu or that of Samory Touré had been defined by their desire to convert animist people to Islam, restore true Islam in allegedly Muslim states, and by their opposition to the French, Christian, invasion. In his advice book for colonial officers, Parfait-Louis Monteil who had first travelled the journey taken by Voulet and Chanoine described the situation of Islam in West Africa in the following terms:

> Islamism, wherever it has settled, and in particular in Senegal, has always been fighting European Civilization; the progress of civilization was always limited by the narrow minded religion of Mahomet, when progress was not stopped altogether. It is to Islam alone, far more than climate that we must attribute the little progress in our settlements of our ideals of liberty and civilization.[71]

Not every colonial officer took this simplistic viewpoint and later on as the French state became increasingly opposed to the Catholic Church, missionaries complained that Islam was favoured by colonial administrators. Starting from similar premises Colonel de Trentinian argued in the 1890s for an in-depth exploration of the power of religion:

> In the shadows and in secret, Muslim congregations are holding the threads of the Muslim world from Indonesia to Morocco. Mystics are claiming to be the holders of a share of divinity and exploit marvellously the messianic ideas and Mahdism which are at the same time the dominant symbols of Islamism and the origin of struggle to the last against anyone who is not Muslim. These men personify the strength of religion, the only one able to raise the masses and oppose some

difficulties to the European powers that do not know or cannot use it to favour their expansion.

De Trentinian in Soudan argued that this force was potentially one that the colonial government could harness and control: 'these men who direct religious congregations—ensure you get their sympathy and when needed use them for the benefit of the civilizing mission and of the Muslim power that we are.'[72]

De Trentinian was not alone in taking a 'native' viewpoint and in arguing that the French empire was indeed very largely a Muslim empire, expanding thanks to Muslim soldiers in often animist territory. De Trentinian argued from the point of view of the imperial power that Islam could serve France effectively and that, should it be alienated, Islam had the potential of being France's worst enemy. From a military point of view, though, Islam was perceived as presenting more of a threat than traditional African states which were all either too small or too weak to put up serious resistance.

The Voulet–Chanoine expedition must be read in this ambiguous cultural context which combined bullish missionary imperialism and doubts on the suitability of Europeans to survive in Africa, or to vanquish fanatical opponents. As the following chapters will show the leaders of the mission were apprehensive at, and hostile to, the societies they encountered. They were acutely aware of the physical risk they were taking. The dangers of living in Soudan were not all imaginary or psychological. Tangible medical evidence had also accumulated. Other tropical wars had shown just how real the risk was. During the Madagascar campaign of 1895, which Vigné d'Octon denounced in parliament on medical grounds,[73] disastrous fever and dysentery epidemics resulted in nearly 6,000 casualties out of an expeditionary force of 15,000. This was a public scandal, which was followed by numerous accounts of abuse of power. Vigné d'Octon denounced these abuse and began a life-long campaign against General Gallieni who governed the island.[74] Gallieni was of course a veteran of Soudan.

If some of these debates on degeneracy, empire building, and race were largely theoretical, they nevertheless impacted and reflected some truth of life on the ground. If Soudan was the place where careers were made or sunk it was because it was one of the most dangerous postings in the empire. Of all French colonies, new and old, Soudan had the highest mortality rate of soldiers with 107 deaths per thousand each year, compared to only 28.6 in nearby Senegal or, in the more salubrious colonies, 2.8 per thousand in Tahiti.[75] It had even more dangerous a climate than Madagascar. This high mortality explained the increased use of native soldiers and the very small proportion of white men in the Voulet–Chanoine expedition. Part of this was based on cost, as a French soldier represented an investment four times higher than a soldier from Indochina, who was himself more expensive than an African soldier—the empire had to be conquered by colonial subjects themselves. When Frenchmen had to be sent, the colonizing soldiers had to be young, 25 to 35, vigorous, sober, and self-disciplined.[76] Medical men were arguing that 'it is not enough to live wisely to live well in the colonies. The greatest caution, the most sober existence did not preserve Europeans from malaria.'[77] This emphasis on fitness rather than experience explained the relative youth of Voulet and Chanoine, 33 and 29 respectively, and their level of excessive responsibilities compared with what they could have obtained in mainland France.

The anxiety over disease haunted the leaders of the mission. Chanoine paid particular attention to his own health and also that of his white officers: 'Keep an eye on Laury, his cattle herd has not drunk properly yesterday even though he denies it, he is letting himself go from the point of view of hygiene and health.'[78] We have few medical reports from the Voulet–Chanoine mission but on 19 July 1899, after the killings of mid-July, Dr Henric, the mission's doctor, evaluated the health of the survivors starkly in his report to Pallier:

Joalland and Meynier are anaemic, Bouthel is suffering from severe recurrent fevers, Tourot alone is remarkably well, Laury is in deplorable condition suffering from deep anaemia, fevers and diarrhoea.

Henric from March 1899 had suffered from hematuric or 'bilious' fever and from April was crippled by rheumatism.[79] Yet in the medical reports of the mission there is one startling omission. Even in his report to the higher authorities, of August 1899, when all the survivors attempted to explain the events and justify the part they had played, Henric never explained Voulet's crime as anything other than treason. Dr Henric did not raise mention of the insanity other commentators wished to ascribe to Voulet.

3

PRIVATEERING FOR FRANCE

> There is no doubt that one day, if we do not let the opportunity pass and if we keep these two countries, the Sahara and the Soudan will become the most marvellously productive French colonies. No other, including Indo-China, will match it.[1]

The author of these lines, Paul Leroy-Beaulieu, was the most prominent economist of the pro-colonial lobby and the (unsuccessful) political rival of Paul Vigné d'Octon for the constituency of Clermont l'Hérault. In this highly fanciful dream of systematic development of the Sahara, apparently rich with untapped resources and water, he went as far as describing the River Niger as the French Nile.[2] To support his vision of potential wealth, he systematically exaggerated the writings of army officers and missionaries who were often equally enthusiastic about the lands they had conquered for the empire. Like many others he then used these assertions to campaign for the expansion of the new colonies. Unverifiable claims established an echoing circle of fancy which ran continuously between the colonial lobbyist and the soldiers, the conquerors and their Parisian backers. Not since the earliest periods of imperialism had colonial enterprise resembled so much a private limited company. In Leroy-Beaulieu's book there is no mention of either Voulet or Chanoine, and their mission is recorded under the names of Joalland–Meynier instead; yet they had been key participants in the creation of information until their downfall.

How did the French army expand and justify the empire? In the 1890s, when political support seemed uncertain the military reached out to civil society and financial lobbies for support and found it in abundance. It gave rise to a uniquely political generation of young officers like Voulet and Chanoine.

Like the great privateers of the seventeenth century, Voulet and Chanoine were propagandists—a role they perfected during a previous mission in Mosse territory. Voulet and Chanoine were often described as old Soudanese, as experienced men who knew well the land and its customs. Yet Soudan was so new that these old hands had less than 6 years of life in Africa between them. In the 'debilitating climate' of Africa this was thought considerable experience. They used their experience of African warfare—as opposed to the demoralizing administration of bush postings—to present themselves as representative of a new class of officers. Much has been said about the fact that the two men came from different social contexts. Voulet was a marine (*troupe de marine*, a unit of embarked infantry serving the navy); Chanoine was a cavalryman. The cavalry was an elite, socially superior group. Indeed Chanoine was the well born of the two. He was the son of a politically astute general. Voulet on the other hand had a more petty bourgeois pedigree as the son of a provincial doctor. His father had few claims to fame apart from a brief university acquaintance with the radical senator Émile Combes, who became premier (président du conseil) in 1902. On Chanoine's side was the inherited wealth of an old champagne dynasty, and overseas service. Chanoine's father had also been a colonial man and among his prestigious campaigns was the pillaging of Peking's Summer Palace in 1860 during the Second Opium War and the first French military collaboration with the Japanese armed forces in 1868.

That these men should meet in Soudan at this point in history was not by chance. Soudan had suddenly become very appealing to ambitious young officers. Until the 1870s, sub-Saharan Africa had been the preserve of the least qualified and most inept officers. The climate was regarded as deadly—as were the social interactions one might encounter. Since military salaries were always low relative to the rank they had to maintain in society—a colonial captain earned between 7,500 and 10,500 francs a year—officers sought to complement the meagre income with a good marriage. To be in an environment where there was no one to marry was a blight on one's prospects.[3] To live in the colonies did entail an increase of wages of about a third on metropolitan wages but everything was more expensive in Soudan.[4] Yet life there could be adventurous unlike that of an officer in France. By 1896 military life for the latter was mostly tedious, spent training and preparing for war. After 1889 sixty per cent of Frenchmen experienced military service as a process of militarization unseen since the Napoleonic era.[5] The French had been crushed in 1870 and ever since had had a lingering wish for revenge on Germany. Yet building forts and training in eastern France, looking after the border with the lands lost to Germany (Alsace and northern Lorraine) was hardly the sort of military career that justified joining a largely underpaid officer elite. In the barracks a culture of barely contained brutality prevailed. If preparations for the next European war seemed dull, life in most colonies was even more tedious as most of them were already subdued and out of the limelight. Only in Soudan was there a moving border, a universe in turmoil, which could be pushed and shaped by young officers. There was no money and hardly any political desire for it but there were opportunities for soldiers in a desperate search for heroism and 'grandeur'. When it came to social promotion the prestigious posts were either in the good cities of metropolitan France or in Algeria. Yet, for a soldier with naked ambition, the place to go was further south.

To understand the war in Soudan one must go back to the conquest of Algeria.[6] Algeria was not only the largest French colony at the time; it represented also the colonial past and present of the French military. Algeria had provided ample opportunities for social and financial promotion since the conquest of 1830. The army had run it as a fiefdom until the mid-1860s and it retained considerable prestige. It had been the African army of Algeria that had backed Louis-Napoleon in his 1851 coup; it was an ex-governor of Algeria, Marshal MacMahon, who became the first president of the new French republic after the military defeat of 1870 and the end of the French Second Empire. Indeed the defeat of 1870 could be attributed to the leadership of the Algerian-trained generals rather than to the hapless emperor of the French.

In the annual parades on July 14th, the soldiers the Parisians most liked to applaud and welcome were the *Turcos*, originally native troopers from Algeria. The Foreign Legion had been created in the 1830s to serve in Algeria and the legend of these fearless warriors has been growing ever since. But, from the late 1870s onwards, Algeria was no longer a land of opportunities. The Algerians had revolted en masse in 1871. The insurrection, led by an 'assimilated' Algerian nobleman, El-Mokrani, had developed into a jihad. Successful at first, the last great Algerian revolt of the nineteenth century was soon crushed by the French army. In the ensuing trial the republicans turned the tables and it was military rule that became accused of fomenting trouble. The political settlement that followed pushed the military south of the main inhabited zones.

In Algeria, the end of military rule meant a hardening of living conditions for the natives. In the early years of the republic the Algerians lost most of their very limited autonomy and much of their land.[7] The reprisals of 1871 were terrible. The chieftains were sent to New Caledonia in 1873, where, ironically, they became instrumental in repressing a Kanak insurrection in 1878.[8] As often in the empire, it was the fate of subjected people to become the agents of further conquests.

Only the land deemed to be the most insecure and worthless remained squarely in the hands of the army: the Sahara. Between the late 1870s and 1898 the French gradually conquered the Saharan lands now part of Algeria and Mauritania. These lands were obviously mostly empty but had played a primary role in African history. The lines of exchange crisscrossing the desert were the routes Islam had travelled during previous centuries.[9] Scholars, saints, and marauding bands roamed this allegedly empty land. On arriving in Timbuktu or Djenné, on the border of the great deserted areas, the French were astonished to find a rich scholarly Islamic culture.

Of all the colonial landscapes of the empire, the desert became the land of moral elevation and cultural shock. Ever since the painter Fromentin had brought back images of the Sahara soaked with light and accounts of his meditations, the desert had acquired a special spiritual quality for those French colonials with any imagination.[10] Yet, even when reading Fromentin's lofty account of the inspirational landscapes and life in the desert, one finds many traces of the extreme violence that had enabled him to stay in this hostile environment. Fromentin had arrived in the empty city of El Aghouat in 1852 whilst it was still reeking of putrefied flesh. The army was in the process of cleaning and occupying it, having massacred its people.[11] Later in the century, at a time when the Sahara was still being conquered, violent clashes occurred regularly. In particular the French found the nomadic people hostile and difficult to subdue. The Foureau–Lamy mission, which was sent in 1898 to meet Voulet–Chanoine and Gentil on Lake Chad, faced considerable difficulties along the way.[12]

In their attempt to control the desert, the French met nomads such as the Tuaregs by using units on camel backs that behaved like Tuaregs, dressed like them, and used the desert as they did: the famous Meharistes.[13] This process of imitation was an example of a consistent policy the French army had adopted since the first difficult days of the conquest of Algeria. Faced with irregular warfare, the French developed irregular warring units recruited among the allied tribes: Spahis and Goums. These soldiers enlisted for a short duration, served mostly near their own land, and were originally paid in plunder. These units were neither entirely trusted nor trustworthy. Yet the French increasingly relied on locally recruited troops.

When they did not, they developed a strategy based on extreme violence. The *colonnes mobiles* created in the 1840s by General Bugeaud in his war against the mystical Algerian leader Abd El'Kadir were mobile units apt to strike anywhere and whose military effectiveness was secondary to the trail of destruction they left. Inspired by the Napoleonic war in Spain where Bugeaud had fought in his youth, these *colonnes* were meant to be a deterrent. On their path the grass hardly grew, trees were cut, and crops burned. This strategy of laying waste to the land, traditionally used by people defending themselves against invaders, had been turned on its head by the invaders. The aim was to strike terror in order to reach a negotiated settlement. In Algeria as later in sub-Saharan Africa, the conquerors practised what they called *aman*, the forgiveness of past rebellion in exchange for compensation and alliance.

By the 1880s the *colonne* strategy had been refined into an art: 'they are small war operations which while executed by small contingents must comprise soldiers from the three arms (cavalry, artillery, and infantry). These expeditions of this kind have the aim to chastize the indigenes who, most of the time, have only limited means of action and defence compared with ours.' Basing his analysis on the muzzle-loaded rifles carried by the indigenous population, Monteil estimated the French soldiers had a 6:1 advantage in firepower. As weaponry developed this ratio of firepower increased further.[14] For the cavalry the ratio was 1 to 4 in 1880: the artillery often had nothing with which to make a comparison.

From their colonial experience in Algeria, the French military had developed a doctrine of violence first as a negotiating tactic. Of course Bugeaud and his subordinates, such as Pélissier, notorious for 'asphyxiating' thousands of Algerians hidden in caves, had been criticized. But judging from their careers, the controversies had not been that damaging. What Bugeaud's techniques of war meant was that conquest could be economically viable if brutality was applied. Originally extreme, the violence of the conquest in Algeria declined as the land became more closely controlled. The army then used bribes and patronage in equal measure to control the more violent tribes. French agents were placed among the tribes like little governors and information-gatherers. These isolated men often managed large territories and groups. This method was not foolproof, however. Every decade almost (in the 1860s, in 1871, in the desert until well after 1900), resistance movements came together and fought the occupier most often in the name of Islam.

Compared with Algeria, Soudan had been the poor military relative. Deep in Africa it seemed like the distant hinterland of Senegal. Senegal itself had only recently become more active as a colony. Originally composed of a few settlements trading in slaves and African products, the colony lost its *raison d'être* after the abolition of the slave trade, and slavery itself in 1848. The inhabitants of Senegal's four main colonial settlements, Rufisque, Saint-Louis, Gorée, and Dakar, had been electing a representative to France's parliament intermittently during the nineteenth century and more regularly since 1879. While only a minority of the inhabitants enjoyed all the rights of French citizens, the inhabitants 'originating' from these colonial sites as well as the tirailleurs were regarded as French.[15] Uniquely these outposts on the coast of Senegal were a part of France. However, Senegal was not a central part by any means, and its oldest settlements, Saint-Louis and Gorée, stagnated both economically and socially when they were overtaken by Dakar in the 1880s.

By the 1850s a hitherto poorly rated officer, Faidherbe, moved in as governor. Under his rule colonialism in sub-Saharan Africa acquired a life of its own. Originally threatened on its borders by the great African kingdom of El-Hajj Umar, the colony began to grow incrementally, often without any central government control. With the death of Umar and the division of his kingdom among his sons, the French were under less pressure and that political vacuum allowed them to grow.[16] Using 'border trouble' as an excuse the French army officers developed a policy of aggressive response which invariably pushed further into the hinterland. This was a classic case of flag-led colonialism whereby the settling of new borders in lands that previously had ignored the concept of international boundaries ensured a constant state of 'insecurity' and a need to endlessly 'pacify' territories. Even though 'pacify' remained the euphemism in fashion throughout the colonial era, and some might say to this day, Voulet accurately pointed out to the Ministry of Colonies: 'Should not one understand conquest by the word "pacification"?'[17]

By design and accident the hinterland was bound to grow incrementally but at a potentially disastrous cost to the French armies. The pioneer governor of Senegal, General Faidherbe, created a native army of Senegalese tirailleurs whose costs he could control and which became the war machine of the French in the region. The Senegalese soldiers were trained and paid by the French but they were far more than regular soldiers. Their wives and children were attached to the military camps. More than a straightforward army the tirailleurs were used as a way of managing the entire colonial society. It is clear that Faidherbe intended to create elites from the native soldier—usually on the basis of who had best resisted the invading army.[18] As in other empires the colonized became the agents of the colonizers, sometimes colonizing themselves.[19] Writing in 1901, immediately after the military colony of Soudan had been abrogated by decree, a year after Voulet and Chanoine had died, Lieutenant Gatelet set out to explain and justify French military rule in Soudan. He began, as in most other books devoted to the region, with a brief and shallow ethnological survey of its people addressed to the French lay and scientific public.[20] The Bambaras were brave and warlike, the Malinkes were artisans more than warriors, the Mandingues were cultivators, the Foulah were 'very intelligent but very proud', the various 'Berber' tribes, allegedly originating from North Africa or even Egypt, such as the Fulbes, Tuaregs, Songhai, and the Toucouleurs, belonged to a superior ethnic make-up that made them more civilized yet unreliable.[21] In Monteil's words:

> the Toucouleur is a Métis race resulting from the crossing of Pullo and Ouoloffs or the other black races that they took as captives. The Toucouleur has all the weaknesses of the Pullo and of the Ouoloff without any of their qualities: the boasting of the Ouoloff without his courage, the duplicity of the Pullo.[22]

In this fairly typical instance, the colonial author defines and discusses race as he would do animal husbandry and uses simple stereotypes, commenting on the essence of whatever ethnic group he chooses to define in his description.

To an extent the colonial officers created the categories they described and, by choosing their soldiers among one group rather than another, invented the martial races they believed existed since time immemorial. This process, which has been documented by historians in every colonial setting, has left its impression across the world since many post-colonial conflicts can be directly related to the colonial favouring of one group over another.[23]

Among this racial make-up the Bambaras were often singled out as exceptional soldiers even if the NCOs were often chosen from other ethnic groups. A pidgin of their language and French became the language of the Senegalese armies. Ultimately, as the historian Joe Lunn has shown, this empirical know-how became a quasi-science with positive reception given to Mangin's *La Force Noire*, which proposed in 1910, for the first time, to compensate for the French fall in population by using African soldiers against German armies.[24]

The Senegalese tirailleurs were thus not only from Senegal, but often originated from the ranks of the enemy, in particular from Samory's *sofas* or from whatever enslaved people could be enlisted on the spot. This makeshift and haphazard recruitment policy explains why Voulet's forces were so ethnically disparate. In a note he described his army as being composed of ten ethnic groups.

In that Babel of languages the Africans themselves more or less understood each other using pidgin Bambara-French as the lingua franca. For anything more complex the officers had to rely on interpreters who became their essential go-betweens. In the Voulet–Chanoine case these men were so closely associated with the two officers that they suffered the same fate. The main witnesses of the events, and the only ones who could have given Voulet's and Chanoine's versions of events, Voulet's translator Koulibali and Sidi Berete, Chanoine's translator, were both executed. Berete was killed by the tirailleurs but Koulibali was executed after a mock trial. In most accounts Berete and Koulibali were essential cogs in the mission's hierarchy. Closest to Voulet and Chanoine they often deputized for them and were even resented as privileged advisors to the two officers.

Indeed the haste with which these men were killed suggested to Commandants Lamy and Laborie who led the two enquiries in the affair that the surviving officers and NCOs had some interest in suppressing them. Their privileged position had made them so closely associated with the two captains that they were deeply unpopular. As the historian Emily Lynn Osborne has noted, and before her, the great Malian author Hampaté Bâ, these intermediary African employees often controlled and negotiated access to the colonial power for the Africans as well as for their employers. Koulibali was described as a power of his own and it was unclear how much he obeyed Voulet and how many initiatives came from him. Ultimately Pallier chose to associate him with the crimes of Voulet and had him executed.[25]

In the midst of this racial mix, not only hierarchies but also a diversity of status existed.[26] Scientists played a key role in shaping racism, as evident in the great anthropologist and craniologist Broca's 'scientific' hierarchy of racial attributes that could be measured for his school of physical anthropology. Explorers visiting Africa were provided with specific instructions regarding the sort of racial information they were meant to bring back with them. Voulet and Chanoine carried the books of Broca in their trunks and they saw the peoples of Africa in set racial terms.[27]

That races were different was a given; that they were unequal was also uncontroversial. Yet this inequality extended to minute variations between groups—the races were not two but many and intermediate groups might appear in the right context. For instance Governor Faidherbe had not hesitated in encouraging the French to procreate locally and to create a Métis race.

If racial inequality was at the heart of colonial rule it was also predicated on extremes of differences and graduations within. Some Africans were French nationals and many Senegalese soldiers could eventually acquire French nationality.[28] Among the NCOs of the Voulet mission there were several who were 'assimilated'. The depth of this assimilation was tested to the full when Voulet organized a mock trial and the execution of a 'French' NCO, Taciny Taraore, and of a tirailleur. Among Voulet's many other misdemeanours, these executions weighed most heavily with his superiors until the murder of Klobb. In Voulet's eyes, as indeed in his fellow officers' eyes, there was no doubt, however, that this colonial citizen was not worthy of the kind of legal niceties a 'real' citizen would have been entitled to. Among the myths of French colonialism, political and cultural assimilation was one of the most central yet most contested.[29] Yet assimilation was the key to the new colonial rule. In competition with other empires, the French had to give a legitimate excuse for their rule. From Faidherbe onwards that excuse was that the French represented the sympathetic rule of law and that its domination would be fairer and more open for the subjected people.

Part of the impetus of empire had been to present to the metropolitan public a series of great opponents and 'enemies of France'. The public stature of Umar, Samory, and Rabah was literally built up by propagandists to explain and justify the constant and often unauthorized military operations taking place on the borders of Soudan.[30] Even though most of these African leaders merely responded to incursions and aggression the French administration set itself up as the solution to their despotic rule. The most notorious military leader of West Africa at the time was Samory Touré. He used a well-disciplined army of soldiers known as *sofas* who were often ex-slaves, or former soldiers of his defeated enemies. Resource hungry in a poor land the Samory empire was destined to be fragile. It relied on extensive slavery which could only be maintained by conquest. Samory himself had been a voluntary slave in order to buy out his own mother. Yet he had risen to prominence. In this rather more porous society there were other examples of slaves rising to the summit of political organizations. Yet the slave trade that had developed in central and Western Africa in the second half of the nineteenth century was broader than this: caravans of slaves were traded across the land. They were mostly composed of women and children as their men-folk had often been killed in the slaving raid.

Samory Touré was the enemy par excellence. His religion, his war methods, and his slaves made him ideally suited to becoming the opponent of the civilizing French. At its most lyrical the administration imagined itself a charitable force: 'France will only use towards them [colonized people] justice, benevolence and humanity. They can see that we have to come to them without the ideas of the black conquerors who oppressed them relentlessly and without pity.'[31] The victors hardly reported on the exactions of the French armies and it took the Voulet–Chanoine scandal to reveal them.

Yet, despite being demonized, Samory was also a model to imitate in some crucial ways. Arrested in 1898 in a surprise attack, Samory was unlucky. Unlike El-Hajj Umar who could compensate his relative technological inferiority with sheer numbers of warriors, Samory arrived at a time when technology tipped most heavily in favour of the French. Between 1870 and 1898 military weaponry was revolutionized. Historians tend to admit the fact with some reluctance, lest they be branded with technological determinism. Yet breech-loaded rifles, automatic weapons, damp-proof metal-cased bullets, smokeless high explosive powder, so-called melinite, shot-loaded guns, and 80 mm light artillery changed entirely the balance of power in Western Africa.[32] In the open field the French soldiers could shoot and kill at 200 m while their opponents' arrows and rifles could only reach them at a fraction of that distance. Samory had attempted to catch up, importing weapons and manufacturing some of his own but his time ran out.[33] Against better armed and drilled Senegalese tirailleurs, Samory lost set piece battles at a cost of twenty soldiers to one. Sheer volume guaranteed disaster. However, killing the French was possible, and there were many instances of failed missions where an entire unit was wiped out: the Flatters mission in the desert for instance, or the Bonnier *colonne* attacking Timbuktu in 1894.[34] Yet in almost every case, these successes were the outcome of a daring ambush by a small cohort rather than the battle of a great king meeting his foes. Ambushes and irregular warfare were an admission of political weakness; they did not have the symbolism of great victorious battles. By 1890, wars were no longer winnable and Samory's power base was eroding away. He attempted to move his kingdom away from the French and reinvent it further to the east; yet nothing could stop the French from tracking him. The fortified villages and towns of Soudan were no longer strong enough to resist shelling and their mud walls crumbled.

Yet some of Somary's tactics were adopted by the victors. French weapons could kill at distance; yet officers felt obliged, sometimes with disastrous results, to lead hand-to-hand assaults to seal a real victory. Their status as war leaders was at stake and their heroism was to be proven in furious charges, after an initial pounding of the enemy. Only after the charge had been concluded could these men claim victory and act as African war 'chieftains'. Voulet and Chanoine corresponded to this warring ideal and both had been noted for their individual courage under fire. Among their soldiers were *griots*, court poets hired to sing the praises of the war leaders.[35] *Griots* reciting poems to music were the keepers of oral tradition, as well as being status symbols of power, in the African societies Voulet and Chanoine encountered.

In Songhai tradition there existed a range of *griots* and we do not know whether Voulet hired cheap *Bini* flatterers or the genuine *Jesere Dunka*, the master *griots* from Malinké whose role was to call upon noblemen to surpass themselves. The fact that they chose to put Voulet in a historical context suggests his poets were court *griots*, who, unsurprisingly perhaps, chose to compare Voulet to Samory himself.[36] When Voulet and Chanoine left Senegal, Samory's adventurous reign was coming to an end, with the French closing on his now itinerant group of faithful tribesmen. As a result his power eroded and when the French soldiers stormed his compound the tired leader asked to be killed. The French decided to deport him to the island of Ogoune in Congo instead and spared his life and that of his sons. He died the following year of pneumonia. His 40,000-strong army was disbanded and the officers distributed them geographically, returning some limited power to some of Samory's sons.[37] Twenty-five hundred of his soldiers were kept as captive workers on the Soudanese railways, while many returned home or joined the French army ranks.

In this context, where a few officers and hundreds rather than thousands of men sufficed to change the political map of Africa, Voulet and Chanoine were living the last imperial dream. It was a dream that only a privileged few could access—while countless others, posted in sleepy settlements of the empire, envied them. Only in Soudan could such junior officers claim to have political agency, and negotiate as a sovereign power with African kings. In 1896, Voulet and Chanoine had made their name through the conquest of the Mosse kingdom and its capital, Ouagadougou (Burkina Faso). This conquest was presented in typical heroic style by Chanoine and their superiors despite some complaints regarding Voulet's methods.[38] At the time not many people objected to the summary beheading of forty emissaries, to the burning and wasting of territories, or to the enslavement of much of the people who resisted him.[39]

This 'adventure' was the triumph of youth and daring. In 1896 Voulet and Chanoine, then mere lieutenants, with Sergeant Laury, 23 regular tirailleurs, and 23 regular cavalrymen, augmented with 180 irregular soldiers, 40 cavalrymen, and a local army of 250 men led by Ouidi-Diabo, king of Borari, and with a claimant to the throne of Ouagadougou, Yatenga Naba Bulli, launched an attack against the Mogho Naba Wagba (or Bukari Koto Moog-Naaba Wogbo, 1850–1904) of Ouagadougou. The excuse for war was geopolitical. The Naba had resisted French advances and seemed to favour British ones.[40] In all likelihood the king had attempted to use one power against another in a desperate attempt to maintain his independence. Accordingly British agents had made some claims over the Mosse in 1894.[41]

Voulet led a daring raid straight to the capital of the Mosse. The city of Ouagadougou resisted for merely two hours and was burnt in retaliation. The Naba was deposed and replaced by one of his brothers. The Mosse king fought against this invasion for the rest of his life and died in exile on British-controlled land. The conquest of the Mosse gives early indications of Voulet's poor judgement in African internal affairs. Acting on his own information and, it appears, manipulated by local leaders, Voulet then decided to execute one of France's allies, the Marabout of Lanfiera, Karamokho Ba, in order replace him with a kin of one of their weak allies, Ouidi.[42] The consequence of the murder of this widely respected holy man was further resistance to the French. Voulet had intervened in a volatile part of the world where traditional powers such as that of the Naba of Ouagadougou were threatened by rising forces.[43]

Yet, by 1897 the campaign was over and Voulet had 'conquered' the Mosse, most of today's Burkina Faso making the desired bridge between Senegal and Dahomey. It is worth adding a caveat to the meaning of the word 'conquest'. It was not complete, effective, or final since it took another 10 years to turn the effective powers of the Naba of the Mosse into a puppet figurehead.[44] The indirect rule imposed by Voulet merely gave the French a freehand to interfere rather than the ability to govern. And on the whole the Soudan colonial world was severely underpopulated by French administrators who relied instead on traditional chieftaincies, creating new ones where there were none, and replacing other rulers with more compliant ones. Heavy-handed and often misguided, this attempt to rule through local potentates would backfire when the ruler lacked real legitimacy or credibility. In those cases the French had to repress yet again their 'pacified' subjects.[45]

In Mosse territory as elsewhere in the new colony the French practised violence systematically and instances of 'exemplary' punishments abound. Anthropologists such as Jean-Pierre Olivier de Sardan have argued that this era marked a radical break for the people of the Niger River. Others like Stoller saw it as a continuation of hundreds of years of violent rulers sometimes backed by terrifying divinities.[46]

This mission of 1896–7 took place at a time when the military perceived the enemy to be no longer the African states themselves, but rather the other European powers and in particular the British. Voulet and Chanoine had been in conflict with the British who had sent Captain Donald Stewart in an attempt to challenge the French presence in this central area.

In a confidential letter of 29 March 1897 Chanoine wrote to the Capitaine Destenave who was the first French residing authority in Ouagadougou: 'I think that it is unnecessary to wait before acting, that is to throw the English soldiers out of Gurunsi and to inform the English that "any intrusion of soldiers in arms of this kind will be considered as a pirate and filibustering Enterprise".'[47] Eventually, after much posturing, dining, and exchanges of formal notes and probably as a result of British difficulties with Samory's armies, Voulet obtained the Mosse and Gurunsi territories for the French empire. Stewart provides one of the few external eyewitness accounts of Voulet's conquest methods. In his report he mostly objected to his taking of slaves. Commenting on Voulet's systematic burning of villages he found it repulsive that French soldiers offered to sell slaves to his constables.[48]

This phase of the conquest propelled the two young lieutenants into the small circle of empire builders. When it came to costs, the conquest of the Mosse had been delivered incredibly cheaply: 100,000 km^2, a fifth of the French territory, were acquired at the cost of 113 wounded soldiers and 20,000 francs. This staggering result was exactly what the soldiers wanted to tell Paris. The inspector general of colonies, Chaudié, praised Voulet for succeeding through 'missions with few staff, living off the land and governing through the indigenous chieftains'.[49] Many previous expeditions had been costly and inefficient and in recent years many had ended in utter military disaster like the Bonnier march on Timbuktu. Critiques of empire and economists objected that the real cost was yet to come and that administration and development would be a drain on financial resources of the colonies if not of the metropolis. Yet the drive to conquer at the smallest possible cost was irresistible.

According to Voulet and Chanoine, results always justified the means. Things had to be done 'considering the variable aspect of African military support. That's why when one is fighting a black chieftain one should not fight a softly, softly war but a *hard* one.'[50] Since the French were unlikely to sustain a high level of military presence they had to impose their rule brutally at the onset.

South of the Mosse, Voulet and Chanoine also invaded a region called the Gurunsi. There the two men supported a local chieftain, Hamaria, of dubious lineage, against another 'alien' potentate, Babato, who was himself an ally of Samory Touré's son Sarankeni Mori. Chanoine was in charge of gathering intelligence and remained. Samory having renounced Gurunsi, Chanoine established a basis of borders with the British sphere of influence. He swiftly repressed any attempt of resistance and established tense relations with the British forces led by Handerson and Fergusson, giving them a refuge after the son of Samory Touré defeated them.[51]

Voulet and Chanoine despised their British counterparts who did not belong to the British army—'We do not face British officers but the officers of the civilian colonial service of the style of Fergusson, men without any honour or loyalty'—and accused them of arms trafficking with the sons of Samory Touré.[52] In fact, like elsewhere in Africa, the colonizers accused each other, often quite justifiably, of underhand tactics and of equipping Africans resisting the invasion of their rivals. The African rulers who had some intelligence about competition attempted to play off one colonial empire against another, often in vain after international conventions established geometrical borders on the map of Africa.[53]

Acting like a little ruler of his kingdom, Chanoine set out to define effectively the borders of northern Ghana while delivering to the Paris Geographical Society the sort of information it demanded. Jules Chanoine, one of the earliest members of the society, ensured that his son's articles got published.[54] The popular press and the travel periodicals *Le Tour du Monde* and its supplement *A travers le Monde* reported the news in glorious terms.[55] Chanoine was then 27 but his level of responsibility in the Gurunsi was nothing short of autocratic and by June 1898 the information he provided relayed the French position on borders and fed directly in the tense governmental negotiations between the British and the French.[56] Meanwhile his rule was brutal to the point that three years later his successors in the area found it difficult to meet, let alone administer, the local people. In the larger settlements such as Bobo Dioulasso for instance, the local people still resisted French tax demands on the ground that they had not recovered from Chanoine's conquest.[57]

Voulet meanwhile returned to Paris to rapturous applause from the colonialists. He had a private meeting with the president of the Republic and set out to write a description of the Mosse. Chanoine and Voulet gave lectures on this new land in Paris and Lille,[58] at the colonial school on 7 July 1897, and to the committee of French Africa.[59] The enthusiastic reception they received in Paris seemed to justify all the privations of living in Soudan. Their swift promotion to the rank of captain was guaranteed but their meteoric career left them vulnerable to jealousy and rivalries. They would have to fend for themselves in the Parisian political jungle.

In the field of politics they faced enemies on the left like Vigné d'Octon who questioned the motives of colonialism, suspecting commercial interests and private motives; but also those on the right who deplored the resources lost to the revenge war effort against Germany or even deplored that the recently defeated nation should inflict on others what it had suffered itself only recently.[60] Old Bonapartists like Paul de Cassagnac or royalists like de Broglie were opposed to the colonial venture and adventurers just as were old socialist Communards like

Barodet of Lyon, or economists and pacifists like Lockroy (who opposed the naked imperialism that had been voiced in French parliament). Yet, these men, even though they remained a thorn in the side of the empire builders, never managed to stop the endless growth of the republican colonial empire. There were also opponents within the army, who were considerably more threatening. The colonial lobby had been led by an old Soudan hand, Archinard, who had driven the great offensive east in the 1880s and he still nurtured the careers of his protégés, which did not include either Voulet or Chanoine. Other colonial officers resented the young upstarts who engaged in Soudan purely for the sake of promotion and carefully avoided the tedious backwaters in favour of the limelight. Most perilous, however, was the fast-changing political landscape of France where governments seldom lasted more than six months and where a merry-go-round of appointments might suddenly remove whatever support one had.

After the collapse of Ferry's government over defeats in Tonkin in 1885 the massive expansion of France's overseas territories had continued in a more haphazard manner, often lacking a real master plan beyond those drawn up in the colonies themselves by officers. New territories were acquired by junior officers such as Savorgnan de Brazza. Brazza established treaties with local kings between 1875 and 1880 on his own authority, and distributed weapons and gifts to create a colony that his government had not fully anticipated.[61] With some limited financial backing, he imposed a colony on the French. After Brazza all new enterprises benefited from a combination of naval, military, and business backing. Even the academies rewarded leading figures of the colonial enterprise with the widely publicized, annual Audiffred prize.[62] Each next step forward had to be costed and assessed before it could be taken.

Yet once a mission was launched there was little that could be done to stop it. The colonial conquest had a life of its own and the distance and disobedience of men on the ground ensured that it thrived on heroic but often unpremeditated advances. Throughout the great imperial drive forward, colonial enterprise was divided and contested, so much so that it is easier to talk of colonial factions rather than a single colonial party. Furthermore, on the borders of empire, individual initiative ruled and often led the game.

In Soudan the drive to conquer was almost always led from by officers on the spot. In 1894 the conquest of Timbuktu was precipitated, with disastrous consequences, by the initiative of Bonnier and other officers against explicit orders from the civilian administrator Grodet. Even though Timbuktu fell into French hands the mission was ambushed and the French army had to send another expedition to seize control of the city. The Bonnier disaster revealed the impetuousness of the colonial drive.

As late as 1901, officers like Destenave could launch attacks on a Tuareg group which amounted to a private war.[63] In the area where Voulet and Chanoine had fought, conflicts continued often until well into the twentieth century. When an unauthorized military expedition, such as that of NCO Martel on the village of Sargadié in 1900, failed it was explained away as a *coup de folie*.[64] The conquest of Africa at this particular stage presented a mixture of unique features: it was led by military men but not necessarily with much military backing or financing. Yet it was enough of an impetus to be labelled, quite justifiably, 'the colonial rebirth of France' by the colonialist lobby.[65] Given the lack of genuine political direction, the men on the spot managed to give the illusion of a carefully premeditated plan.[66]

There were some people who had grand plans and, even though they did not rule France, they influenced significantly the conquest of Africa. A private committee which contained a number of decision-makers, the Committee of French Africa, funded part of every mission. The committee had been created by republican nationalists in 1890 in response to a previous mission, the Crampel mission, which aimed to conquer the hinterland of Congo and create a company modelled on the British Royal Niger Co.[67] In 1899, the committee was presided over by the journalist Auguste Terrier, who used the press to popularize the narratives of his colonial correspondents with spectacular and savage illustrations drawn from sketches or photographs (see Figure 2). The prior secretary of the committee, the journalist Harry Alis, Terrier's brother-in-law, was a secret agent of Leopold II of Belgium and promoted bullish colonialism in the spirit of the Berlin agreement of 1885.[68] (Leopold II, initiator of the extraordinary private colony of the 'free state' of Congo, has remained the most controversial figure of capitalist colonialism, and the abuses of Congo which became known in the 1890s remain controversial today. Leopold's predatory regime committed crimes specifically to extract as many resources as possible from the colony.)[69] The committee was small with only about thirty members and fewer than 2,000 supporters but it yielded considerable influence on the relevant politicians.

The Paris Geographical Society was dominated by another arch-colonialist, Baron Hulot, who used the *Bulletin* of the society to convey his opinions and relay the news of successes of young officers.[70] Julien Chanoine received the Caillé medal for daring explorers from the Commercial Geography Society in 1897; the Lyon Geography Society also rewarded his work. At this time geographers and colonialists agreed on their reading of the world. Soldiers, explorers, and travellers were often one and the same. Some travellers like Stanley were armed to the teeth; other explorers were officers on leave or on mission.

According to Octave Meynier these networks operated like a sort of freemasonry convinced of the importance of the civilizing mission and motivated by the potential financial outcomes of colonization.[71] A kind of feverish activity was constantly fed by news and returning officers. This enthusiasm was nurtured and fostered by the officers themselves. Julien Chanoine identified a number of deputies supporting them: Etienne, Lemyre de Villers, le Herisse Merlou, Alphonse Humbert, d'Agoult, and a friend of the president, the senator Siegfried.[72] Throughout the mission he sent flattering and begging letters asking one or another member of the committee to intervene in the political web of intrigues he imagined to be at work against him in Paris. His last letter was a forceful if desperate plea:

> Dear Sir, you and we have different souls and other feelings than these bad Frenchmen, we will oppose their evil plans. We will continue to move forward, sticking to our mission and not deviating one line from the instructions written and signed by the minister of colonies with the approbation of the minister of the foreign office. Back us like the committee has always done. Protect us from this back stabbing!! The committee can trust us that our interests are those of France, just as much as we trust you to support us.[73]

After Voulet and Chanoine's death, their heir and successor in the field, Joalland also resumed the correspondence with the Parisian backers of the expedition, summarizing in characteristically bullish terms how he had won back his men:

> I only had to resume their moral education, talk to them about duty, inculcate the principles of discipline and devotion—fifteen days later I announced that the mission would start again its march eastwards but that all the women and the herd of captives would remain in Zinder with 100 men under the orders of Sergeant Bouthel . . . good bye dear

sir and if the Joalland–Meynier mission could make people forget the atrocities of the mission Voulet–Chanoine we would be grateful.[74]

The journalist Terrier certainly did his best to grant him his wish. Soudan occupied a particular place in the geographical imagination of these elite lobbyists. To make its conquest and development a higher priority, new branding strategies and new concepts as promisingly catchy as they were groundless were developed. Since the 1880s colonial officials had deplored the poor development of trade and urged the need to enable traders and entrepreneurs to gain access to the markets and resources of the African hinterland. In Charles Colin's pioneering words: 'What will [trade] become when we take seriously the task of demanding from this land everything it can give?'[75] Like most enthusiastic colonialists the emphasis was on untapped riches and underdeveloped wealth, among which native people featured only as intermediates or an associated human resource.

These entrepreneurs of empire were constantly looking at other colonial enterprises and in particular jealously regarded the British colonial successes as worth imitating. Thus Terrier also used the idea of the 'Niger, the French Nile' to advocate investments and colonial drive in the new colony to match British investments in Egypt.[76] In actual fact the enterprises launched, sometimes at great expense, in the new colony often had very limited success. In the words of Bismarck, France had colonies but no colonists, despite a sudden surge in colonial propaganda in the 1890s.[77] Before the First World War the entrusting of merino sheep to the White Fathers was financed by the Chamber of Commerce of Roubaix, the great textile city of northern France. The sheep died. Irrigation plans and hopes to develop a new cotton-producing region that could match Egypt or India were less disastrous but never delivered as much as was hoped by the colonial lobby.[78] It took some creative accounting to demonstrate that within five years of the conquest the colony paid its own way. The new governor, Colonel de Trentinian, endeavoured to demonstrate rapid progress.

The superior officer in the military colony of Soudan in the period of Voulet's expeditions, Trentinian had a thorough colonial pedigree. He had distinguished himself in the repression of New Caledonian Kanaks with the help of deported communards in 1878.[79] Since then he had invested his career in the development of Soudan and managed the threatened colony like an enlightened despot: he organized schools and the teaching of French, reformed property law, set up border guards, and banned corporeal punishment in schools.[80] His modernist ideals led him to invest heavily in motorized transport in 1898–9, when by that stage Soudan had one-fifth as many cars as existed in the entire United Kingdom. Conscious of their isolation in Paris as well as in the heart of Africa, the military rulers attempted to project a modern image that would yield quick returns and feed the empire with new goods to compete with products from the British Empire.[81]

Grand plans for irrigated fields of cotton, flocks of acclimatized animals, and schools targeting the African elites as well as various study missions were welcome and reported positively on the agricultural and mineral potential of the colony. The Soudanese railway, built at great expense but also thanks to forced labour, promised to open up the new territories. As Voulet and Chanoine headed towards Lake Chad, a scientific mission composed of engineers, botanists specializing in latex production, cotton dealers, and coffee dealers as well as advertisers and painters reported on the 'progress' of the colony.

Other ministries could be involved either on scientific grounds or merely on the basis of networks and group solidarities. Thus, the Foureau–Lamy mission leaving North Africa to meet Voulet received much of its financing from the Ministry of

Education. This mission was designed to reconnoitre the Saharan routes between Algiers and the Niger but it was also meant to explore the commercial possibilities of the desert. Geologists, businessmen, and politicians were part of the expedition and its military leader was in no way the most familiar name. Fernand Foureau was a civilian explorer who had exploited his connection and experience in the field of exploration to assemble the large group that took his name. This progressive image was to be troubled by the reports from Voulet's mission. The colonial fantasies woven by the colonialist lobby and de Trentinian were bluntly rebuked by the accounts of the massacres. De Trentinian had feared this and so had many of the Soudanese officers.

Even as he embarked in Bordeaux, Voulet knew that his expedition, commandeered from Paris, would be unwelcome. The local leadership attempted to prevent the mission from taking place and as late as the 12 July 1898 the governor general of Occidental French Africa, Chaudié, wrote to the minister in a last ditch attempt to block the departure of the mission by foreseeing its failure:

> It seems to me that after the intense armed activity period that Soudan has been through in recent times... that it would be opportune to stop for a while in order to pacify and organize the newly conquered territories. This mission... is increasingly taking the features of an expedition. Captain Voulet, in order to safeguard his column or in order to go forth, will have to be waging war as soon as he will have left the territories under our authority, and even in our territories the constitution of a convoy of 800 porters will not be without serious difficulties and will cause deep trouble across the land. If recruiting them is difficult, feeding them is worse if not impossible. They will be driven by hunger to steal what they could not get, to pillage the villages. If the mission leader wants to do the same by requisitions he will have to use the same means, porters will run away and he will have to use violence.[82]

This letter, like many others, directly and accurately predicted (perhaps in a self-fulfilling manner) the obstacles that Voulet and Chanoine would meet. Voulet and Chanoine were bypassing normal channels of command and threatened the status quo which favoured the military over civilian colonial administrators. Soudanese officers feared for their fledging colony and resented Parisian intervention.

In this revealingly frank telegram, the governor shows that he knows full well how colonial missions operate and the portrayal of violence to come is undoubtedly meant to remind the Parisian patrons of Voulet what the nature of colonial war was. This ominous message also shows quite clearly that the expectation of violence was well understood in Paris and in Soudan. As we will see later, it also implies that the 'scandal' of that violence cannot be understood simply as a shock of discovery.

The harsh recruitment drive led by Chanoine in the Mosse territory in the autumn of 1898 demonstrates that these fears were justified. Even though Chanoine 'could cross this land without noticing any difficulties', de Trentinian commented that the requisition of men, cattle, and food created shortages and a general fear of the French administration.[83] On the other side of the debate Voulet and his supporters argued that these bad omens were likely to act as self-fulfilling prophecies if it became known that the colony was not behind the expedition. In the 1898 political climate the military leadership of the 'Soudanese' feared that their reign may be threatened. Originally they resented the Parisian expedition and its resources, but ultimately the failure of this mission signalled the end of military rule in French Soudan on 17 October 1899. 'Their' colony was then carved up and divided between the hinterland of Senegal, Ivory Coast, and Dahomey, leaving the military with only the desert areas of the north and north-east.

Voulet had some 'African' credentials but his backing was exclusively Parisian and like Foureau's his adventure had the highest possible political backing. Unlike Foureau's his mission remained primarily military and his backing was much narrower. The bulk of his finance came from the Ministry of Colonies where he had much support with only 30,000 francs from the minister of foreign affairs.[84] In fact in the 1902 report of the 'Court des Comptes', the audit of the French Republic, the mission was identified as being rather opaquely financed.[85] With the help of Chanoine's political connections the entire package was set up reasonably swiftly but perhaps not entirely legitimately.

Yet in the same way that seventeenth-century privateers set up their corsair activities, Voulet was left to fend for himself without much help from anyone, not even in logistical terms. For instance, Voulet had to purchase his weapons from the army with the budget allocated to him by the Ministry of Colonies. Two years after his death, the mapmaker Bonere was still chasing his unpaid bills.[86] With little more than 100,000 francs coming from the Ministry of Colonies special funds and a few thousands from the French Africa committee Voulet had to prepare for war up to 3,000 km away from his base in Soudan. The other main mission sent in 1898 was the Foureau–Lamy mission which benefited from a legacy of 500,000 francs, additional funds from the Ministry of Education, and support from the army. With his money, Voulet had to buy his own weapons: some 200 obsolete 1874 rifles, 200 1892 cavalry rifles (mousqueton), 60 sabres, 200 machetes, 180,000 rounds of ammunition, an 80 mm mountain gun with 125 shells were bought after some tough negotiating with the army.[87] In the end he could not afford the two Hotchkiss machine guns he listed.

At one stage Voulet complained that the army was charging him more for each rifle than if he had set up a shooting range for a provincial sports club.[88] When much of the material arrived it had been damaged in transit as a result of poor packaging and the weapons and ammunition had to be dried in the sun. On arrival in Bamako, 150 of the rifles were found to be unfit for purpose, 80 were repaired on the spot and 70 had to be exchanged.[89] The huge mass of luggage of the mission taxed all the resources of the colony. It took 100 Lefebvre iron carriages to take the goods to the Niger, where Voulet asked for 100 camels on departure from Timbuktu; only 27 could be found. These logistical issues meant that the mission relied very heavily on human portage at a greater cost for the local people.[90]

Throughout the mission Voulet obsessively accounted for ammunition and funds, keeping a stringent eye on expenditure. In February 1899, he estimated that he needed a further 500 rifles, 400,000 bullets, 150 scattering bullet shells, 100 melinite shells, and a small gun to complete the mission.[91] Sending his first demand on 25 January he then lobbied feverishly to ensure that the ammunition should come from the south with the Bretonnet mission sent from French Congo. Despite this lobbying the resources were not forthcoming and the response from the ministry was a flat refusal to indulge Voulet. Yet Voulet could see his resources diminishing daily in the many skirmishes his mission encountered. Responding to the dismissive note of refusal from the ministry, Voulet took a critical tone which reflected his unease with his political backing. Suspicious of politicians and civil servants, Chanoine and Voulet suspected a Parisian or Soudanese plot to make their mission fail. In a telegram sent to Terrier, later found in his papers, Chanoine took an authoritative tone: 'Act vigorously against the hostile ministerial office and against Gentil, send supplies requested to the point in Chad held by Bretonnet.'[92] Ultimately Bretonnet was ambushed and his expedition massacred on 3 November

1899,[93] while Voulet and Chanoine never made it across to Lake Chad to meet him.[94]

This absence of decent funding has been used by historians such as Muriel Mathieu to explain, if not justify, Voulet's constant plundering. The argument would have more weight had the colonial columns not lived off the land elsewhere. The resources of colonialism were spent on people rather than logistics and the old customs of living from theft and imposing taxes on local products saw a revival. One of the main resources targeted was the native men themselves. The French acted like a predatory state, increasing the slave trade.[95] The soldiers themselves were mostly recruited locally and trained on the spot with limited resources. Voulet's mission was a perfect example of a motley crew partly composed of Senegalese tirailleurs, which were the organized regular French forces in Western Africa, as well as convicts released to serve in remittance for petty crimes and those partly recruited by Chanoine from villages in the Mosse territory for the purpose of the campaign.[96] The new recruits, many of whom had been fighting the French the year previously, were literally held in captivity until they were far enough from their homeland to be regarded as safe. Other irregulars, principally cavalrymen, were recruited from local warring tribes.[97] The Voulet–Chanoine mission, despite its considerable size and equipment (including portable artillery), conformed to that rule and improvized. Interpreters gave the officers' orders in the two, three, or more languages spoken by the recruits.

Voulet and Chanoine were convinced that they were the target of intrigues and plots to depose them. This heightened their sense of self-importance and their grievances against colleagues and the administration were widely shared. Lieutenant-Colonel Klobb himself had written to General Chanoine in 1897:

France is always seeking to make any savings on its budgets it can; it seeks to conquer colonies but without opening its purse and *in such a way that the officers who are not well loved by our governments can get neither profits nor honour.*[98]

Mixing honour and profit in the same complaint was not surprising in the military context of the late nineteenth century. French officers were then supposed to maintain all the appearances of upper or middle class respectability with the very limited means of their salary. Colonial ventures, in particular in Algeria, had, in the past, been the key to profitable positions, speculation, and retirement plans. The limited speculative worth of Sahel in Soudan frustrated the interests of these men. One of the great architects of the new colony of Soudan, General Archinard, who strongly opposed any kind of civilian involvement, summarized with some truth the republican policies:

To feed public enthusiasm with a few well advertised but pointless travels, a few successes that cost little; to profit from this enthusiasm to obtain from the public or the state some credits to use in the colonies and then use these funds to turn them immediately into benefits for some individuals seems to be the colonial policy that has the most supporters today [1894], yet it is the one that gives without doubt the worst results.[99]

Archinard wanted full, long-term, in-depth investments to develop simultaneously the economic and military infrastructure. Archinard wanted bridges and cotton fields, trains and roads, cities and settlers under the benevolent guidance of disinterested officers. This utopian take hid Archinard's notorious thirst for glory and his self-aggrandizing designs. In Africa alone could soldiers enjoy power on the same footing as Napoleon's men had done.

Another characteristic of African conquests, as I noted earlier, was that its officers were very junior considering their absolute power in the field. Even de Trentinian was merely a colonel when he governed Soudan. The main explanation for their low rank was the limited military resources at their disposal. At the height of their mission, including all the soldiers recruited illegally, Voulet could claim to have only 600 fighting men at his disposal. Joalland moved on with even fewer soldiers. Yet with 500 men a sultanate could crumble, a whole region could become part of the empire. If the means of conquest were modest, the ensuing 'pacification' took place with virtually no resources at all. The administrators complained of the huge demands made on their pitifully understaffed settlements.[100] Gentil, who set out in October 1899 from French Congo to meet the 'Klobb' mission and the Foureau–Lamy mission, complained in a bitter letter to the minister of colonies:

> Not only do I have to face a difficult situation, to create an administration, to make war, to feed a large number of staff but I have to supply the Klobb column and the Foureau-Lamy mission—how can I do this when we do not even have the necessary supplies, when the wine supply for Europeans is down to 25 cl per week and that bread is only available on Sunday?[101]

Similar complaints came from all corners of the empire; yet, despite limited resources, the imperial forces continued to deliver vast regions. Gentil also used this argument to cover his systematic exploitation of the Congolese wealth:

> I am fully aware that some of the measures I will take are illegal from our administrative point of view, they seem necessary to me over all others because they will be admitted by the natives.

He thus justified the sort of slavery-like forced labour and trafficking of ivory that would bring about an inquiry on him a few years later.

Given the dangers of life in the bush, anaemic and dispirited colonels and generals stayed away and only paid a few irregular visits to their subordinates. This distance gave space for daring initiatives, bordering on systematic disobedience which would be rewarded if they resulted in a significant gain. The army suffered from systematic 'mission creep' and the politicians in Paris chose either to ignore this or to seize the fruits of unexpected successes. Yet international political dangers lurked in the free enterprising imperial march forward. In Fashoda, in 1898, a small French mission led by Commandant Marchand advanced as fast as it could towards the Nile. The intention was to cross the continent and set up a presence on the upper shores of the Nile.[102] It was there that Kitchener met Marchand during the war against the Sudanese Mahdi. Kitchener had Anglo-Egyptian claims to make and his army vastly outnumbered the light colonial force led by Marchand.

The meeting, while cordial, raised vividly the prospect of a colonial war between the French and the British. The biographers of Kitchener are unanimous in attributing surprising diplomatic skills in a man of few social graces. Despite conflicting claims on the same stretch of land the encounter was relatively good-humoured. Kitchener was a linguist and had served with the French in 1870; Marchand was much his junior and knew his position to be indefensible. Sending Baratier to Cairo to get fresh orders, Marchand eventually accepted that this claim on Fashoda was not one the French government would go to war over. Declining offers to return to France via Egypt, Marchand trekked back across the desert to French land in Djibouti.[103] Ultimately the French reluctantly abandoned their pretensions on Fashoda in exchange for a settlement on the

Niger. This settlement suited both parties since they could both claim to have united their African territories into coherent masses.[104]

In France the Fashoda incident was regarded as a national humiliation and only with hindsight can one read it as the beginning of the constructive negotiations between the two empires which brought about the *entente cordiale* in 1904.[105] In 1898, only a few high-ranking politicians could have foreseen any lasting friendship with the British.[106] Amongst the colonial officers, so infatuated with their self-importance, the humiliation of Marchand was an insult to each of them.[107] In his private correspondence Chanoine erupted with angry Anglophobia and forecast an invasion of what is now Nigeria and Ghana from Soudan.[108]

There was among the French military a strong Anglophobic culture dating from the seventeenth century, shared by army officers fed on Napoleonic mythology. Trafalgar and Waterloo remained painful memories. Ironically the two nations had not only been at peace since 1815 but also constructive allies in the Crimean War in 1853–6, and in Lebanon and in China in 1860. Franco-British interests were not that dissimilar in their common suspicion of Russian attempts to reach warm seas nor in their distrust of the German Kaiser, Wilhelm II. In Africa where neither Russians nor Germans really mattered, the rivalry between the two empires could be made a personal crusade. Voulet and Chanoine saw their mission as a race against the enemies within and against the British agents operating in northern Nigeria. In June 1898 the borders of the British and French territories on the river Niger had been fixed. This decision involved a multitude of people who then ignored the existence of either empire; if it had a geographical basis, it was the logic of mapmakers rather than actual knowledge of the sites. Voulet's role was therefore to establish ownership of these lands while finding out what they were, and who they might have belonged to before the French. This topsy-turvy logic was the product of extreme imperial arrogance at a time when victory was never in doubt and when policies could be shaped in theoretical terms by Paris- and London-based politicians.

The military men nevertheless nurtured a distrust of conventions which had no material existence on the ground. Local potentates might be tempted to submit to the wrong people and occupation would then turn to possession. If fear of the English was a primary mover of officers in the field, they were also fearful of civilians. The logic of empire had shown that military rule could always be pushed aside by civilians who distrusted the military. Despite the paradoxical yet considerable prestige of the army in post-1870 France, anti-militaristic forces were thought to be at work. These might come and dispossess the army of its mission and deprive its officers of autonomy and of the opportunities of progressing rapidly through the ranks. While in France it could take ten years or more to move from lieutenant to captain, in Africa success and sudden deaths provided the required vacancies and glory. Voulet was a lieutenant when he seized Ouagadougou; he was a captain two years later. Chanoine who began the mission a mere lieutenant became a captain in October; Joalland who reached Zinder as a lieutenant was made a captain before his return to France.

Under civilian rule this symbolic capital would be lost and their more cautious rule would close the battlefields of adventure for ever. This deep-seated hatred of civilian rule was borne out of experience. Algeria had been lost to the settlers and their politicians; Soudan was so near established colonies that its autonomy would always be at doubt. A civilian governor, Grodet, attempted to rein in the military during his controversial rule in 1893–5. He was ultimately unsuccessful and was replaced by de Trentinian. But this return to power was short-lived and 1898–9 became the apex of French military power in Soudan. As governor of Soudan, General de Trentinian knew this. From his capital in Kayes, very far to the west of the territory but also sufficiently close to the sea to have fresh news and act upon it, he sought to present a modern vision of his colony (see Plate 3 and Figure 4). In 1898–9, while Voulet and Chanoine were enslaving men and women to enable their slow progression, the governor started an ambitious programme of public transport and a network of communication which, though built using forced labour, were presented as liberating technological progress.

The train line built by the prisoners of war, the soldiers of Samory, progressed painfully through Kayes, and many of de Trentinian's modernist aspirations remained just that. Nevertheless these aspirations reflected the diversity of colonial attitudes and contrasting approaches to governing. When Voulet and Chanoine launched their expedition they were leaving an unsecured frontier with the associated frontier mentality. During the expedition this frontier land attempted to present itself as a colony with a model of good military government. The news of violence to the east and its graphic portrayal in the metropolis could not have come at a worse time. The days of Voulet and Chanoine were numbered and the sort of African adventure they sought could not be part of modern colonial rule.

4

OFFICERS AND GENTLEMEN?

It is a powerful charm that comes not only from a free and independent life but also from this innate desire in man to be a creator; this is a need that we can only satisfy fully in Africa where everything is still to be done. The more one suffers to create, the more one loves one's work.

Still, some people sometimes feel sorry for us for sacrificing the best years of our youth to a savage land! Those who think like this, understand neither the meaning of life nor that of youth![1]

Albert Baratier, who wrote in 1913 a series of anecdotes on the colonial conquest, was representative of that generation of colonial officers who had chosen to serve in the empire. In an about-turn, the image of the colonial officer had changed from being sloppy and less gifted of men described in Chapter 2 to that of the salt-of-the-earth.[2] They claimed to embody a colonial spirit, a culture and attitude to the world that would match the civilizing mission assigned to them. Yet on closer examination the colonial world proved to be less a character-forming school for the new men France needed than a dysfunctional society ruled and divided by conflicting ambitions.

In 1898, the colonial enterprise of army and navy officers had at last found its legitimate place in the media. Acutely aware of the importance of publicity, the young officers were masters at image shaping. The pictures were posed and they provided the text. (See Figure 5.) Popular magazines such as the heavily illustrated *Journal des voyages et des aventures* created in 1877, or the older and less nationalistic *Tour du Monde*, the populist luridly illustrated *Petit Journal*, and the glossier expensive weekly *L'Illustration* used stock colonial images to sell copies.[3] Highlighting the savagery of the natives and the natural ascendant of the Europeans, these newspapers worked on established stereotypes of racial superiority. In their tight uniforms and under the glare of artificial lighting the men of the colonial missions gave a gallant image of the nation embarking on its civilizing mission. Who could better represent France than these young men risking all for the flag, the advance of civilization, and the alleviation of African suffering?

Historians have noted how the colonial enterprise was reshaped and presented as a manly activity in which the elite of the nation flourish. Conquest and safari were twin fantasies that grew in importance for those at home through press coverage, including publications intended for boys. A product of military schools and competitive examinations, the officers fitted well with the ideals of a regenerated army. The other protagonists in the picture appear as a think tank and not as adventure seekers. In this picture, as later in the individual reproductions printed by the *Illustration*, the men appear young yet wise, with perhaps a hint of a superior air in the case of Chanoine. Within a year of this picture being taken Voulet and Chanoine had disappeared from the colonial pantheon and their group portrait seemed strangely ironic. In the portrait published by the *Illustration* in 1899 (see Figure 1) after the scandal had become public knowledge, the images of Chanoine and Voulet already seem to have faded. Centre to the picture, Joalland incarnates the sort of virility his superiors do not. Voulet looks sheepish; Chanoine with his kepi to the back of his head and his eyes half closed looks like a vicious pantomime villain.

In their actions and in the final hours of the Dankori massacre, they had toppled from an impossibly idealistic pedestal. As men as well as soldiers Voulet and Chanoine were now compromised failures. From being ideals of manhood in a time of an alleged crisis of masculinity, Voulet and Chanoine had become models of brutality and barbarity, allegedly as a result of their mental and moral failings.[4]

If they had failed as men as well as soldiers it was perhaps because the ideals themselves were almost unattainable without some careful editing of the colonial story. Told crudely and without respect for the convention of heroic narratives, their adventure could only seem sordid and alien.

The myth of the colonies as written by the colonists themselves or by later historians, which echoes even in the work of recent public commentators such as Niall Ferguson, was that it was built mostly by honourable men whose intentions were almost unfailingly elevated. Indeed many men were honourable and well intentioned. For France the main herald of this ideal of a genuine encounter between the civilizations was no less than Marshall Lyautey, whose image probably loomed largest over the colonial enterprise.

In many ways Lyautey belonged to the impeccable pedigree of officers and gentlemen promoted by the Republic. Unlike most officers, Lyautey was also an inspiring writer, confessing a genuine interest in the civilizations he encountered as a conqueror. A friend of the cross-dressing convert to Islam Isabelle Ebherardt, he had more eclectic interests than most colonial administrators and his philosophy, steeped deep in the conviction of French superiority and genius, advocated, condescendingly perhaps, collaboration between unequal 'races' and the eventual assimilation of the imperial subjects to the French nation.[5] Assimilation was then regarded as a very distant ambition for which few resources, if any, were ever mobilized. Lyautey shaped afresh the new image of colonial officers but he was not alone and he was building on a tradition which had had its heyday half a century earlier in Algeria.

Then, the French colonial service was keen to represent itself as more culturally sensitive than that of the Indian Army.[6] Coming through the ranks of Sedan, his master and patron General Gallieni had also cut a gallant figure. Major generals of the First World War such as Joffre and Charles Mangin also learned some of their trade in Soudan. Joffre had avenged Bonnier in Timbuktu, and Mangin had a long career in Soudan from which he had derived his theory of 'black force'.[7] They were later glorified to such an extent that some of this cult has reflected on their colonial years.

Joseph Gallieni, now primarily recalled as the last minute saviour of Paris during the first battle of Marne in 1914, played a crucial role in Soudan as a lieutenant-colonel and his theoretical and practical writings on war in Soudan were regarded as the authoritative account on efficient and humanitarian warfare. In his key book, Gallieni emphasized the need for effective warfare at little cost to the colonial soldier.[8] Trained in Soudan's warfare techniques, Gallieni alienated his peers by criticizing their methods but he also learned from his superiors such as Archinard the need to control information and orchestrate his own propaganda.[9] He then applied this very effectively in Madagascar where, after the invasion of 1895, he served as governor, in effect the absolute viceroy of the new colony. Publishing an official journal, Gallieni put particular emphasis on pomp and circumstance, parades and displays of power. In many ways this could sum up much of the philosophy of governance fostered in Soudan at the time. In some sense the military regarded power in what they considered to be a primitive society as being personal and immediate. In the words of Viscount Melchior de Vogüé of the French Academy and the French Africa Committee, these officers had to be renaissance men: they had to be 'at times, soldier, engineer, physician, botanist, astronomer, cartographer, doctor, chemist, trader, diplomat; a little like illusionists when needed and always psychologists, like a professional novelist'.[10] The technical expertise was to be combined with the art of the storyteller and the cunning of the stage magician. Monteil allegedly based his success on his ability to offer a dilemma to the Africans from which he always found a successful way out. His use of modern technology was also occasional and sensational. These virtues were allegedly the ones all French colonial officers possessed.

This ability to combine skills was presented as uniquely French. There were other models of colonial men competing with the French one but the French emphasized that theirs was more subtle and honest than the Germans, less haughty and more sensitive to the local conditions and psychology than the British. Unlike Western societies or civilian-ruled colonies where a web of power could be found in a complex administration which contained a balance between rights and duties, taxes and obvious social benefits, the frontier colonies were likened to feudal Europe (in the understanding of feudalism of the late nineteenth century). The exercise of power was infrequent because of the very limited administration the French could afford for these distant colonies; therefore it had to be spectacular when it did take place.[11] In the census of 1904 there were 311 Europeans for about 4 million indigenous people in Western Soudan.[12]

To use the terms of Michel Foucault, sovereign power had to be establishd in these moments of violence. In his famous study of power in Western Europe, *Discipline and Punish*, Foucault notoriously begins with the detailed and almost pornographic description of the sufferings of a failed regicide, Damien, who was pulled apart by horses and then ritually displayed for a crime of lese-majesty. The spectacular violence of this public execution was meant to highlight simultaneously the heinousness of the crime against the king and God as well as the unlimited power of the sovereign king.

Many officers in the colonial setting behaved along similar lines. Served by unreliable and often rebellious troops and auxiliaries,[13] isolated at their outposts or on their campaigns, they reflected on how they might gain the natives' 'respect', and they ventured that this respect could only come from two things: distance between the mere mortals and the colonizers, and power in all its glory and violence. From their experience of Soudan in previous campaigns, Voulet and Chanoine knew the scale of what they were undertaking and repeatedly reassured the ministers that they were the right men for the task:

> My knowledge of the men and situation in Soudan, resulting from a stay of over 5 years in this part of Africa, enables me to assess rigorously the efforts needed from the local people. The fact of having conquered the Mosse, to have managed in 8 months to impose French influence on people and chieftains who were hostile in the first instance, are considerable advantages towards local indigenous folks who will always accept to lend their support and help to Europeans they know and who have prestige.[14]

The idea of prestige was one that recurred in most of their reports, implicitly to explain their violence. In Voulet's words prestige and fear are inextricably linked. Writing from Tibiri in March Voulet explained his policy in these terms:

> In France we are used to regarding black men as mediocre in terms of wit and intelligence, they seem to us always ready to accept Europeans as their superiors. They have shown quite the opposite here, how

little they fear us, how much they despise us and that we have no other prestige than the power they attribute to us. European prestige vanishes when the natives think themselves more powerful.[15]

Voulet notably dismissed any idea that technology could be regarded as a basis for prestige. Chanoine also stressed that this respect was a fragile capital easily squandered by being too close to the soldiers. 'In Soudan we live off prestige alone.'[16] Voulet (who had originally served as a private, not an uncommon thing in this transitional era when the French army valued service over education) took great care to establish a distance from native NCOs, and even French ones. From 19 April 1899, Voulet decided that officers and NCOs would no longer eat together.[17] Maréchal des Logis Tourot was disciplined for being too close to the native soldiers on more than one occasion. Ultimately that proximity to his men saved his life on 14 July 1899.[18]

While for some observers this isolation seemed to be a classic symptom of Soudanitis, it is likely that Voulet and Chanoine sought to anchor their authority by an ever stricter adherence to hierarchy, mimicking the examples of royalty found in their readings and in contemporary Soudanese society.

From February onwards Voulet and Chanoine became almost unapproachable, being surrounded by an entourage of African soldiers (Hausa cavalrymen for Chanoine). Their translators served as necessary go-betweens for them. Even the French officers found it difficult to communicate with either man. Joalland later complained of this distance. It has been used by historians and biographers as a key indicator of their growing insanity. In some sense it did seem to go against the grain since, as many historians have noted, colonial work was one which favoured homosocial and homoerotic bonds.[19] Their isolation and violence has been criticized as it jars with forms of ideal colonial governance developed at the time.

For instance Lyautey and his colleagues stressed that the military were engaged in a humanitarian form of colonialism which required strenuous self-discipline from army officers who could combine the talents of explorers, warriors, administrators, and anthropologists. Listening to all parties before making irreversible decisions, the army officers of the conquest were to promote the values of homosocial loyalties. Masculinity was displayed by constituting a family *à la mode du pays*, in the mission's case composed of slaves. All the officers of the mission had such 'wives'.[20] Pallier was thus asked by his colleague from Say whether he had managed to 'break', like a horse, his new sexual partner.[21] The French NCOs had their own spouses selected among the captives and guarded jealously. In fact the sexual tensions between the soldiers and the NCOs led to at least two executions.

A tirailleur NCO, Taciny Taraore, was executed near Sansané Haoussa for risking a relationship with Sergeant Major Laury's woman. In the final report, Laury was blamed roundly. He 'has had a despicable attitude in the Taraore affair. He has shown a complete lack of moral sense in keeping the woman.'[22] What the investigator found unsettling, beyond the illegal execution of a French soldier, was that he should have kept the tainted woman and not removed this threat to the morale of the mission. It is unclear what would have happened to this woman had she been left behind.

Another tirailleur was also executed for sexual indiscretion towards one of the women of Chanoine's household. On 16 March 1899 'Tirailleur Moussa Kone was unfairly condemned for a relationship with one of the women of Captain Chanoine. Joalland proclaimed Voulet's threats to all the women and servants assembled on the site of the execution that anyone behaving like tirailleur Moussa Kone [would meet the same fate].'[23]

Closing ranks around their women was at the centre of two criminal acts against tirailleurs which, in themselves, would have been enough to cause a full enquiry had the facts become known. The final report argued that the execution of the NCO had been almost clandestine.[24]

Even though the mission acted at times like a gathering of sexual predators, there was a strong homoerotic component too.[25] In their day-to-day interaction the officers were in a society of men; with few women visible or made public, these officers had to be 'good comrades'. Among the qualities of a good comrade, one had to be caring, sensitive, and forthcoming, *prévenant*, and even 'loving'. To be a charismatic leader, a 'chef', in distant lands one had to be loved to be obeyed. These qualities were demonstrated by the observation of etiquette, encouragement, and attention to the medical and mental condition of one's comrades. The good officer was one who cared for the condition of his fellow officers primarily, and, time and circumstances permitting, that of his troops, starting with the regular soldiers and then irregular ones. Loyalty based on respect and deference could turn into worship and love. Joalland was obviously bowled over to be asked by Voulet to follow him. The loyalty that a common enterprise generated could not be unmade easily. The sharing of meals, small celebrations such as the bottles of warm champagne drunk on 14 July 1899, and long deep conversations cemented the union of groups of gentlemen.

Against this model of what a good comrade should be, all members of the mission, Voulet and Chanoine included, fared differently. Dr Henric was deemed to have had an equivocal position in the group as he was prone to gossip and to factions. Voulet had virtues that eased comradeship and fostered friendship and loyalty, whilst Chanoine was often described as arrogant, cold, and aloof. Writing soon after the death of his superiors, Joalland wrote a devastating indictment of Chanoine which he later retracted but which reflected his views at that moment in time:

> Chanoine was better educated but without any of Voulet's qualities. He was a perfect brute, selfish, ambitious, cruel in cold-blood and by pleasure, insolent towards all and a coward in battle and in illness. It is because I think he was a coward that I do not believe that he was Voulet's accomplice.[26]

Yet, according to Joalland again, it was in the last few days of the expedition, after Tibiri, that Chanoine mollified his harsh image. Perhaps more confident that the mission was on track he 'became an excellent comrade: joyful, affable, one did not find in him the insufferable and aggressive chief of the banks of the Niger and of Birnin Konni'.[27] The campaign was probably going according to his plans by then: villages fell one by one and the mission was moving relatively smoothly towards Zinder. The 'affable' man was at that time responsible for the hanging of little girls and women but he was working on his subordinates. Later on, his character became more needy when he knew of but did not prevent Voulet's plans; meanwhile he betrayed symptoms of intense stress.

In his hour of need he allegedly changed his character to benefit from the male companionship of officers. These qualities had to be combined with their almost exact opposite of daring, decisiveness, and courage. The officers of Africa were meant to lead by example rather than direct from afar. They had to take arms and confront danger, leading charges and not weaken under fire. In his guide book for aspiring officers, Monteil stated the virtues of the French officers: 'we had all the qualities to colonize and they can be summarized under three headings: we are frank, honest, and energetic; frankness commands sympathy, honesty commands friendship; and energy commands success'.[28]

In all cases virtues were about command and command was virtuous in itself. It seems that the conflict between Voulet and Klobb was based on their high conception of honour.

The following letter, which was endlessly copied and became the main evidence that Voulet had rebelled, related to the comradeship of officers as well as to an individual sense of honour:

Even before you addressed me the proof of your authority to take command, you sent me two notes ordering me in rude terms. This is the evidence of your ungenerous feelings towards me. You must realize by now that you have insulted me in coming like this, pushed by your unlimited ambition to steal the fruit of my work but you are misguided in thinking that I will accept this abasement. Therefore I am honoured to inform you that, first I keep command of the mission; second I have 600 rifles, third I will regard you as an enemy should you continue your march forward, fourth all my men have been consulted on this situation . . . I am resolved to sacrifice my life rather than submit to the humiliation you are threatening me with but I also prefer to risk all.[29]

It is revealing that this transcription of Voulet's letter should put so much emphasis on feelings and in particular on the lack of comradeship between Klobb and Voulet. Its feverish conclusion and its sudden change of tone also reveal how unhinged Voulet had become. To refuse to abase oneself was not dishonourable and Voulet played up the virtues of the military to the extreme.

So did Klobb. When Klobb walked to his death despite menacing shots being fired in his general direction, he conformed to this stereotype. That his second in command should have taken an equally suicidal posture and face danger with the same equanimity was also to be expected. Even Voulet and Chanoine died the good death of gallant officers. Voulet went to the camp in the full knowledge that his chances of seizing power were slim; Chanoine single-handedly charged the mutinous soldiers shouting, 'France, France!' In both instances the acts had suicidal connotations. In the spirit of their military training these men embodied the virtues of a manly officer. Their comrades all stated their admiration for this behaviour. A good death almost atoned for their crimes, the most important of which, in the eyes of the French people, was the killing of another good officer, Arsène Klobb.

After Klobb's death, little was said of the other killings. Yet the brutality that had been so dominant in the mission had been troubling observers ever since the start. According to the role model set out in the colonialist literature the officer was meant to be impartial, compassionate yet dominated by the demands of the mission, paternal yet authoritative. In this patriarchal model the officer had to rule like a benevolent despot over the native soldiers, imposing calmly the benefits of the rule of law on the unruly children of the empire. The pedagogic value of punishment had to be put in context and explained to the punished. Voulet and Chanoine used flogging abundantly. Flogging in the French army and navy had been abolished since 1790 and the creation of citizens' armies in the revolutionary years. Yet the usage of varied corporal punishment was common in the colonial armies, When mission organizers found it difficult to find volunteers they even advertised that corporeal punishment would not be applied in their force.[30]

Even in France the emphasis was on absolute passive discipline and the 'abolition of the will'; a set of petty punishments and humiliating duties ensured that soldiers were 'broken' into uncritical acceptance of all orders they received. This culture of obedience and loyalty was everywhere in the military and it made the contesting of orders or the criticism of a superior's behaviour almost treasonable offences.[31] A culture of conformity prevailed and stifled any attempt at critical individual judgement.[32]

The military code reserved capital punishment for a narrow range of crimes primarily in times of war: abandoning a position under enemy fire, robbing a wounded soldier and inflicting a new wound, assaulting a superior officer with a weapon in a premeditated manner, murdering a civilian, his wife, or his children, refusal to obey when facing the enemy, or open betrayal in time of war.

Voulet stated to his men that after Say they were in effect on a war footing and that these laws would apply.[33] Crucially, nevertheless, they implied a constituted tribunal which Voulet only once attempted to organize. His interpretation of the vague military law was increasingly arbitrary and random since none of the acts of violence committed by his troops against the civilian populations were ever punished.[34] The punishment regimen applied in the colonies was not unknown in France and newspapers campaigned in the 1890s against excessive and collective punishments. Voulet and Chanoine were not operating in a moral vacuum: there were rules, and excess was portrayed as a scandal in newspapers such as *l'Intransigeant*.[35] Even in the colonial world their attitudes were harsh.

Soon after the mission left Timbuktu, the soldiers were heavily punished for petty violations of the military code. At this stage, some went back to Klobb to obtain protection from this unusual discipline. Unwilling to disavow Voulet in front of his men, Klobb washed his hands of the case, acted like a good comrade, and supported Voulet. Soon afterwards physical violence against the soldiers multiplied.

One could see this aloofness and violence as exemplary of what went wrong in the expedition. Yet another explanation, more consistent with what both Voulet and Chanoine wrote beforehand, exists. Voulet and Chanoine believed firmly in the virtue of exemplary punishments. Through example, power could be displayed brutally but infrequently. Neither men believed that Africans had innate qualities on which discipline could be established. Instead they understood African politics as being of a primitive monarchical type. They wished to obtain fanaticism from them of the kind they observed in their opponents. They sought to earn admiration and prestige through fear and rewards in order to obtain devotion and loyalty that could compete with the loyalty and respect granted to their enemies, the local chieftains, and Tuareg:

> The black population will never become ours until they are certain they have been freed for ever from their savage oppressors. This deliverance can only come from the power of our weapons. A fighting spirit [*esprit de lutte*] is no longer in their soul which has been shaped to accept all tyrannies. Never by themselves will the Songhai emerge from the most servile submission to combat their masters (the Tuareg).[36]

These lines, written by Chanoine as he was crossing the Mosse territory on his way to Say in the autumn of 1898, clearly expressed two central concerns shared by many officers in Soudan. The first one was that war the French way had to be decisive to win over the local people. Voulet explained this in other terms when he wrote to the Ministry of Colonies that the only effectively humanitarian war was a brutal, decisive, and short one. Pallier's report, endorsed by all the members of the mission in August 1899, associated the two men closely:

A number of women and children were massacred on [Voulet's] order [in Birnin Konni] but our attitude, apart from that of Chanoine, at the massacre of Sansané Haoussa had made our feelings clear; during the following meals our freezing cold attitude irritated Voulet, who complained about us to Chanoine who responded: 'you are wrong to tell them, they are not used to it, when they will understand that we are attacked and that these people are hostile, they will come to [our methods].'

Pallier then argued that 'his usual theory was that by taking terrifying measures one would put them off resisting and one would prevent far greater bloodshed'.[37] Pallier and his colleagues took great care to distance themselves from Voulet and Chanoine but this is not what other evidence reveals. Even though Pallier, like Joalland and others after him, talked of 'moral sufferings we had to endure' he nevertheless defended or qualified some of the practices attributed to his superiors. For instance in other passages of the report, Pallier does not condemn some of the brutal practices of the mission:

Tirailleurs had orders to bring back the hand not of the porters they shot but of the enemy killed in their raids, and that in order to check their stories because they had the habit of exaggerating their successes enormously.[38]

Reflecting Clausewitz, Voulet and Chanoine sought absolute victory and submission. They understood any attempt to extemporize or negotiate as akin to rebellion. This explains but does not justify their extreme brutality towards villages which reluctantly gave a portion of what the conquerors asked for. While there is considerable evidence from a wide range of sources that the imperial conquest was brutal, the reality of its violence was always minimized or censured in the French media as well as in the archives. A good example for this self-censorship comes from the difference between the manuscript and the printed version of Sgt Ernest Bolis, who served in the French Foreign Legion between 1889 and 1905.

In the manuscript of his memoirs Bolis relates without any negative comments that wounded prisoners had been beheaded and scalped. In the published book the scalping is commented on negatively and the wounded are described as already dead. He makes no mention of the beheading.[39] In the manuscript he talks of the beheading of men and the crushing of women's heads under the feet of elephants during the Tonkin campaign of 1892–3.[40] These disappear from the published book. Similar editing out is found in every published account. In the public domain the conquest was narrated in gallant terms, as a test of the race and gentlemanly quality of French officers and soldiers. Since the colonial world was so central to international relations, it was also perceived to be a public arena where representation was everything and one had to fear anti-French propaganda. The Germans had tried one of their officers; there had been scandals in Togo land [41] and in south-western Africa. Rumours of atrocities in the Free State of Congo abounded.

In 1891 a French photographer from Lyon, Joannès Barbier, was given exceptional permission to travel to the new colony of Soudan and take pictures, some of which would be printed as illustrations in the prestigious middle-class weekly *l'Illustration*, the French equivalent of *The Illustrated London News*. The pictures, appearing on 11 April 1891 (Figures 6, 7 and 8), were taken in the immediate aftermath of the execution of prisoners of war; the army acknowledged the killing of 36 soldiers of Samory, in Bakel.[42] The photographer took his picture after artistically arranging the heads in a jar (Figure 6). The sensational pictures of corpses abandoned in the sun or thrown into the current, not to mention the pictures of the heads, were accompanied by a strident and unusually violent article in an otherwise conservative periodical.

'It was decided that an example shoud be made, to terrorize the soldiers of Ahmadu and to stop the villagers around Bakel from being hospitable. The unfortunate inhabitants of the villages near Bakel found themselves forced to become executioners in order to avoid being executed—a real man hunt took place.' The liberal news magazine then concluded in pithy fashion: 'War explains many things we will hear—in this case we do not believe so. We cannot admit that war justified a panic which led to the arming of non-combatants in order that they should kill their brothers; we do not accept that war justifies encouraging slavery, murder and the worst passions.'[43] This approach to colonial brutality was not new—similar words had been penned forty years earlier about previous conquests—and similar words were expressed in 1899 during the Voulet–Chanoine scandal. Yet this indignation was never enough to begin a public debate or a scandal.

When the picture appeared in the press the colonial officials were appalled, not so much by the executions themselves as by the breach of censorship. The enquiring telegraphic note sent to Captain Roix, in charge of the post, made clear that he would not be punished for exercising these measures if he could explain them in a few lines; however, he had to answer for the circulation of the picture:

> Requirements—repression can and must obey some observation of general rules which must be that outside the battlefield, they maintain some judicial form for instance a court-martial and avoid any kind of disgusting display which would make us look like Ahmadu or Samory against which we are fighting.

adding in conclusion:

I understand full well and I attempt to make others understand the special circumstances of Soudan where you must get obeyed and discourage any spirit of revolt over an immense territory with very few soldiers.

Softer methods inspired by a recent example were then advised. If anything this dispatch revealed how prevalent extreme violence was.[44] The officer's response was terse and to the point. 'It was impossible considering my staff to keep in my fort the people I had executed, had I left them free I would have run a risk. I have acted according to my conscience.' He then confessed that while he thought the arranging of heads was in bad taste he had not felt like stopping the photographer's enjoyment: 'I made him notice that selling these pictures would be immoral. He promised me in front of the officers that he would never sell them and that he would keep them as a personal souvenir.'[45]

In the corridors of power in Paris the events had taken considerable importance until the French ambassador in London, William Waddington, confirmed that the image had had little currency in Britain. Had it been taken on by the British media, the event would have become seriously embarrassing. In fact the arrangement of heads in a jar had played against the credibility of the picture which was taken as a photomontage by anticolonialists. It was nothing of the sort but the picture was no longer credible.

One may wonder why the French government seemed to care only if other governments did. The explanation is simply that the colonialists knew their enterprise to be less holy than they claimed it to be. Even though they had no qualms about justifying the means by the ends, they knew that the government and public opinion were fickle in their support for distant and brutal conquests. The national glory earned abroad was a lesser currency than that earned in Europe and, by the 1890s, people seriously called for humane rule at home and abroad. To be a barbarian in the colony was a stain on the homeland rather than on the colony itself. Furthermore, colonies were deemed to be hungry in resources and uneconomical. De Trentinian summarized the dominant administrative wisdom:

> The total of all troops in Soudan is absolutely insufficient to support our political action and administration if the latter was not exercised benevolently, tactfully and determinately ... so that in full knowledge of the facts we can moderate our demands every time we can without undermining our prestige or the civilizing mission that is entrusted to you.

He then advised the good administrator to apply authority delicately and using in-depth studies of the ground first:

> carefully study these people, ethnic groups, the principal leaders of the different areas (cercle) of your region, their past, their character, their tendencies and whatever cultural influence under which they labour, so that finally the means of bringing them to you will enable you to conquer them morally.[46]

The moral conquest was the second phase of domination based on violence.

Some historians have, since Hannah Arendt, agreed that some colonial practices would eventually be applied in total war and that colonialism represents another Western totalitarianism alongside Nazism and Soviet Socialism.[47] In a sense this is nothing new. The anti-militarists blamed military violence against strikers on colonial experience and, after the First

World War, parallels were made between the excesses of German rule in Africa and their behaviour in Europe. This stereotype grew with time and in particular with Nazism. Writing in the aftermath of the Second World War, Octave Meynier, who survived the Klobb–Voulet encounter and became one of its first historians, made what he perceived to be a necessary distinction:

> The methods employed by the actors of the great colonial epic were, in general, inspired by the purest French spirit. From Faidherbe, Gallieni, Archinard or their putative heir Colonel Klobb, one can see them just as equally energetic and without pity for the tyrants, the bloody slave traders who devastated Africa in the nineteenth century as they were benevolent and accessible to the small people... Their human measures were not, alas, those of their subordinates. Some were officers without any pity in their hearts, young chiefs with an absolutist mindset who were thinking like Germans on the advantages of terror to ease conquest, protesting that the true humanitarian war is the shortest one, thus the most pitiless.[48]

This 'German' perspective was immensely convenient in 1947 since it enabled Meynier to cast aside Voulet as one of them, but it contained a kernel of truth. The years between 1890 and 1900 had been a time of debates between factions in the French army. Much of the debate was on the role and responsibility of army officers towards their soldiers and the nation at large. Partly inspired by the dramatic increase in the number of conscripts and by social Catholic ideas, some urged a dramatic departure from Prussian-inspired methods and brutality.[49] This new approach was by no means the dominant view in these years until the arrival of the radical minister of war André in 1900. Prior to that shift there was a general feeling that officers should embrace a cult of action. Voulet and Chanoine were precisely the sort of men of action readers recognized in their superficial reading of Nietzsche. As a journalist put it: 'Soudan has been a tough school in which the most robust energies were forged. A great people who wants to live and prosper needs schools like this.'[50]

In some respects, the fashion for German efficiency was a dominant feature of a country poised for another conflict. The violent episodes of German warfare in Namibia or harsh rule in other German colonies were emerging when Voulet and Chanoine became monikers for cruelty and were cause for comparison.[51]

Voulet and Chanoine modelled themselves as hard men. The Songhai kingdom both Voulet and Chanoine referred to as a model was the great native kingdom which dominated the region in the fifteenth and sixteenth centuries before the arrival of Moroccan invaders. This great civilization was perceived by the French in Soudan as being the basis from which the people of the Niger region could arise again in opposition to more recent political regimes dominated by more nomadic Muslim jihad leaders. According to anthropologists, the Songhai notion of kingship was based on the almost godly nature of the sovereign who could embrace the whole kingdom in his gaze and punish without pity those who did not respect his rule. For instance the anthropologist Paul Stoller makes the point that Voulet and Chanoine's violence was perceived to correspond closely to forms of monarchy in the Songhai kingdom of the fifteenth century and in particular to the memory of the ruthless empire-builder Sonni Ali Ber. The fearsome deity Dongo and its mortal avatars, the Songhai kings, would return.[52] In the mythology of Songhai, Dongo as the one who could be a force of evil can also be the best healer. In their sudden surge of mindless violence Voulet and Chanoine, almost one entity, became an African version of the wrath of God. If the

Soudanese could make some sense of this extraordinary violence in their own religious and historical terms, so could the soldiers of the mission.

For their own soldiers Voulet and Chanoine were compared routinely to the Almany, Samory Touré. Indeed Chanoine saw their mission as taking place in a Muslim political system based on fear and duplicity:

> We, the civilized, in our immense pride believe all the blacks are prostrated before us in deep admiration and we think that they take us for gods or supernatural beings; that's what comes from the stories of travellers who have not travelled much and who tell lies or who have not seen or understood or who think that they will seem more interesting if they write that they were taken for gods or wizards. Hence all these sentimental theories go so well with the government's miserly policies and make so many of our enterprises fail from lack of weapons and ammunitions.
>
> In reality, most blacks are not much impressed by our science, it is God's will; but what they are surprised by is our immense naivety and our imperturbable trust in their lies... when one fools the chief one despises him, in a Muslim land submission is made from fear; one does not fear those one despises and as one hates the master, the cursed Christian, one is always near revolting whether openly or not.[53]

Voulet agreed to this view and in his reports of January to April 1899 repeatedly referred to the need to rule without contest, stating even 'the locals are only just beginning to take us seriously'.[54] This was the interpretation the French had given to the immense dedication of the soldiers of the Muslim kingdoms they had defeated. The French saw El-Hajj Umar and Samory as bloodthirsty tyrants and yet their soldiers were willing to die for them. Chanoine like many others in French Soudan could see no harm in imitating their previous enemies. Voulet and Chanoine's perspective on colonial war was the direct continuation of Bugeaud's and Faidherbe's in the sense that it followed to the letter the guidelines on expeditionary *colonnes* and the strategy based on adapting to local warfare.[55]

They even went further back. They had another model to hand which related to their own education: Julius Caesar. Voulet had ordered a number of books that would constitute a small library for the mission. The library contained the accounts of major travellers of the region, Barth, Perron, Monteil, Stanley, Houant, and Lini; several anthropology manuals such as Havelague, Hartman, or Broca's famous *Instruction pour des recherches anthropologiques*; and medical guides on diseases including Laveran's treatise on malaria and Burot's book on soldiers' diseases. The less utilitarian books included a narrow selection: Rabelais, Pierre Loti, Alphonse Allais, 12 copies of the Qu'ran, Daudet's adventures of *Tartarin de Tarascon* and its sequel, Flaubert's orientalist novel *Salambô*, and a twenty-volume encyclopaedic dictionary.[56]

Some were light-hearted reads such as the absurd humour of Alphonse Allais, but the books ordered in largest quantity after the twelve copies of the Qu'ran, probably intended to be available to all French soldiers of the expedition, were Julius Caesar's *De Bello Gallica* in French translation, the works of Sallust, and Quintus Curtius's Latin life of Alexander the Great. It is difficult to understand today how relevant and immediate the knowledge of ancient Rome was to nineteenth-century Frenchmen. Throughout their secondary education the privileged few whose education continued beyond the age of fourteen were fed a constant diet of Latin. Together with Cicero, Caesar was deemed to be the most accessible and pedagogically useful of classical authors.

Reading Caesar in a colonial setting was not as strange as it may seem. Indeed the parallel between Roman and French colonization had been made for over sixty years in Algeria. Napoleon III during his visit to Algeria had paid much attention to the Roman remains found there and had made a clear comparison between the colonization of Algeria and that of Gaul, making the essential claim that if the French were the result of brought-in civilization, they could now act in the same manner towards the North Africans. The Gallo–Roman assimilation, which had been so effective as to imply the disappearance of the Gallic Celtic languages, seemed a viable model for assimilation of the colonized into the colonizer's polity.

By 1899, this comparison seemed a cliché and many military men objected to the assimilation agenda, preferring instead to advocate the renewal of local culture according to a more British imperial rule. If the Romans were the model it followed that the natives were like Gauls. What had been done to the Gauls could be done to the colonized people.

Julius Caesar seemed an important example from a military and political perspective. Napoleon I had written an extensive commentary on Caesar and Caesar's campaigns were taught in the military schools that Chanoine and Voulet had attended, together with more recent strategists such as Napoleon and Bugeaud. Chanoine, and after him his brother, had been trained to be an officer directly from school.[57] Meanwhile Voulet had risen through the ranks. Yet to make this difference of education an essential difference is to misread the military culture of *fin de siècle* France. According to William Sernam only one-third of French officers had followed Chanoine's prestigious route. The vast majority were in the Voulet mould and this empirical training was not lacking in prestige.[58] Training in the army remained primarily practical rather than based in theory. Indeed academically trained officers like Captain Dreyfus were deemed suspicious. Many generals owed their entire career to their daring and courage rather than any academic study.

Rising from the ranks meant that education could be gathered along the way, which Voulet, the son of a medical doctor,

1. Portraits of Voulet and Chanoine (26 August 1899).

2. African warfare according to the *Journal des Voyages, 1902.*

290. Afrique Occidentale - SOUDAN — KOULIKORO — Buffet et Hôtel Terminus
du Chemin de Fer de Kayes au Niger

3. Kayes *c.*1900.

4. Boats in Kayes *c.*1900.

5. Picture of Voulet and Chanoine scrutinizing the map of Soudan in 1898.

6. Heads in a jar (*L'Illustration*, 11 April 1891).

7. Bodies of captives (*L'Illustration*, 11 April 1891).

8. Dispatching corpses in the river (*L'Illustration*, 11 April 1891).

9. Portrait of Colonel Klobb, 1902.

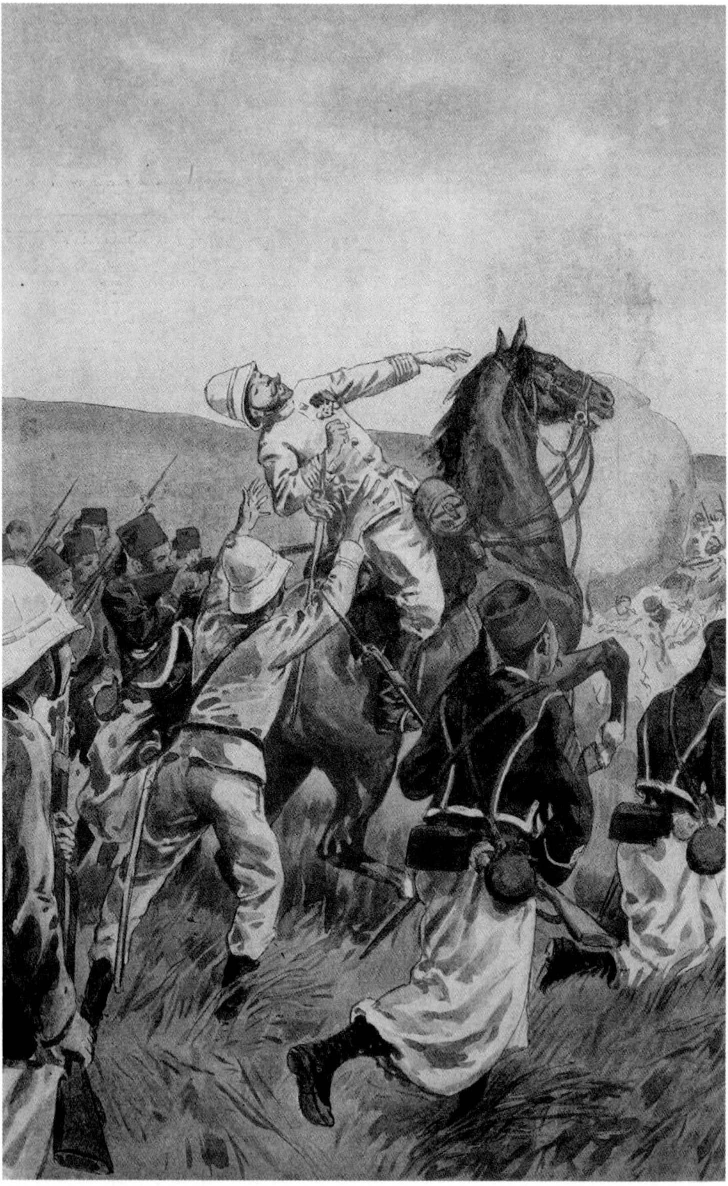

10. Death of Commandant Lamy, 1900.

11. Village de Liberté *c.*1905.

12. Voulet and Chanoine's porters in 1901.

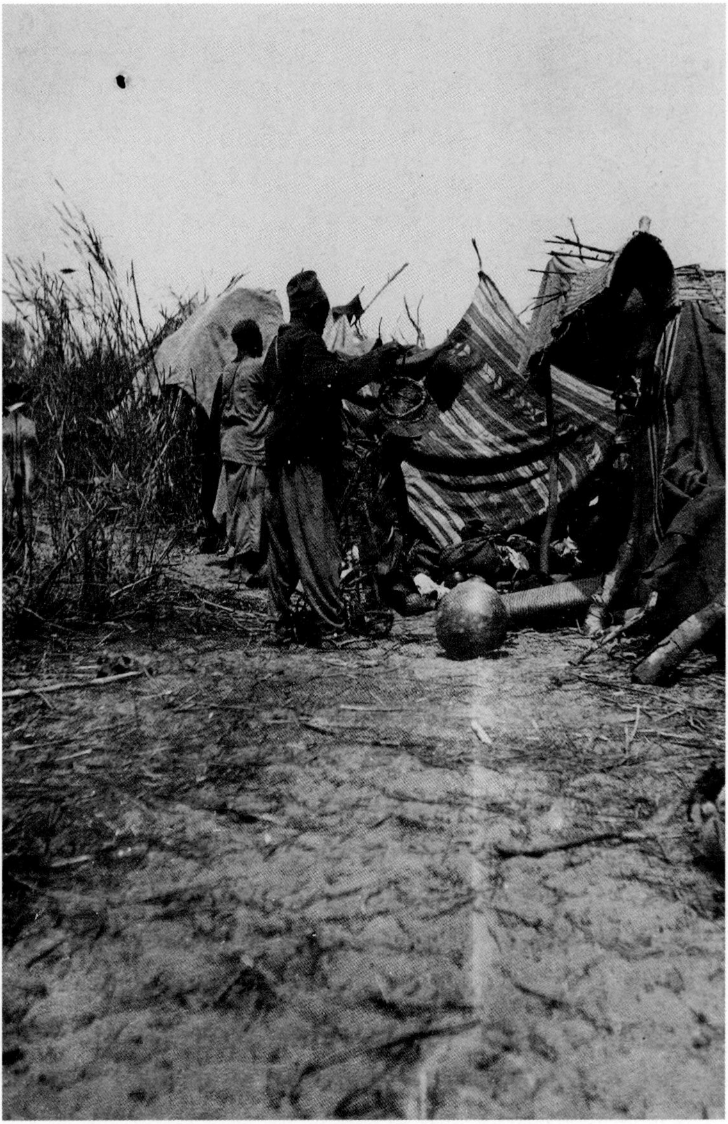

13. Chebaré, the soldiers of Voulet and Chanoine in 1900.

14. Portrait of Jules Charles Chanoine (*Assiette au Beurre*, 1902, p.1124).

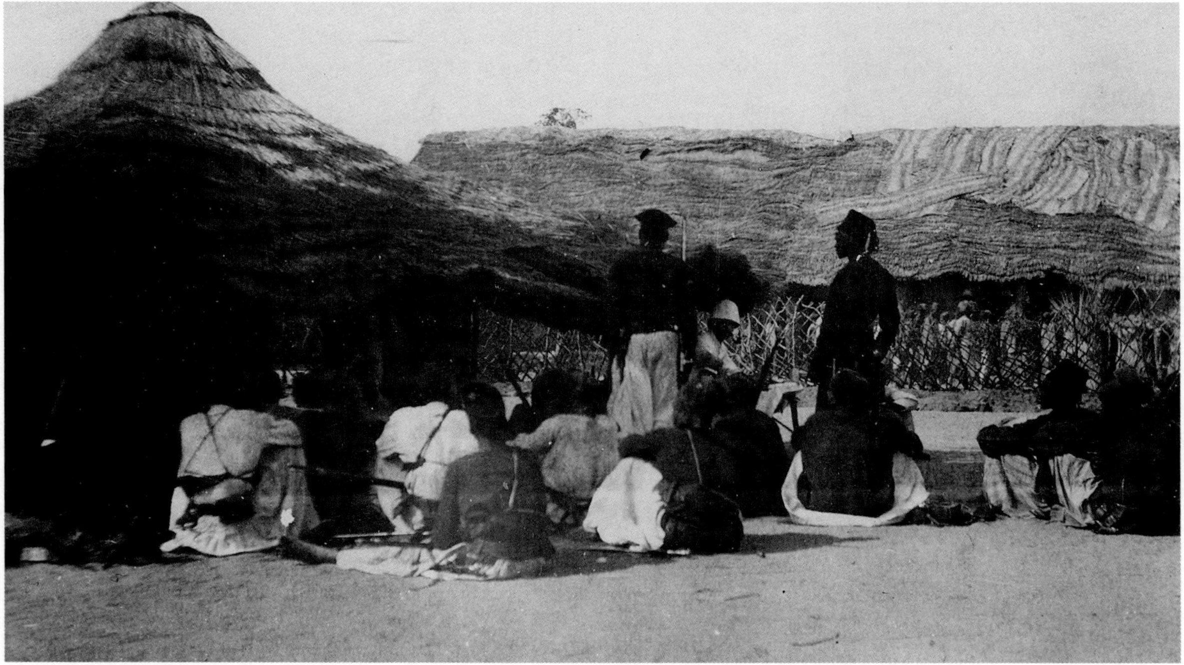

15. Say, paying the soldiers, 1901.

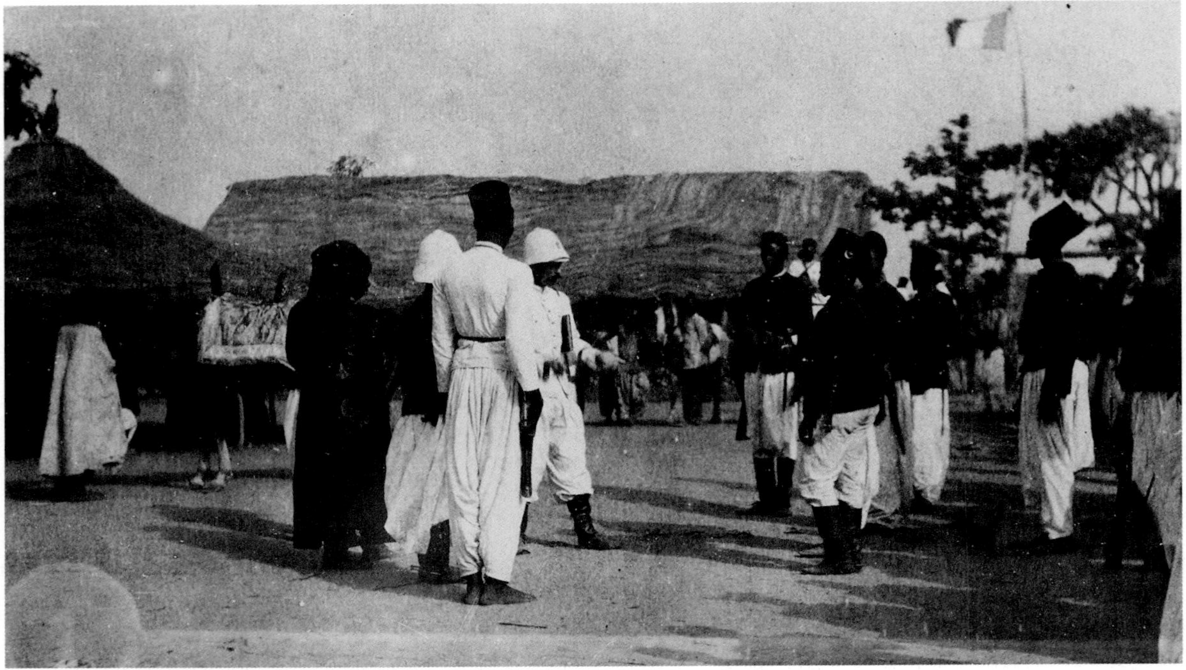

16. Joalland saying farewell to his NCOs, 1901.

17. Say: Joalland and his followers, 1901.

18. The tombs of Voulet and Chanoine, 1909.

had done, completing his empirical education with the appropriate officer training at the École Militaire d' Application de l'Infanterie. There he was trained on the lessons of 1870, which denounced the defensive strategy followed in this disastrous campaign, and other historical lessons, some of which were based on Julius Caesar. Caesar was not simply a general; he was an empire builder and ultimately the political model for all ambitious military men. The term 'caesarism' was used in France at the time to denounce any general who might be tempted to follow in the footsteps of military dictatorship.

If one reads *De Bello Gallica* one is struck by the absolute brutality of the conquest. Cities were burnt and vanquished armies were taken into captivity, tribes allied to the Romans were rewarded, and Gaul in its entirety was peppered with military settlements linked by a road network. West Africa was deemed to resemble Gaul in 58 BC. Similarly divided and without any central leadership, the tribes of Soudan were under threat from foreigners, their military valour was no longer what it had been. Like the Romans the French advanced along clearly defined axes of communication, building railways and freight ships, methodically carving the region into tribal and administrative chieftaincies ruled from afar by French officers. The comparison, however superficial, was appealingly clear. It illustrated how violence could lead to civilization. To Caesar all was forgiven in his triumph as he brought into the Pax Romana the chronically warring tribes of Gaul. Caesar it is true alternated examples of his *clementio*, his pitiful generosity, and his reprisals. His rule was one based on absolute submission which would then lead to political assimilation since one of the consequences of Caesar's victory was that the Roman polity embraced the Gallic elites.

Heroic models and epic storytelling also abounded in the other classical texts taken on this mission to Lake Chad:

Sallust on the conquest of North Africa and the defeat of Jugurtha and a life of Alexander the Great, the conqueror of Asia Minor. The epic mode fitted the soldiers' sense of self-importance and it reflected directly the real autonomy that they enjoyed in the field. In their books and stories this generation of officers consistently defined their role as that of empire makers. Reading each other's writings and emulating the rather grandiose language of the great colonialists Archinard or Faidherbe, the officers became intoxicated by their own legend.

Any notion that Voulet and Chanoine might have gone native would be doubly insulting—both for the 'natives' and for these men. They were applying to the letter a philosophy of colonial war based on mimicry and adaptation. Chanoine like many others in French Soudan could see no harm in aping their previous enemies.

The soldiers themselves had sometimes served with Samory and they could relate to empire building and raids as well as extreme instances of violence. They were all firmly trained in this tradition. When interviewed by a missionary White Father in the 1930s, one of the few Mosse survivors of the expeditions of 1896–9 recalled Voulet as a hard man worthy of respect. Whatever had happened to Voulet and Chanoine in reality, the soldier was right. Their action and their rule never really died and the Africans remained fearful of the possibility of such absolute violence. As Stoller has pointed out this fear could take on supernatural form. In Niger there were many cases of the haunting presence of colonial violence. With a delay of some twenty years, men acting under the possession of *Babulé* spirits were compelled to mimic French soldiers; later called *Hauka* the spirit possession took highly ritualistic forms whereby European spirits modelled on Frenchmen were mad ones. The violent possession of Songhai men led to riotous and subversive scenes halfway between theatre and politics. Eventually the *Hauka* spirits migrated south with the workers from Niger and became common in the Gold Coast (Ghana) where they are well documented. In some sense the mindless violence of the early colonization remained like a carnival of brutality and the *Haukas* represented it through what the French anthropologist Jean Rouch called 'the mad masters', *les maitres fous*, in his pioneering film of *Hauka* possession in Ghana. These possessed spirits appeared in 1925 living through the trauma of conquest and world wars. Eventually and ironically these 'European' spirit possessions were repressed militarily by the French themselves. Ever since, anthropologists have been divided on the matter and most eventually agreed with the colonial powers that *Haukas* were forces rebelling against the colonial presence. As often in other circumstances, a traumatized people found religious solace and political organization in the same movements which combined an understanding of the difficult time they went through with messianic hope.[59]

Voulet would have used terms that echo the shock and awe strategy of more recent conflicts. They knew violence to be the tool of rapid subjugation and they knew something of African rulers, enough to imitate them in order to establish their authority. Folk tales were known to Voulet and Chanoine who like all colonial officers acted as local correspondents to learned societies. By the mid-1890s Soudanese folklore was collected by the French who then attempted to relate its stories and traditions to medieval fables and stories. Observing the power of the despised yet feared *griots* and blacksmiths they sought to understand the power of words and glimpse at the often incomprehensible world view of their new subjects.[60] They appreciated that any hope of imposing themselves on the basis of their technological superiority was doomed: 'To the gramophone and camera brought by the mission', Voulet wrote 'the only words of admiration we receive are these few words: "in truth white men have good blacksmiths [*forgerons*]".'[61]

Western technology failed to have magical purpose and offered no protection. Yet magic was part of the idea of power. Voulet and Chanoine could relate to their soldiers' fears and beliefs through their interpreters. It seems that they took magic and local religion seriously. During the expedition they responded violently to an alleged cursing of a tribute of Kola nuts offered by Birnin Konni. Joalland and other survivors explained, without any sense of European rationalism, that a curse had to be responded to and that magic entailed repression. In other circumstances, the French expedition encountered witchcraft in war and the officers showed some sensitivity to the magical dimension of their power.

All this might have been rewritten in lurid prose and the power of literature might well have built an epic story. Had Klobb not met Voulet and Chanoine on 14 July, their story would have been the success story it was meant to be. Step by step colonial officers invented a world to which they also contributed, shaping and expanding endlessly. For the most ambitious ones, like Klobb, Voulet, and Chanoine, this experience was a life-changing moment which, in the right context could dramatically accelerate a career and ensure some lasting fame.

Their world was undoubtedly isolated and dangerous but it was also the land of opportunity. Thus Klobb rejoiced when he heard of Voulet's approach: 'This mission will enable me to achieve my plans and to take possession of the part of the Niger we did not have yet; I am therefore glad it is happening yet I fear that it may not have any other usefulness.'[62] Chanoine like many of his peers could talk of 'my policy' and of signing treatises with local potentates and regional powers.

Of course some men fell along the way and they were commemorated accordingly. In most cases 'Our Africans' were really these men whose unpreparedness only matched their own self-confidence.[63] These setbacks were only temporary and the constant logic of the imperial mission was never to negotiate durably on a defeat.

Death was invariably associated with chivalrous images and the death of Colonel Klobb was no exception. In Octave Meynier's account his death puts him on a pedestal close to martyrdom, at a level enjoyed by few military men except perhaps Gordon of Karthoum a decade earlier.[64]

As soon as the first shots were fired the colonel was wounded to his right thigh, Meynier was shot in the stomach. He pulled his sabre.

'—No, no Meynier put your sabre back,' the colonel said softly while rubbing his wounded leg.

Meynier was just letting his guard down when a bullet hit him in the chest and threw him to the ground, dead. Sergeant Mamadou Ouahe seeing the lieutenant dead asked for the authorization to shoot.

'—No, no shooting,' replied the colonel, immobile on his horse, looking straight ahead, admirably calm and composed. Almost immediately a new salve shot him dead with a wound to the head.

This early version of the events, written from the witness accounts of a handful of survivors who had reached Say in disarray, contains some major errors, notably that Meynier is killed, but it fixed durably the image of Klobb as a composed sacrificial figure refusing to be dragged into civil war.[65] This narrative of the events was then relayed in the press and in official reports. It contained a number of strange features. Klobb's quiet acceptance of his death; his heroic attitude to suffering recalled Christ at the point of his arrest. Indeed Klobb demanded from Meynier the sort of resignation to fate Jesus asked from his disciple Peter. The stance described in remarkably precise terms seems to be entirely made up. Other soldiers' accounts differed significantly and revealed that between the realization that they were ambushed and Klobb's death virtually no time elapsed. The surprise had been complete.

Beyond Klobb's death, another character was built up as a heroic and saintly officer. Commandant Lamy, military commander of the Sahara mission who had crossed Africa towards Lake Chad from the north, presented an alternative model of gentlemanly behaviour and self-sacrifice.[66] After Voulet had been deemed to have failed, the command of his mission was transferred to Lamy. A coded telegram stated new instruction for his mission:

> Because of grave accusations against Voulet and Chanoine for cruel acts committed by them, Government has sent from Soudan Lieutenant-Colonel Klobb to take command of mission. If you meet mission before Klobb, I instruct you in agreement with minister of war to notify Voulet and Chanoine that they are relieved and that you are put in command until Klobb meets you. You will continue towards Lake Chad according to Voulet's instructions... Beware that road to Say will be dangerous for the return of Foureau because of cruel deeds inflicted on people by Voulet. The two missions could unite under same command towards Lake Chad.[67]

Eventually Lamy died in battle against Rabah, the key Muslim potentate and slave driver of the Chad region. Dying on the battlefield, Lamy became the incarnation of self-sacrifice while his diaries exemplify the intellectual and moral depth of a model French officer.[68] In this process of heroicization his opponent was devalued:

How could we compare the loss of such a soldier and great patriotic figure as Commandant Lamy to the elimination of a negro as vulgar as Rabah . . . the moral worth of this bloodthirsty brute was negligible, less than nothing, meanwhile the services that the nation and civilization could expect from a man such as Lamy were beyond limits[69]

Of course Lamy himself had ordered a number of executions along the way. On 14 August he wrote in his diary: 'I am worried, bothered. The guide, Klelil who did not seem very sure of the way has been accused of being a traitor and shot. The death of a man in these circumstances is always difficult to accept. Was he even a traitor?'[70] His mission did not take prisoners when attacked and bayoneted any captives when triumphant,[71] but these incidents were edited out at the time and Lamy's death lent itself to a glorious reinvention. In the illustrated press, Lamy was thus pictured on horseback shot by the enemy while supported by his faithful soldiers (Figure 10). The picture was closer to the fate of Klobb than that of Lamy who was shot leading an assault on a fortified town. Yet, mainly through his death, just as Voulet and Chanoine had been demoted from heroes to villains in the space of a few weeks, Lamy became the redemptive figure the colonial enterprise needed.[72]

5

SLAVING AND AFRICAN WARFARE

> Throughout the width of Africa, the arms of the French Republic are protecting the traffic of ebony wood [black Africans]. Since the capture of Samory and the dispersal of his bands, French officers and their bands are the only providers on the human flesh markets. They are surrounded by harems, herds of human cattle: they put down the decrepit elders; they separate the women from their offspring, they sell the mothers in the West for one hundred and fifty francs and the children to the East for two francs (forty sous). On their return to France after a good career as slave traders, having paid their debts with their profits on the price of slave meat, they become proud members of the antislavery societies and present humanitarian essays to the Institute of Moral Sciences competition.[1]

Urbain Gohier's vibrant and pugnacious preface to Paul Vigné d'Octon's equally emphatic denunciation of French crimes in Africa contained a measure of exaggeration but also a kernel of truth. Its main allegation of an institutional slave trade was probably seen as defamatory by most French people and like the book itself, set aside in all but the most radical circles. Yet the gradual accumulation of a large crowd of captives is one of the salient features of the Voulet–Chanoine expedition—to many it explained its slow and relentlessly violent progress. One should try to understand the rationale for this accumulation of 'impedimenta', as Joalland called the wretched captives, against the background of growing 'humanitarian ideals' taking place at the end of the nineteenth century.

Denouncing the French army for slave trading was going against the spirit of twenty years of anti-slavery campaigning supported by the Catholic Church.[2] Since the 'crusade against slavery' had become a central cause of the Catholic Church, the archbishop of Algiers and Tunis, Cardinal Lavigerie, had begun drawing attention to the plight of African slaves and the role the French army ought to play in this new crusade.[3]

In the renewal of the anti-slavery campaigns, the French had been at the forefront but they worked with pre-existing movements which had been firmly led by the nonconformists in Britain and the USA.[4] In France the anti-slavery cause was one most often associated with the republicans rather than the Catholics and the leading figure had been the abolitionist Victor Schoelcher.[5]

In the 1880s and 1890s, slavery was represented as the plague of Africa, and as the main cause of backwardness in its civilization. Not only were the slaves victims but their attitude of servility was deemed to ensure that slavery would perpetuate.[6] Self-righteous Frenchmen often complained bitterly that liberated slaves seemed to understand wealth only through the ownership of other slaves. The great enemies of the French conquest were always presented as slave-trading states. The great Samory Touré was represented simply as a trader of slaves; in Dahomey (today's Benin) the young king and his army of amazons were condemned as slave owners, barbarian fetishists practising human sacrifices, and slave traders. Further inland, the fledging kingdom of Rabah of Burnu was also denounced as a slaving operation. There was some truth in that. Rabah had originated from Darfur and had established the economy of his territory on slavery. Further south in eastern Congo, a slave trader, Tippo Tip, ran a proto-state entirely geared towards the exporting of slaves to Zanzibar. He was an opportunistic adventurer rather than an African monarch and he lacked the kind of stature and respect the French gave to Samory Touré.[7] In the French media, slavery was always one of the most heinous crimes, second only to human sacrifice and cannibalism. In imperialist propaganda, the abolition of the slave trade was one of the pretexts that would warrant the 'humanitarian' intervention of French arms.

Even Voulet repeatedly used the word 'humanitarian' to explain the need to conquer and repress the activities of nomadic slave traders. In his January report of 1899 he concluded:

> from the point of view of humanitarian and political interest, France must establish its effective domination on the Niger from Timbuktu to Say; from the humanitarian viewpoint because we will thus prevent the final destruction of the populous and prosperous urban centres that the Tuareg will certainly destroy in a near future by their exactions.[8]

The archived copy of this report was partially underlined in blue, more than likely signifying the Ministry of Colonies' approval.

The fight against the slave trade was also used to explain the Mahdi's jihad in Egyptian Sudan and Darfur. It explains why Gordon's defeat was viewed as the heroic death of a man fighting greedy Arabs.[9] In Congo, the Free State set up by King Leopold II of Belgium was also using this rationale, supported by missionaries, to justify its sudden and vast expansion across the continent.[10]

To the east, the British in Zanzibar scrutinized the sultanate's trading and applied pressure on local slave traders such as Tippo Tip in the great lake region while utilizing their campaign against slavery as a justification for their increased political presence.[11] Livingstone, a few years earlier, had painted the atrocious picture of a continent emptied of its people by warring raiders. Slavery in Africa was at the heart of all political conflicts but was also a response to the growing pressures applied on Africa from outside.[12] Citing Livingstone, the anti-slavery militants described slave traders as hyper-criminals, associating their polygamous way of life with unrestrained lust, greed with the violence of slave capturing.[13]

The terms of this attack on the social evils of a greater evil were sufficiently secular for an anticlerical feminist to embrace. Hubertine Auclert's ferocious denunciation of Islamic society followed the tropes of clerical anti-Islamism almost unconsciously down to the denunciation of slavery in Islamist households.[14] Using the struggle against slavery as a vehicle enabled the geopolitics of Africa to be summarized in an easily comprehensible manner. Who could and who would object to a struggle against slavery? Who could object to saving women, children, and the elderly from the grip of social exploitation? This Manichean representation was of course problematic where native Christian slave-owning societies were concerned and Menelik's empire which used slave trading to finance its conquests never fitted the stereotype despite Italian attempts to portray Ethiopia in the same light as Sudan.[15]

The main artisan of this anti-slavery propaganda was dead by 1892; yet his influence remained central in French politics. Cardinal Charles Lavigerie, who had given a pan-European impulse to the anti-slavery campaigns of the 1880s, had managed to convince Pope Leo XIII that the Catholic Church should be at the forefront of the anti-slavery struggle. Lavigerie had become aware of African slavery through his work in Algeria where a few slaves still lived and through his missionary society, the White Fathers, characteristically dressed in the fashion of Arabs, in *gandoura*, and almost invariably bearded. The priests were sent on missions to Africa, often finding themselves in fierce competition with other missionaries. They settled in isolated locations, soon building their dispensaries and schools next to their church and compound. They often immediately followed in the steps of the French army and in other places pre-dating French or Belgian colonization.[16]

In central Africa, near the river Congo, the missionaries encountered slavery at its most rampant. Like Stanley before them they met the long processions of women and children enslaved by the traders of Zanzibar. In Zanzibar slavery was not abolished until 1897, the struggle was led by a fundraising campaign to purchase slaves and install them in 'villages of liberty' or settle them near newly established missions (see Figure 11). In some instances the struggle was real and armed men were called on to defend missionaries and defeat slave-traders raiding the hinterland of Africa. Catholic pioneers such as Captain Joubert devoted their lives to this war.[17]

Since most of the traders were Arabs, the struggle against slavery gave new impetus to Lavigerie's campaign against Islamism. If Lavigerie was relatively content making friends among Protestant anti-slavery campaigners; he retained his venom for Muslims. For a long time, Lavigerie's hopes of converting Algeria had been thwarted by weary military administrators. Convinced that the French administration would do nothing to undermine the Muslim status quo, possibly even favour Muslims over Animists or converts to Christianity, Lavigerie used the struggle against slavery as a means of heightening awareness of the threat posed by Islam in his view.

Lavigerie's aim was the abolition of the slave trade, enslavement, and slave ownership by Arabs and marauding traders. The trail of destruction these late traders left in central Africa had been immense. The traders benefited from the same technological superiority that also enabled the Europeans to conquer these lands. As a result slaves ended up in other parts of Africa or in the Middle East. A significant portion were 'freed' to become indentured servants. Indenture service had been a key tool for plantation economies struggling to convert from a slave to a free workforce. An indentured servant was essentially living under conditions similar to that of the slaves of old; yet, unlike slaves, the servants could capitalize their small income and, at the end of seven years of work, could return home. The French territories overseas used indentured service extensively. The servants came from India or from mainland Africa. Notionally, liberated slaves could be signed up for service and the slave trade fed on this practice.

None of these subtleties made it to the public arena. Instead the picture was painted in garish tones, with lurid descriptions of murder, torture, cannibalism, and mindless violence. The slave-traders were the enemy the Western powers had to defeat and to defeat them fully was only possible through colonization. Lavigerie was thus unashamedly imperialistic; yet his imperialism was undoubtedly Catholic and he even envisaged private warfare if the great powers could not be convinced to step in.

In his preaching from the 1870s Lavigerie clearly argued that the causes of French colonial armies were 'the triumph of honour, of humanity, of justice over the most monstrous barbarity'.[18] In France, Catholics were in the political wilderness and had not taken part in any constructive manner in the new Republic. Lavigerie, backed by the pope, was to be instrumental in 1891 in reconciling Catholics to the new regime. After twenty years of republican rule, some Catholics saw that the only way of ensuring a future for their ideals was to embrace a regime they loathed. The *ralliement*, as it became known, was not entirely successful as many Catholics remained royalists whilst Republicans feared the Catholics within the Republic even more than when they were outsiders. For all his conflicts with the French state, Lavigerie had a grander vision. For Lavigerie and his allies the game was played on the world stage and Lavigerie was undoubtedly one of the first princes of the Church to see the future of the faith outside Europe.

Pope Leo XIII made the struggle against slavery a universal religious priority for missionaries and the faithful alike and the Catholic clergy evoked an African crusade, an armed mission aimed against the barbaric Africans and what Lavigerie called 'Islamism', the political regimes and societies ruled by Islamic law.[19]

In Congo, Lavigerie faced another entrepreneur, King Leopold II, who was central to the scramble for Africa and carved out for himself gigantic territories the size of Europe with the help of privateers such as Stanley. Even though Lavigerie publicly declared his admiration for Leopold, privately he strongly opposed the capitalistic intentions of the king and his coterie of 'free masons'.[20] Ultimately private enterprise proved unable to lead the anti-slavery crusade since the governments of Europe had seized the initiative from them. At the 1885 international congress in Berlin, European powers declared Africa an empty land, a Res Nullius, up for grabs since no one owned it. This was half-recognition of what had already taken place and half a new programme. To add a layer of respectability to the enterprise, the white man's burden was used as a cloak; colonization became justified as the enfranchisement of Africans from themselves.

Never was the urge to intervene in the name of freedom so freely justified. Who could contradict an enterprise devoted to human happiness and freedom? However, the humanitarian logic of the colonial enterprise was in stark contrast to the means employed to achieve the conquest.

Livingstone and Verney Lovett Cameron's writings and the reports made by Stanley provided the sensational platform from which Lavigerie renewed his campaigns against the evil of 'Mahomedism' or Islamism.[21] In the 1870s Stanley described his encounters above Stanley Pool with the proto-state of a major slave trader, Tippo Tip, whose trading networks led across the continent to the Sultanate of Zanzibar.[22] From Zanzibar slaves were traded to the Arab peninsula and served in plantations in the east of Africa. Presented crudely the slave trade of central and eastern Africa appeared as the last great evil of the age, one conspicuously serving the interests of Muslim leaders and societies. Lavigerie estimated the slave trade of central Africa at 500,000 slaves per annum. Based on Cameron's reporting, he ventured the figure of 30 casualties for each traded female slave. This would make 15 million victims of slavery. Even in more sober analyses, it was clear that the extraction of slaves was extremely bloody and figures vary as to the numbers killed in slaving raids. In some cases it might have been as low as one live slave for every three dead, or as high as 1 for 10 or indeed up to 30. Slaves often fell victim to the abject conditions of their captivity. Furthermore the moral picture of slave traders associated all the tropes of Orientalism: unrestrained lust, greed, and cruelty.[23]

Thus to describe French officers as slave traders was no mean insult. Yet Vigné d'Octon did not face duels on the matter (perhaps because he was a fine fencer himself),[24] the book was not condemned, and in parliament no one really challenged his evidence. Voulet and Chanoine had, the year before, unwittingly exposed the murky economics of French colonial expansion. After all, they had up to 800 slaves in tow when their trail ended.

Listen! Our indigenous troops either need to be increased or renewed, the commanders of the 'cercles' [military and administrative districts] receive the orders for recruiting in their districts a fixed number of subjects; at the same time they receive the important funds required by this operation. From that moment in those posts the register of volunteers is open, which means that all the caravans of slave drivers are welcome to present their wares to the commander. From that moment also this sort of traffic is no longer called 'slave trade' but *acts of enfranchisement*, the slave is no longer a slave but a volunteer.[25]

Despite the militant tone of his writings, Vigné d'Octon knew his facts and, over the previous fifty years in Western Africa, the French had often used the slave trade to feed their own military needs—they were not alone in this in sub-Saharan Africa. By 1899, many if not most of the Senegalese troops were bought out of slavery this way. Their freedom was then limited to the demands of the long service they now owed the French army. They found their matrimonial match either among women of the same origins, freed slaves themselves, or through conquest by enslaving or stealing the slaves of others. Chanoine in the Gurunsi thus instructed:

in Balélé you can use here our Samos prisoners dressing them properly, giving them some muskets you will buy in Fontankès, four in Balélé and four at Ona-Loubala. I'll set them up by getting them married locally so that they do not desert, their mission would be to show the French flag to every traveller coming by, that would not stop us from having a local agent who would be a man of the village.[26]

In this manner and at the cost of a handful of primitive weapons and some cloth, Chanoine used ex-slaves to staff the border of the empire. 'Setting them up' would be done under duress with local women bought from their families by a mixture of gifts and threats.[27]

At that stage and on the ground, polygamy was not objected to by the French army and the payment in kind, of female slaves, was considered normal by the French.[28] The custom was meant to mirror that of local chieftains. When the Sultan of Zinder was deposed by the French a full census of his harem was undertaken.[29] Of the 81 women of his household, 69 were slaves or captives taken by force, another 5 had been bought on the market, and only 4 were what the French recognized as legitimate free wives.[30] According to Joalland, 'Voulet had for a principle that one had to force feed [*gaver*] the men in order to get from them the maximum of loyalty and work. A good principle, when you do not have to undertake a long campaign.'[31]

As Thompson has shown this domestic arrangement was crucial for the material organization of French colonial troops. Meynier even argued that 'the presence of this *smala* does not provoke any disorder. The "*moussos*" are tough and follow gaily the squads.'[32] Captured women and 'freed' slaves formed the indentured backbone of the colonial army.[33] Without this parallel society of tirailleurs, the French colonial armies would have been unable to operate on such low budgets and during such long campaigns.

The observers and travellers to Soudan soon picked this approach to slavery and republicans as well as conservatives shared the 'localist' viewpoint:

Yes it is awful to say it but the black slaves in our possession at this time at least do not want our pity... It is so true that in

Senegal and Soudan captives have never taken advantage of our protection or of the 1789 principles we peddle about to gain their freedom. He knows that he only has to enter our outposts to become free and put himself under the protection of our washed out tricolours to be enfranchised on the spot—he does not come! If you drive him there under duress he escapes to return to his chains!!![34]

The naïve or disingenuous republican witness of colonial rule imagined a consistency in practice which was far from the case. Faced with a variety of situations of slavery, captivity, domestic subservience, and the complexities of African extended kinship, the French defined slavery narrowly as being either of a domestic kind (*de case*) or the result of trade or war. On the one hand, domestic slaves were not liable to be enfranchised easily since their familial bonds seemed complex and eminently variable; on the other, trade slaves were identifiable assets liable to be confiscated.

When slaves escaped, the French administrators followed the rules applicable to all economic assets. In most instances they chose to return escapees to their masters. As Martin Klein has noted, French attitudes to slavery were a mixture of realpolitik and, at times, an embrace of the pleasures of slave-owning societies.[35] It seems that on the whole they stopped short of becoming fully fledged slave plantation owners, with some significant exceptions. As late as 1895, Governor Grodet discovered a plantation staffed by 120 slaves belonging to Commandant Quiquandon and working for his sole benefit.[36] At his request the commandant was recalled to France where he obtained promotion shortly afterwards. The slaves were 'liberated' and resettled.

Apart from brief anti-slavery interludes such as the one of the civilian governor Grodet, the practice of returning slaves was a way to cement a protectorate and maintain a fragile economic and social order. The principles of the rights of man and citizens first proclaimed in 1789, if they were widely shared at all among the military, fared poorly in this context. When considering slavery, sub-Saharan Africa presented a dilemma. Some even alleged that Victor Schoelcher, the French Wilberforce, had given his support to this toleration of slavery.[37]

The dilemma of slavery originated from the absence of a labour market from which the colonial administration could recruit either soldiers or workers. Facing societies without a class system or economies intelligible to Western economists, even liberals concurred in thinking that slavery and polygamy would be slow to disappear and that rushing their abolition might be counterproductive. While economists argued that colonialism would expand the liberating effects of free trade and the beneficial effects of a market economy throughout the world, they also admitted that these changes would be gradual.[38] In most instances market economics were suspended in favour of monopolistic concessions given to enterprising capitalists willing to invest in remote areas which presented the risk of low returns. If the capital was not free, neither was the labour market, even in well-controlled areas. In the era of breakneck colonialism forced labour was universally applied in French colonies. Though the living conditions of forced labourers were akin to that of slavery, the colonialists reassured themselves that this work served the higher interests of the empire. In Soudan forced labour applied mostly to the building of roads, railways, and towns, the digging of wells, and the planting of commercial crops. The most common form of forced labour, however, was human portage itself. Even where there were no slaves, there were few genuinely freemen. Frenchmen on the ground accepted slavery as an African reality, not imposed on Africans but the product of African social organization. In 1898–9 none of the French officers thought the complete abolition of slavery possible. Archinard in the 1890s defined the French policy, quoting General Gordon of Khartoum for his moral authority:

> I think it is pointless and dangerous to pretend to abolish slavery, we would empty the country around us. It is true . . . that slavery appears over there under seducing guises but for one who has seen things closely and for a long time, for someone who does not simply consider anecdotes or children's stories, slavery is nevertheless a deeply sad and demoralizing thing. We must fight against it but we can only debate our choice of weapons and the time to use them.

He then argued that ending war among Africans would dry up the supply of slaves, that better modes of communication, currencies, and transport would reduce the value of slaves as a means of exchange and transport. Finally he argued in favour of a gradual enfranchising process using freedom villages.[39] This gradualist approach had the benefit of keeping the local elites on side and of maintaining the use of slaves in the developing economy. Yet French officers knew that the anti-slavery struggle was one of the key elements of any civilizing mission and the spirit of the scramble for Africa had been cloaked in anti-slavery propaganda since the 1880s.

The French tolerance of slavery was not unique among colonial empires and in Nigeria the slaves were formally enfranchised by the Master and Servant proclamation of 1903, roughly at the same time as their peers in French Soudan.[40] Yet slavery was so deeply entrenched that whatever status replaced it resembled slavery to the point of being indistinguishable from it. Sierra Leone retained slaves formally until 1927 despite being a country created for the benefit of freed slaves.[41] In the French colonies slave markets operated openly until the 1920s and it is still unclear whether servitude has disappeared completely from Western Africa.

In their private life (and the French evidence in this respect is sketchy), French officers seem to have had first pick among the captives. The Voulet–Chanoine expedition was thus not behaving entirely outside the norm when it built up its large captive population, estimated at around 800 women by the time it stopped near Zinder. Even if historians have identified a 'swelling' in the number of available slaves as a result of their action, this swelling was commensurate to the dimension of the expedition.[42] These women were primarily captives allocated to the soldiers themselves and to the auxiliaries recruited by Chanoine whose salaries were due to come out entirely from the spoils of war. They were increasingly carrying loads of their own and helped with the management of the cattle. Sergeant Bouthel even suggested that female slaves 'freed later on could be given as a reward for the convoy drivers and be the nucleus of [porters] at the inevitable moment when we will have to replace donkeys with men and women.'[43]

After the expedition stopped in Zinder, the large cohort of captives had an uncertain fate. There is some evidence that Sergeant Bouthel freed many of them.[44] Other sources show that many captives were reclaimed by their families or previous masters; however, the sources are unclear as to who stayed in Zinder and how many returned on the same tracks with Pallier and Henric and the 'unreliable' units. As often the lack of information in sources reflects the lack of importance given to slaves and to their disregard as people.

Any claims made about slavery were disingenuous. The conquest, with its own logic and its own realpolitik, had begun well before the new humanitarian ideals were deployed.[45] The impetus given to the conquest had propelled the empires towards a largely unknown hinterland. These campaigns were led with geo-strategic aims in mind and few concerns regarding slavery or the civilizing mission.

Perhaps as a result of limited human resources, the missions invading Africa were prone to demonstrative violence, as shown in Chapter 4. French soldiers were supposed to be used to slaving warfare and slaving warfare was a means of attaching them to the cause of the French. Since in most of tropical Africa beasts of burden were unable to survive, porters were used instead. These men and women, loaded with up to 25 kg on their head and backs, were notionally not slaves; yet as requisitioned and unpaid servants their conditions were similar (see Figure 12). Chanoine roamed the Mosse to find the porters he needed, he then parked them, undressed despite cold nights, in guarded compounds each night. The sick and dying were left behind; those who attempted to flee were beaten up with the same ruthlessness one would find under the slavery codes of the eighteenth century.

These porters were treated harshly in every expedition that required them. In the controversial expedition of the 'Mount Kongs' which took place in 1895, led by Lieutenant-Colonel Monteil, the conditions were somewhat similar to those of Voulet's mission.[46] The Kong expedition was a disastrous campaign against Samory which also faced sustained resistance in the Baoule region. In what ended in a difficult retreat, in itself a genuine French defeat, the survivors chose to describe individual skirmishes as victories.[47] Neither the official accounts nor the propaganda ever described the plight of the terrorized porters.

Porters who refused to serve had the soles of their feet burnt before being hanged. Some were hanged slowly to strangle them above a fire.[48] Evidence for this level of brutality towards native porters is scant. Chanoine executed ten deserters on his way to Say for instance; yet official figures for the mortality rates speak volumes: the attrition rate among porters of colonial missions was over 25 per cent.[49] Even Cazemajou was accused of atrocities when he took 350 porters with him and lost a third along the way, killing those who could not or would not walk.[50] After Cazemajou's death his behaviour was never mentioned again.

The load the porters carried, it was often argued, hardly exceeded that of soldiers on campaign (about 20 to 25 kg), but their rations, clothing, and medical care were grossly inadequate for the distances they had to cover. The Voulet column lost dozens of its men to illness, starvation, and thirst. In the Voulet mission two standards were applied: 'there was an order to kill the prisoners who refused to carry their load but this was not applied to the men recruited in Soudan among the Mosse.'[51]

Tied together five by five, the porters were under armed guard. In the normal portage scheme the porters were hired for a portion of the journey and replaced with fresh ones on a regular basis. Yet Chanoine was accused of refusing to send back the porters hired for one portion of the journey.[52] The evidence was that they were eventually freed after a couple of months. Yet each time some were freed others had to be enslaved: 'Send me some porters to replace each group of twenty I set free.'[53] Freemen alone survived if they stumbled or collapsed under their burden.

Yet in a letter to the member of parliament Étienne, on 25 March 1899, Voulet showed blatant hypocrisy or the most astonishing naïve cynicism:

> in a humanitarian ideal we have substituted animal portage for humans carrying boxes on their heads; thus we have now 40 camels, 200 donkeys and 100 bullocks ... we maintain our cattle to about 200 heads. In these conditions the march is obviously slow as we have the great satisfaction of saving human lives. Everyday we have to find 40 tons of water.[54]

At the time when Voulet wrote it is true that the great decimation of his porters was a thing of the past but the transfer to animal carrying was only as a result of raiding and slave trading for animals. Each animal was worth several slaves as the oral evidence recalls.[55] At that stage Voulet and Chanoine exchanged human cattle for horses and load-carrying animals.[56]

This constant violence against human herds must be read between the lines of most hagiographic records. Officers were often shocked by one another's actions but an element of solidarity prevented leaks which might further harm the whistle-blower rather than guilty men. Typically the men closest to the murders of Sansané Haoussa were reluctant to put to paper what they had seen: 'I will be happy to make some things known to you that I do not want to write down.'[57]

It took Voulet's conflict with his base of Say for many of his deeds to become officially noted and sent as a confidential report to Kayes. In Kayes nothing happened until Péteau leaked information to the press. It is unclear whether the Crave report of February 1899 would have made it to the archives had Voulet survived and succeeded in his mission. In fact the administrative process worked in reverse.

When Paris sent a telegram asking for an officer to be sent after Voulet, the administration constituted a file to establish that it was already aware of his actions and was building up a case against him. On 28 April de Trentinian wrote in the margins of a report: 'the Voulet mission horrors, who can tell them to me? Send to policy office.'[58] The limited level of scrutiny did not mean there was no intelligence as to what was going on in the field. Far from it. There was intelligence and rules were routinely ignored but colonial officers exploited a degree of discretionary tolerance. At any time the trap could close on them. So why take such risks?

On the whole, until 1899 the risks were minimal, and until Voulet and Chanoine the sanctions were so small as to seem insignificant. Military censorship was applied strictly to all correspondence out of Soudan and the fact that Péteau managed later to get his detailed letters leaked to *Le Matin* and Vigné d'Octon was in itself a remarkable event.[59] As well, self-censorship ensured that little information ever saw the light of day. Self-censorship relied on collective solidarity and on a common sense of beleaguered identity. When Granderye using the evidence of Delaunay wrote an irate and scandalized political report from Say on 1 March 1898 which denounced the killings of Sansané Haoussa, he was punished for it. His superior officer wrote in the margin: 'this is an act of accusation not a political report'; he was then called to order and taught how to write 'proper' political reports.[60] Subsequent reports from Say made no further mention of Voulet except to mention that Chanoine had contributed to the pacification. To regular and sometimes loud denunciation of their methods the French officers responded that they had no choice. The state had not given them the means by which to apply the expansionist colonial policy.

Yet the Voulet expedition, under-resourced as it was, carried ice-making equipment, loads of trade cloth and jewels which could be used to bribe chieftains and buy slaves or peace treaties, bottles of champagne, and the trappings of civilized life. A phonograph with records and blank cylinders, a camera with all the necessary equipment to develop photographs in the field, and a multitude of other objects travelled on the heads of Mosse men. The cumbersome and largely unnecessary quantities of items Voulet had purchased for his expedition had to be carried at the cost of many human lives.

If slavery was part of the structure of military expedition it was also the product of a successful campaign. The captives were slaves. This was the 'African' logic of war which was not to be contradicted. When the chieftain Samory Touré was captured in 1898, 40,000 people were captured with him and disposed of at the whim of colonial officers to quasi-universal approval in France. The auxiliaries of campaigns against Samory and the campaigns of 'pacification' were paid in slaves.[61]

In a notorious incident in 1894 the commander of Soudan supervised a vast redistribution of captives seized in Bosse which reached not only the soldiers of the column but also the collaborators and employees of the military administration of Djenné. Voulet did not act any differently. His last moments were in the company of a woman, probably one of Chanoine's sex slaves, but he had one of his own too. In fact his officers went as far as to blame some of his crimes on his African wife.[62]

The tirailleurs could expect to obtain wives or tradable human beings which could then be exchanged for a necessary complement to their insufficient military wages. Only through systematic slavery could the French army sustain its already small permanent army afoot. The French government knew this but the financial constraints were always more important than any moral concerns. In this sense, the mass of slaves accumulated by Voulet and Chanoine was normal considering their lengthy journey. It was proportional to the duration of their campaign.

The Pallier report of August 1899 was the official version of events agreed on by the officers of the mission and the answer to the Péteau report found among Klobb's papers. In answer to Péteau it listed the villages and towns seized:

Lougou, Birnin Konni. Much of the action took place in 'British territory' but Chanoine acted with a sense of impunity: from the 9th to the 24th May, they were raiding 15 to 20 kms around the main convoy, burning the many villages that were there. The captain was responding to the manoeuvres of the Sultan of Sokoto. We were it is true on English land, but we had the firm conviction that the Sultan of Sokoto would hide from the English the destructions of the Column in order to keep up his prestige and strength.[63]

At one stage Chanoine raided a village a mere 50 km from Sokoto itself. The long list of raided villages included towns of 3 to 12,000 people. In every case 'all the villages, all evacuated were burnt, the few individuals we met were taken prisoner'. Guides who lost their bearings or refused to show the way were executed. In Tibiri, Voulet executed the women of the chief who had run away. On 1 July in Karankalgo Chanoine had 150 women and children massacred in reprisal for their resistance. In other instances the slaves were used as informers. Chanoine thus wrote a short note to Voulet on 1 April 1899:

you have entire families captive; send the father [as a spy] and promise to free the rest of the family on his return as a reward; then you will need to send 2 from each to check the results.[64]

Yet the need to take the captives with the column was to become a logistical nightmare. Unable to feed them or provide enough water, the column deviated from its planned route, raiding further and further ahead and aside of the path, gathering yet more slaves in the process. For Voulet and Chanoine the killings were neither uncommon nor objectionable. When the report of Sansané Haoussa was written, it reflected the economic reality of slavery. Voulet explicitly targeted slaves in his reprisals: 'The women were not all old said [the chief], many had only had one child ... and one man was a freeman from Sansané Haoussa. The tirailleurs skewed them with their bayonets until they had all fallen then they cut their throats'; the orders were given by Mhmadou Koulibaly, Voulet's interpreter.[65] In a late report, filed in May 1899, from Lieutenant Salaman, who denied witnessing any violence until the French colonial border, described the scene of Sansané Haoussa in these terms:

On 15th February, I arrived in Sansané Haoussa where I found the remains of about one hundred beheaded bodies—1300 metres from the village, 300 metres from the river—the ground was covered with the bones scattered and torn by the hyenas, a blood trail of thirty metres and 1 metre across was still visible. A common grave of 2 metres by 70 cms contained the bodies of the freemen (40 I was told) buried by orders from the chief. It was impossible for me to get to know the reasons behind *these rigorous measures*.[66]

The rigorous measures were exaggerated since the freemen had not been killed. Indeed it seems that, in the early massacres at least, Voulet took care to kill slaves and to regard it in the same way as he regarded the punitive destruction of other assets. As a matter of fact claims made by the chiefs of villages on the banks of the river Niger were primarily for compensation for lost income rather than for any hope of judiciary retribution.

In their previous campaigns, Voulet and Chanoine had had the latitude to fight their wars according to these methods and they were rewarded for their successes, regardless of the means. In 1898 human life was cheap in Soudan for the conquerors who benefited from an advantageous exchange rate between francs and the local currency of cowries. Cowries were shells from the Indian Ocean which were the stable currency of pre-colonial West Africa and were very slowly replaced by the colonizers' currencies.[67] In 1899 the cowry was in decline, worth only 1/1000 of a franc. Part of the problem of using shells as a currency was that their bulk was considerable in proportion to their value. Cowries were fine for small transactions but not very convenient for long-distance exchanges crisscrossing the Sahel regions. Slaves were more convenient and represented a considerable volume of cowry value. In this sense slaves were not only a product but also the large denomination currency in West Africa. In the more peaceful time of the German traveller Barth, earlier in the century, a slave was worth 33,000 cowries, the value of three slaves being equal to a full load of a camel.[68] Since then cowries had declined considerably in value and the Niger economy had suffered from massive inflation. Five thousand cowries were only worth a 5-franc silver coin by 1895. According to economic historians, by the end of the century a slave was worth between 60,000 and 140,000 cowries.[69] Despite the greater supply of slaves due to wars, slaves held their value better than the shells. A slave was therefore worth between 60 and 140 francs on large markets. In Chanoine's private papers one finds his calculation dating from his stay in Gurunsi and from the rates noted at the market of Sati:

> A captive is worth 20 to 40,000 cowries, 60,000 for exceptional ones, making an average price of about sixty francs. A load of gunpowder is worth one captive; a good horse is worth up to twenty captives; a bar of salt 100,000 cowries or two to three captives, half a bar of salt equals one good captive.[70]

These prices were low and reflected the surplus of slaves generated by the conquest itself at its frontier. For instance, in 1894, near Kayes, the administrative capital of Soudan, Mrs Bonnetain bought a slave girl for her daughter for 180 francs (approx. £7 4*s*), away from the main slave trade.[71]

Brought back to the income of the tirailleurs serving with Voulet (Figure 13), each slave in their possession was the equivalent value of their full wages for 100 to 200 days of service paid at the going rate of 80 centimes per diem. Slaves represented the most valuable booty for the soldiers, and auxiliaries received no other payment. But it was also a temptation for the administrator running a post with as little as 180 francs in the coffers.[72] In the early days of the colonial wars, one-third of the booty was reserved for the army and funded its social infrastructure.[73] In their campaigns Voulet and Chanoine followed this custom and retained ownership of about one-third of the captives for themselves and for the mission, thus imitating old military practices inspired by Samory Touré.[74]

Even if one does not consider the acquisition of slaves purely from the point of view of material enrichment, the slaves contributed to the status of the colonial armies. In the slave economy of the Niger region the numbers of slaves increased as a result of Samory's wars and so had the status of slave owners who could dispose of their captives.

Some of this freedom to dispose of slaves was a direct result of colonial intervention. The wars and social disturbances of the past twenty years had undermined traditional restraints on slave owners in the rampant chaos of war. Even though commentators often told edifying tales about the soft nature of African slavery whereby slaves could be made free and were treated like family, the realities within one category of slaves varied dramatically, depending on the circumstances and the owner. The debates on the history of slavery in the Muslim world have since been controversial and hotly debated. The nature of the slave trade and the fact that it was often not explicitly condemned by Islamic scholars or rulers has been a source of criticism in the West against the image of Islam. In the Maghreb, the French used the abolitionist excuse to impose their protectorate on Tunisia in 1881.[75]

Even while Voulet and Chanoine were establishing their human chattel, the governors of the new colony were attempting to reconcile the reality with the directives coming from Europe. True the army had become sensitive to religious pressure and set up the widely publicized *villages de liberté* which were represented as utopian communities (Figure 11).[76] The *village de liberté* were a symbolic and controversial directive from the navy minister Jauréguiberry in 1882. These villages were meant to be a space controlled by the colonial administration where ex-slaves could be re-located and where runaway slaves could be enfranchised. In reality, these villages, created with no real budget to support them, were often pressured to provide free services to the French administration. Soldiers and porters were recruited from them at a much heavier rate than from slave villages or local chieftaincies.[77] The slaves themselves originated from different ethnic and linguistic groups and these villages were no more functional free societies than the colonial resettlements of Liberia and Sierra Leone. The villages were a camouflage for the reality of slavery and, more often than not, served a purely rhetorical purpose. In the same way, the language of slavery disappeared from reports, an omission meant to paint a virtual world of liberty.[78] De Trentinian thus reformed the language and coined the phrased 'not-free' (non libre) which would replace 'captive' which was itself an alternative to the word 'slave'.[79] De Trentinian also regulated the settlement villages in a directive of 1897 which ensured the villages were located close to the administrators who were likely to need the manpower.[80] The local administrators attempted to answer the demands of anti-slavery campaigners while returning high levels of taxes and services that depended on forced labour and slavery.[81]

Occasionally a French administrator attempted to push the anti-slavery agenda. In 1893–5 a new civilian governor was put in place, Louis Alphone Grodet, who decreed, to the astonishment of the military, that the slave trade should be abolished immediately and that slavery should be phased out.[82] Grodet was, ironically, perceived by the military to be tyrannical. When he sentenced Lieutenant Mangin to thirty days house arrest for distributing slaves amongst his servants and interpreters, Grodet was acting almost provocatively.[83] In effect his humanitarian intentions were directly contradicted by the need to keep costs down.

As a historian of these villages, Denise Bouche reminds us this was merely one phase in a long series of edicts and laws, endlessly reiterated, which underlines the fact that slavery resisted humanitarian laws and that abolitionist intentions tended to have limited currency on the ground. Facing growing opposition Grodet did not last in the hostile political context of military Soudan.[84] His liberation policies, which were never abolished officially, were nevertheless moderated greatly in their application. The subsequent governor, de Trentinian, who held the position for a long period between 1895 and 1899, circulated a memorandum which qualified any literal interpretation of the directive.

Historians have since debated over the abolition of slavery in Burkina Faso, Niger, and Mali, the three countries resulting from the partition of Soudan.[85] Some have argued that colonial rule eventually led to the enfranchisement of most slaves but most agree that this occurred almost inadvertently. In French West Africa as in neighbouring British colonies the administrators were concerned that the abolition of slavery would lead to the economic collapse of the plantations and their large tax-generating farming. The contradictory tensions between absolute ideals and the practicalities of colonial rule meant that in West Africa administrators attempted to evade the matter, inconsistently targeting slave traders and neglecting household slavery, hesitating to return slaves to their owners but often reluctant to accept them as freemen.[86]

In 1905, mostly in the Banamba region, household slaves began to walk away from their masters to return home.[87] In the first instance colonial authorities were more concerned with maintaining the taxable income of their subjects and the slaves were returned. The following year the movement became more important and the French were unable to respond other than by recognizing that slavery had effectively ended spontaneously in this region.

This quiet revolt seems to have been the result of the slaves understanding that French rule was in contradiction with itself and that their masters, unarmed and without legal backing, no longer had the means to keep them in servitude. This unique moment, associated with other episodic population moves, has enabled some historians to declare slavery abolished in law by 1906. More recent micro-studies show that this is at the very least an incomplete portrayal of an enduring situation.

In other areas, slavery endured. The families of ex-slaves remained of lower social status, and domestic servants were retained as servants without real wages or rights. Slavery was and remains a problem in these independent nations. The importance of French initiatives has minimized over the long term since the French only ever abolished slave trading after a final flurry in the 1890s.

To argue that the French administrators were unanimous in Soudan would be to miss important divisions that explain how Voulet's conduct became a scandal in the spring of 1899. If some of the most prominent figures of Soudan, such as Colonel Audéoud who covered for de Trentinian during his illness in 1898, were responsible for the siege and pillage of Sikasso (Mali) on 1 May 1898 where the defeated population was distributed amongst the tirailleurs, some army officers were shocked and some even resigned when facing the reality of colonial practices. The missionaries were likewise shocked as they tended to view freed slaves, mostly isolated individuals lacking a home to go back to, as potential converts:

numerous caravans of captives coming from Sikasso pass between our house and that of the sisters; for the last few days, they pass every day. It is said that the Lieutenant Governor has taken 3,000 captives and had distributed them among his soldiers. Thus the market of Ségou is abundantly supplied now. This is how they are reducing slavery in Soudan.[88]

Vigné d'Octon thus did not lack evidence and his sources were from reliable witnesses. Yet his findings and his book, *La gloire du sabre*, were ridiculed and labelled a novel or fiction. Despite its sometimes sensationalistic tone, most of Vigné's work was grounded in facts. Lieutenant Péteau was the denunciator of Voulet and Chanoine within their own expedition. Péteau had been in charge of one of the warring units raiding widely alongside the convoy. It seems that the social tensions between Voulet's entourage and his African wife in particular were at the origin of Péteau's disaffection with Voulet.[89] As the enquiry showed, he had committed some violence himself, burnt at least two villages, and executed a number of guides. In his report from the village of Laboré, Péteau listed the number of women he had seized, along with 14 new slaves among whom 4 were chillingly described as 'useless'. In his balance sheet he then reported that this result had been obtained against 419 bullets.[90] From the enquiry that took place in 1900 it is likely that these 'useless' slaves were executed like 'all prisoners too old or too young to carry loads'.[91]

Yet after his dismissal from the column, Péteau found it necessary or convenient to attack Voulet and Chanoine on their record. His narrative of the exactions that had taken place fed the anticolonialists and Vigné in particular. This about-turn reveals more than most the schizophrenic nature of the colonial enterprise in which the discourse ended up so far apart from observable realities. Péteau was deemed to be a fine officer before he went with Voulet, with several courageous acts to his name. With Voulet he abided by the harsh rules of the mission without ever expressing to Joalland or his peers any kind of deep-seated disapproval of Voulet's methods. This disapproval would have been odd since so many of Voulet's violent acts were then perceived to be within the norm of military action in hostile territory, perhaps on the brutal end of the scale but still within the range of permissible acts. That on being dismissed, with his career damaged for good, Péteau found that a denunciation of violence would cover him and explain his conflict with Voulet shows that a man returning to civilian life was acutely aware of the moral relativism under which he had laboured previously.

There were norms that applied to warfare and Péteau like any other officer knew them. There were rules of engagement and there was a language, almost a law, that could be used to condemn what was taking place in Africa. In 1871 when France admitted defeat it immediately complained of the unacceptable levels of violence that had been inflicted on its population by the German armies. The violation of the rights of people had an even longer legal history. The crimes of the French armies in Spain and Germany during the Napoleonic wars were still contentious. Similarly the violent acts committed by Lord Admiral Nelson were still being evoked at a time when Nelson had become an unassailable hero for the British. All these precedents and the new international rules had shifted the norms of war, altering deeply what could be viewed as legitimate war by European public opinion. From the beginning, humanitarian campaigners sought to establish the principles and mechanics of international tribunals able to judge violations of the laws of war.

The logic of the Geneva Convention was that it would bind civilized nations. The non-Western powers who had signed early such as the Ottoman and Japanese empires were all engaged in a rapid process of Westernization. In a colonial context, the terms of this international law system were seen as less applicable. Yet in the logic of the convention, it only took one signatory for an entire conflict to be ruled by the terms of the international agreement. This had been the case as early as in 1866 when Prussia applied the convention while fighting Austria, who had not yet signed the treaty. The assumption in the minds of the legislators was that the treaties applied from nation to nation—in times of civil war the Geneva organization found itself in difficulty—in times of colonial wars when the state organization of the territories invaded was deemed to fall below the threshold of civilized organizations Geneva laws ceased to apply.

Yet the principles of humanity invoked in the legislation were by no means particular to the West. They were framed in universal terms—Christian ones, and the Red Cross in this sense was not only a Swiss flag in reversed chromatic order—and humanistic ones. These principles applied because the rules of humanity knew no borders, and wars were not justification for inhumanity. Yet the colonial context seemed to present an unknown territory for such lofty principles. Why should there have been such silences? One explanation, the one always used in such circumstances, is that there was no news of what was taking place there. Undoubtedly the colonizers were the propagandists and they wrote their own legendary accounts of their exploits.

Journalists and human rights campaigners were not rushing to the colonial sphere. Some did occasionally visit these places, at great expense. Tocqueville had been critical of the method of colonization in Algeria but only to propose his own views on the best ways of doing it. One had to wait for Albert Londres to have a violent critique of colonial rule in sub-Saharan Africa. Vigné d'Octon and others had to rely on second- and third-hand accounts. The missionaries who could have provided the information, the same missionaries who were so remarkably efficient at stimulating anti-slavery campaigns, were publicly silent. They were silent because they had to be. The French state was engaging in a *Kulturkampf* of its own, a struggle against the Catholic Church between the late 1870s and the separation of churches and state in 1905. Anticlericalism was the trading stock of radicals and republicans. Catholics taking orders from Rome were accused of being anti-national, and the church was denounced for its conservative or even reactionary views.

True, the great republican leader Gambetta had once proclaimed that 'anticlericalism is not a product for export'; yet the missionaries felt under considerable pressure to toe the line. From the late 1890s the correspondence of the missionaries was subjected to self-censorship. The *diaires*, annals of events in the missions, had to focus on edifying examples rather than anything controversial.[92] Despite this edict, the journals do contain critical comments on atrocities committed.

This is not to say that the republicans condoned what was taking place in the name of the Republic. It was obviously difficult to voice openly criticism of the regime that had embarked on this immense colonial campaign but considerable republican groups were devoted to the promotion of human rights at a particular moment when these issues were dividing France most deeply.

At an international level, humanitarian policies were in the air. In Britain they were primarily attached to the legacy of Gladstone, who promoted what some might now call 'ethical diplomacy'. The British media had been freer and more authoritative longer than any other country in Europe. The *Times* was a standard-bearer of journalistic independence. In 1898–9 the main story of violence in the United Kingdom related to another violent adventure, set in South Africa with the unequal struggle against two small, slave-owning Boer republics, Transvaal and Orange.[93] Most of continental Europe had taken sides in favour of the underdogs and the difficulties encountered by the British army, as well as the outbursts of violence committed by British soldiers, were relayed in the press. Yet in Britain itself active networks of liberals were campaigning in favour of the Boers. British liberal activism was not limited to the British Empire. The Anglo-Irish campaigner Roger Casement reported atrocities committed in order to extract cheap raw latex in South America and in Congo.[94] If the Belgian Congo soon became a byword for the most ruthless and extreme form of colonial exploitation, the French Congo colony created by an idealistic adventurer, Savorgnan de Brazza, was equally threatened. Drawing a parallel with its Belgian neighbour, Brazza's last act was to inquire into the dysfunctional colony where hostages were routinely taken to obtain submission, where production was extracted without pay, and where violence was part of a developing strategy which contributed to a grave demographic crisis in central Africa.[95] Brazza, who alone had the stature to carry through a full enquiry into French colonial exploitation, died before he could produce his report (Brazza's widow believed he had been poisoned while in Congo); a committee composed of the leaders of the Soudan and Madagascar colonial expansion quietly agreed to silence his revelations.

All these stories filtered through; yet despite their multitude and their recurrence they did not amount to a systematic critique of the empire. Each one seemed to be a revelation, a scandal, an event rather than a symptom of a more pervasive disease. The newspaper *L'Illustration* was somewhat premature to regard 1899 as the closure of the 'heroic age of African exploration' as many further instances of violence occurred in the following decades.[96] Strung together they could be considered as a pattern of inhumanity across Africa.

Incidents before and after 1914 would feed this approach. The news of the war against the Herero people of Namibia, exterminated relentlessly by the German expeditionary forces, followed close on the heels of Voulet–Chanoine, the Belgian Congo, and the British concentration camps in South Africa. A kind of moral relativism ensued.[97]

Were the Western powers all bad then? More interestingly it is worth asking why *some* of these acts which were in a direct continuation of myriad other atrocities became newsworthy in Europe. One way to approach the sudden surge in barbarous violence is to consider it as the expression of a new set of norms and the realization of some self-scrutiny. Voulet and Chanoine were committing atrocities at a moment when notions of abuse were being defined; they behaved in a moral vacuum, the existence of which was no longer acceptable.

Later on, when colonial abuse motivated resistance as in the great insurrection in San and Bobo-Dioulasso, the administrators were sufficiently astute to apportion the blame on the Africans themselves and to silence durably the memory of the huge insurrection of 1915–16.[98] Yet in that war, a mere fifteen years after Voulet's death, the same destructive rampage tore through these regions—war was raging in Europe and the destruction of dozens of villages and the killing of thousands of Africans (perhaps 35,000) counted for little.[99] The whistleblower Péteau, who had partaken in this violence with no apparent moral compunction, was nevertheless astute enough to engage with the moral imperatives of a humanitarian moment on his return from frontier colonial warfare. The challenge of the turn of the century for European powers and their soldiers was that their societies were expecting codes of conduct which were a long way from that of their armed forces—they expected much from these soldiers who were meant to deliver simultaneously immense empires at a low financial cost while reflecting a highly idealized version of civilized men.

6

CONSPIRACY THEORIES AND SCANDALS

> There is a grim irony about that terrible tale of mutiny and murder in the French Soudan. Captains Voulet and Chanoine were to be superseded and brought to the coast, there to be tried by court-martial on charges of gross misconduct. Considering what we know of French court-martial and their ways, there may be some explanation for the fact the two officers should have preferred to shoot down Colonel Klobb and his lieutenant and take to bush ranging rather than give themselves up to the tender mercies of one of those tribunals. A curious aspect of the case is the light it throws on one of the hitherto unexplained mysteries of the Affaire [Dreyfus]—that namely of General Chanoine's sudden resignation of the portfolio of War. It is now stated that the General, who had taken office to support Revision, was terrorized into resigning by the threats of the Nationalist journals to make public the story of his son's atrocious treatment of the natives in the Soudan. Thus, as all roads lead to Rome, even so everything that happens where Frenchmen are concerned brings us back, somehow, to the Affaire.[1]

This deeply ironic analysis of the Voulet–Chanoine affair may have been wrong as to Voulet's motives on 14 July 1899, but it nevertheless casts the scandal in its rightful place. There was a criminal trial in the making and when it came to military justice, all roads led to the Dreyfus affair.[2] France in 1898–9 was in the final throes of the notorious miscarriage of justice of the Jewish officer Alfred Dreyfus.[3] Alfred Dreyfus had been framed for an act of treason committed by another officer in 1894. The case against him was a document found in the German embassy. To cover up for their lack of evidence the French military secret services forged documents and rigged the trial of Dreyfus. This scandalous mistrial, the cover-up, crude forgeries, and layers of conspiracy precipitated a unique political and cultural crisis of international resonance which received extraordinarily extensive coverage in the European and American media.[4] Over the years a number of family members, intellectuals, and writers began unravelling a web of lies which reached to the heart of the French military organization. The newspaper *l'Aurore* published Emile Zola's *J'accuse* in January 1898 in which he denounced the lies and military conspiracies which had sentenced and kept an innocent man in prison on the aptly named Devil Island, Guyana, for treason.[5] The trial and condemnation of Captain Dreyfus split French public opinion and led to the new expression of racial and political anxieties. Anti-Semitism had found in France and Algeria its first virulent populist expression.[6] The historian Pierre Birnbaum even went so far as to call 1898 the anti-Semitic moment.[7] Dreyfus and Jews in general were presented as enemies of the nation and as enemies of its most virtuous institution: the national army. The Voulet–Chanoine affair came at a most inauspicious moment for the French military, precisely in an era of socially divisive scandals. What made this colonial tragedy a scandal was its association with the key figures of the Dreyfus affair—yet it is also this association with the Dreyfus affair which ensured that it was eventually hushed up and its enquiries buried in the archives.

Through a remarkable effort of propaganda, the French army had been thoroughly rehabilitated after its infamous defeat of

1870. Yet in the 1890s it was at the heart of this crisis as it was revealed how this institution harboured racial divides, how its leadership ignored common principles of justice and the rule of law. By 1898, following the campaign led by Reinach, and in *L'Aurore* by Gohier, Clemenceau, and Zola it became clear that the trial of Dreyfus had been a conspiracy and that there had been a cover-up which had lasted for several years. The army leadership was compromised and so were the governments that had ruled since the start of the affair.

In 1898 one of the central protagonists of the Dreyfus affair at this late stage was none other than General Jules Chanoine, father of the young man sent to Africa. Jules Chanoine had a relatively moderate political profile, mostly known for his knowledge of Japan and China.[8] The nationalists were not overwhelmed by the man. Under his caricature published in 1902 by the fierce journal *L'Assiette Au Beurre*, the legend taken from a nationalist newspaper was lapidary: 'une tourte de choix' (a first class fool) (Figure 14). On 17 September 1898, General Chanoine had become minister of war, replacing the anti-Dreyfusard General Zurlinden who had resigned, like his predecessor, over his opposition to the revision of Dreyfus's trial. Jules Chanoine was expected by the premier, Henri Brisson, to deliver such a revision of the trial. In the first few weeks of his term in office he became responsible for the fate of Dreyfus.

Against all expectations, far from seeking the revision and rehabilitation of Dreyfus, Chanoine ensured that Dreyfus's supporters would be silenced. In particular he sought to silence one of the few officers, Col. Georges Picquart, who had campaigned for Dreyfus and eventually leaked the evidence of Dreyfus's innocence in 1898. Far from being the moderate figure everyone expected him to be, Chanoine revealed himself to be an arch-enemy of Dreyfus. In a notorious and riotous session in parliament, Chanoine responded to the insults of the arch-nationalist Déroulède by a melodramatic statement that he would 'put in [parliament's] hands the responsibility of defending the interests and honour of the army' in a sonorous gesture of betrayal of his political patrons. Some on the left interpreted Chanoine's political gesture as the aborted beginning of a right-wing coup.[9] It seems likely that he had not thought through his resignation as a political act and had more simply refused to become alienated from the majority view in the French army which strongly opposed Dreyfus.

Chanoine was intimately connected to the Dreyfus affair. He had, it was alleged, a familial connection with Col. Hubert-Joseph Henry, one of the men who had falsified documents in order to frame Dreyfus. Henry committed suicide after his arrest in August 1898. Furthermore, Chanoine was acquainted socially with the real traitor, Esterhazy, also imprisoned during the summer of 1898, whose family home was located near Chanoine's.[10] If one adds to this the constant pressure from the right-wing press, the anti-Dreyfusard culture of the army, and the anti-Semitic politics of his class Chanoine was unlikely to favour the return of the Jewish officer from his prison island off the coast of French Guyana.

Such was the impact of the affair that between 1898 and 1899 the talk in French politics revolved around nothing else, contributing to the rapid turnover of governments. Brisson fell because of Chanoine on 26 October 1898, his successor Dupuy appointing a civilian, Charles de Freycinet, as a replacement for these politically unreliable officers as minister of war. Dupuy himself fell in June 1899. Eventually these unstable governments were replaced by a centre-left government led by Waldeck–Rousseau which lasted three years and was the Third Republic's longest serving government. Waldeck–Rousseau led an unlikely coalition which included France's first socialist minister and a notorious general who was nicknamed the red-heeled marquis, Gaston de Gallifet. Gallifet was a hated figure on the left and many remembered that he had been one of most cruel participants in the massacre of Parisian insurgents in 1871. In May 1871, Gallifet was alleged to have whimsically selected people for random executions among the mass of prisoners. Yet these enemies of yesterday were all decided on solving the Dreyfus affair once and for all.

During the summer of 1899 Dreyfus was awaiting an appeal trial which took place in Rennes and eventually found him 'guilty with attenuating circumstances' to the bafflement of most observers and despite a mountain of evidence proving his innocence. The 'attenuating circumstances' were nevertheless a climbdown and a reluctant prelude to his pardon and eventual rehabilitation. All these events took place while Voulet and Julien Chanoine roamed the lands of West Africa. In France the political climate changed fast and the ranks of their unconditional supporters dwindled in the ministries. Their highest ranking patron, the president of France, Félix Faure, himself died on 16 February 1899 in the arms of his mistress, Marguerite Steinhell, to be replaced by a moderate Dreyfusard, Émile Loubet.

The Voulet–Chanoine expedition was therefore set in a particular context of violent confrontation focusing on the honour of the army. When the first revelations emerged, the pressure mounted for a revision of the Dreyfus trial; when the news of Klobb's death arrived in Paris, Dreyfus was being retried in Rennes and Jules Chanoine was standing as a witness against him.

After the killing of Voulet and Chanoine in July 1899, Gen. Chanoine attempted to salvage his son's reputation and, with the backing of the right-wing press, sought to present his son's death as that of a hero betrayed by his superiors:

what one needs to note in his correspondence, is that he knew how to take initiatives . . . how he corrected through his clear thinking and decisiveness all the confused and irresolute aspects of the projects put in his hands by the same ones who would claim his achievements for themselves.[11]

Among the many enemies of Voulet and Chanoine, one stood out in particular: Lieutenant Péteau, who brought about the scandal. The records show a deep unease between Péteau, a Tonkin war veteran who had risen from the ranks to become a lieutenant, and the officers from Soudan. In his operation diary Chanoine showed that much of this tension came from a class dissention:

on the observation that he was still thinking like a NCO and regarded his leaders like enemies, Lieutenant Péteau raised his voice further stating how insulted he was.[12]

In fact Péteau had been following the same path as Voulet and was using colonial missions to overcome his lack of formal military education. Eventually it was Voulet, not Chanoine, who dismissed him.

By telegram Voulet signalled to Paris on 13 February 1899 that Péteau was returned to Kayes on the grounds of being rebellious and incapable.[13] The letter was rather more explicit:

his habit of disputing and criticizing almost openly [orders], this tendency to indiscipline, his ignorance to an extraordinary degree of his duties as a subordinate officer towards his superior constituted already for Europeans and natives alike a nefarious example. To these grave weaknesses one has to add the lack of the primordial qualities of any soldier and especially officers. Thus, Lieutenant Péteau, instead of inspiring calm and patience, tenacity and endurance to the natives tended to exaggerate every obstacle . . . [he has] neither enthusiasm nor the drive [*allant*] indispensable to those who want to obtain good results. Being constantly occupied mentally by the ailments that might afflict the Europeans in the Soudanese climate, he exaggerates the risks and his constant worries about his health are making him forget his military duties.

He then detailed how depressed Péteau seemed. If someone was suffering from Soudanitis, it seems that it was Péteau. The letter finished with the clash between Péteau and Chanoine.[14]

The clash was about a minor incident where Péteau accused Chanoine's cavalrymen of being indolent and lacking discipline. Accusations flew both ways but Chanoine was a captain and Péteau his subordinate. They were furthermore in a warring zone and Péteau could face court martial for arguing back. One might be surprised to find so many references to indolence or moral collapse in a marching unit. Yet as pointed out in Chapter 1, the column by late January 1899 was not so much marching as crawling. The halts lasted days, sometimes weeks. Since October 1898 the mission had been very slow moving. All the accounts include reports of boredom and dispirited feelings at one stage or another of the mission.

Voulet and Chanoine dismissed Péteau with a sense that he might become dangerous. Chanoine thus instructed his father that 'one should be careful that this individual does not seek to undermine us by some indiscrete leaks in the newspapers or in any other way'. In a footnote to this letter, the father added that Péteau

avenged himself with calumnious denunciations, welcomed in Paris by the government with a shocking interest which then used it to end a mission that had become a nuisance and in order to *satisfy* their base private vengeance.[15]

General Chanoine saw the death of his son Julien as punishment for his anti-Dreyfusard stance. In August and September 1899, Péteau added to his previous accusations and had a letter published in *Le Matin* which set the blame squarely with Julien Chanoine while arguing that Voulet had become mad: '[Voulet] is a man of straw . . . his insignificance hands him over, hand and foot, to his accomplice and he leads away with him the generous hearts which he has deluded. Blood maddens him, and casts over his conscience a thick veil which conceals from him the horror of his daily tasks.'[16]

In September 1899 while still unaware of his son's death, Chanoine wrote to his colleague the Lieutenant Governor of Soudan, Colonel Vinard, to warn him that

> Mr Péteau is said to have been and probably is the correspondent of several socialist deputies. This fact and the current state of minds [of the Dreyfus affair] probably explain why his letters are so violent and remain unpunished.[17]

The conspiracy theory had been in existence from the outset of the mission. In truth Voulet faced the opposition of the Soudanese establishment and was well aware that many resented him. Throughout the months of March, April, and May Voulet sent explanatory reports and detailed political analyses which explained his stance and justified his acts. It is obvious that he expected that a campaign against him had been started by Delaunay and Granderye in Say and he tried to discredit them. His reports were lengthy and detailed, of the kind that had been published on his return from Ouagadougou a couple of years earlier. Yet circumstances changed dramatically and his reports either did not arrive at all or arrived late, taking two months and twenty-three days to reach Paris in the case of the report from Tibiri.[18] They saw the absence of communication as further evidence of the gradual collapse of their backing in Paris.

They may have been paranoid but Voulet and Chanoine certainly guessed rightly that there was no longer anyone in a position of authority interested in backing them. When Klobb arrived to investigate and take control of the mission, he embodied, in their eyes, the social and political enemy. In killing Klobb, Voulet engaged in a private act of civil warfare. This was precisely how the event was understood in the media. The 'Drama of Dankori', the killing of a colonel by his subordinates, was read as an integral part of the Dreyfus affair turmoil. Establishing this political and media context also highlights how news travelled and how Africa became integrated in the French debates of the period. For the right-wing press the issues at stake were clearly a fundamental conflict in French society:

> To undermine the son meant to lower the father in favour of *Dreyfus*! A few months ago, the newspapers of the nationless were preparing the ground; a few vicious articles first, quite vague to start with, then increasingly precise, launched the campaign which ended in this masterstroke . . . we mistrusted this contradictory narrative, woven from disparate elements in order to have an impact on the trial of Rennes [i.e. re-trial of the Dreyfus case in August 1899] . . . Anything happens under the African sun. An act of madness is almost natural. Why should the state see to change this isolated instance of delirium into something else that would support the insults and denunciations against all our officers, why should it feed strange collaborators the weapons of a war of lies which were reproduced as if they were truths and which strike the army and mortally wound France? . . . The [Judeo-Masonic] syndicate in its hatred against the army collects relentlessly every indiscretion and feeds it to the sensationalist press: delighted to collect bad rumours it ensures that the relations of the mission with Paris should become venomous, then, having created an incident it

made it bigger in order to exploit it further. Thus the son disqualified was to be used to undermine the father in favour of Dreyfus![19]

The impact of the Dreyfus affair in Africa is not a well-known aspect of this otherwise comprehensively studied crisis in French politics and society.[20] The affair had by 1899 been running for a number of years and had divided and united French politics in extraordinary ways. As a crossroad in French politics it caused some ex-Communard revolutionaries like Rochefort to become rabid nationalists and anti-Semites, while some previously anti-Semitic socialists like Jean Jaurès travelled the other way. Many historians have noted how nationalism and militarism became 'right wing' when, twenty years earlier, the right was primarily known for its pacifism and its reluctance to engage in any talk of military revenge against Germany.

The Dreyfus affair raised essential issues about democratic rights and the limits of the state. Dreyfus had been framed by his peers and by the military secret services as the spy identified in the German embassy. Mysteriously the real spy, Esterhazy, a man whose profile fitted perfectly the actual crime, was set aside. Esterhazy of Hungarian origins was in severe need of cash to pay for his dissolute and lavish lifestyle, he was seen in the company of the military attaches of Italy and Germany, he was keen to study secret documents at home, and his handwriting even resembled that of the document found in the German embassy. Dreyfus was a family man whose handwriting resembled nothing like that of the secret document, he had no need for money being from a rich Alsatian background, and his diary conflicted with information the spy had given his German master. By an extraordinary twist of logic his accusers found that if Dreyfus could have forged the handwriting of Esterhazy, that Esterhazy could not forge his own handwriting, that Dreyfus might have tried to cover himself by framing Esterhazy, and that his Alsatian origins were suspect.[21] More importantly for many he was Jewish, whereas Esterhazy was an aristocrat, albeit a dissolute one. The trial of Dreyfus fed and was fed by the rise of organized anti-Semitism.

Contrary to legend Dreyfus was neither the highest ranking, nor the only, Jew in the French army. There were some in Soudan who were most highly praised, even by Catholic missionaries.[22] What the Dreyfus case showed was that the army was not the mirror of the nation. Its hierarchy was able and willing to bend the law. Its *esprit de corps* was a fig leaf which served private interest and conceit. In a very hierarchical society the Dreyfus affair called to account the highest authorities of the nation and for the first time intellectuals such as Reinach and Zola dared to challenge the elites of the nation before their fellow citizens.

The more the army authorities tried to cover their tracks, the more the debate became a debate on citizenship and loyalty. The Dreyfusards called for the rights of men to become central in French politics, the anti-Dreyfusards argued that the rights of one man had to be put below those of the nation. Some went so far as to argue that had Dreyfus been a man of honour he would have accepted his sentence rather than bring the army into disrepute. As Christopher Forth has pointed out the debate was not only about race it was also about honour and manliness.[23] Dreyfus the Jew was opposed to real men such as the young class of officers fighting in Soudan for the glory of France.

The two stories were taking place in the same media and were fuelled by the writings of the same journalists. Of course the newspaper that had printed the famous *J'accuse* letter of Émile Zola was none other than *L'Aurore* of Clemenceau which had also been printing Vigné d'Octon's regular columns since 1897. In these articles later summarized in *La Gloire du sabre*, Vigné d'Octon targeted a number of individual officers beyond Voulet and Chanoine. Before the Péteau leaks he mostly focused on Gallieni's harsh rule in Madagascar. The Voulet scandal fitted into this campaign not because it was sensational, but because it represented a condensed version of all the crimes that Vigné d'Octon had attributed to military rule in the colonies. His short book was printed by Flammarion, which under severe political pressure, withdrew its imprimatur from the 6,000 copies already printed. Vigné d'Octon had to find a publisher willing to give its name and to distribute the book.[24] The debate that Vigné d'Octon and his friends were bringing to light was not necessarily about the nature of colonialism but rather about the actual human rights of soldiers and, almost as an afterthought, of native people. Some historians have doubted the anticolonial credentials of the baker's son. His opponents accused him of attempting to profit from the empire he denounced; he claimed that they were seeking to tarnish his name or to bribe him.[25] Beyond the dirty tricks atmosphere surrounding Vigné d'Octon's forays into anticolonial denunciation, the truth was that the idea of empire was not at stake so much as the means by which it was established. The forms of violence, the lack of process prior to executions, the sadism, and the cover-up were the scandal.

Ultimately it was the murder of Klobb that made the story worthy of a full campaign regarding its origins. On the right the deputies were querying why these two junior officers had been given such crushing responsibilities that they had lost their minds; on the left it was the lack of governmental control over frontier colonies and Soudan in particular.

In a climate of general suspicion of the army's hierarchy the Voulet–Chanoine affair seemed like another cover-up whereby the administration would seek to turn a symptomatic failure into an isolated incident. Vigné d'Octon alone attempted to show that these events were intimately connected to violent events beforehand and to a general culture of cruelty in the army. In this he met and became associated with anti-militarists such as the anarchist Elisée Reclus, whose books *Guerre, Militarisme* and *Patriotisme, colonisation* published in 1902–3 had an echo in the ultra-left. Yet the more systematic and devastating attacks on the economic basis of colonialism such as the liberal critique of Hobson, in *Imperialism: A Study* which later inspired Lenin's own classic text, were not central to this sudden fluster of criticism of the empire.[26]

The Dreyfus affair had, more than any other before, raised the issue of human rights. A league devoted to the protection of the 'rights of man and citizen' had been created in 1898 which soon federated large numbers of republican and left-wing Frenchmen to become the largest organization of its kind in the world. Men like Victor Basch engaged themselves in a life-long campaign for the defence of victims of abuses of power and the defence of fundamental individual freedoms at a time when the Republic seemed to favour order over liberty.[27] Rennes and the last phase of the Dreyfus affair in 1898–9 revealed the injustice and arbitrary power of the state in its most naked form.[28] The league raised the debate from the incident to the level of principles. It was not the fate of Dreyfus the individual alone being questioned but the system that thought it could crush an innocent man and get away with it. The lies and deceit spun around the spy story revealed a cynical culture of power in the French army. In the history of the Republic, a generation after the establishing of the regime, the army seemed still disconnected from democratic values.

As mentioned in Chapter 2 the Dreyfus affair followed a major threat to parliamentary democracy: the Boulanger affair. General Boulanger, supported by a motley conglomerate of left- and right-wing anti-parliamentarian groups which ranged from the anti-Semites to the ultra-nationalists, from survivors of the Paris Commune of 1871 to monarchists, had presented a genuine threat. His tactical indecisiveness and the swift and brutal repression of his support groups effectively undermined this movement. What struck the commentators then and since was that this military officer had obtained so much support while stating so little.[29] The triumph of image over content, the power of image over mass politics scared many politicians who had remained wary of the military ever since.

In 1898 many foresaw the imminent collapse of the French Republic. Riddled with dissent, undermined from the left by the rise of organized labour movements and ultra-leftist organizations such as the anarchist terrorists, tainted with corruption scandals, the centre-left politicians, disparagingly labelled opportunists, were under threat. In this situation the role of the empire was a paradox. On the balance sheet it appeared as a massive credit to the regime. It had cost relatively little to create a colonial domain on which the sun never set and which was second in size only to Britain's.

In the detail of the empire were the devils. And from the empire might come the downfall of the empire. On his return from Fashoda, Marchand was greeted like a hero by the right and many expected him to become a new Boulanger.[30]

The Republic survived Fashoda, but the architect of its imperial ambitions, the Anglophobic Gabriel Hanotaux and enthusiastic supporter of Voulet, lost his position when the Méline Government fell to be replaced by the more Anglophile Théophile Delcassé, who had little real enthusiasm for the mission.[31] In the tumultuous politics of the Third Republic this barely amounted to a sea-change but in its more subterranean workings it corresponded to a more pragmatic approach which signalled the end of adventure and unilateral imperialism.[32] From 1899 the French started to negotiate more positively with the British, who were themselves experiencing a reality check in the shape of the Boer War.[33]

Marchand returned to a hero's welcome as did his 'Senegalese' soldiers. They were feted and entertained but Marchand was no political adventurer and hopes placed on him were disappointed. For Voulet and Chanoine these events echoed throughout Africa as an example of what a weak policy might be. Chanoine had prided himself on keeping the British soldiers at bay and on establishing solid claims for border tracing in the Gurunsi region; Voulet seemed a little less obsessed about British interference but he nevertheless shared Julien Chanoine's geopolitical views. From the deepest bush Julien had a powerful echo in the shape of his father. Jules Chanoine shared his son's distaste and defiance of the British in Africa. In his eulogy for his son, Jules described him thus: 'he showed the same attitude that Marchand later displayed at Fashoda'.[34]

He might not have shared Julien's enthusiasm for war against them but he nevertheless complacently reprinted all the correspondence which revealed his son's unbridled Anglophobia. In his introduction he portrayed these immature and utterly unrealistic prospects for an African war, which would begin by the rapid invasion of Britain's West African colonies, as the demonstration of his son's foresight and breadth of vision. Comparing him favourably to Marchand his eulogy was obviously reflecting paternal myopia. Yet the Fashoda incident undoubtedly changed the perspective on warfare in Africa. From a purely political viewpoint it made any interference with the British sphere of influence extremely damaging.

When Voulet failed to go through the desert areas north of the 1898 convention boundaries which drew a semi-circle 100 miles exactly north of the sultanate of Sokoto, Chanoine resolutely launched his column south of that border boundary, straight into British-claimed land. The villages he then sacked and burnt were all nominally dependent on Sokoto and thus, rather indirectly and very loosely then, on the British colony.

This had the potential to become another Fashoda in itself. Jules Chanoine became convinced that this fear of a new conflict with the British government explained why the government sent Klobb after Voulet. There is no evidence of this in the archives, and in particular the order would have been the object of considerable discussion between the Foreign Office and the Colonial Office. Yet in the climate of international tension and in view of the turbulent political atmosphere of 1899 the conspiracy theory seemed plausible to the colonial party. The credit given to the rumour of extreme violence and the media attention that ensued in the *Aurore* newspaper, which was then not supporting the government but was the herald of Dreyfusards, seemed a strange coincidence. The government decided rather more decisively than usual to take prompt inquisitive action. On 17 April 1899 it sent a telegram asking for a swift and discrete enquiry to be launched; three days later a second telegram asked for Voulet and Chanoine to be placed under arrest. This dramatic turn for the mission took place under no obvious duress and without new information having reached Paris. It remains difficult to explain why two orders were issued in such swift succession and why the latter aggravated the disciplinary measures so urgently.

The immediate consequence was that Klobb was stopped and killed rather than Voulet. Furthermore a rogue army might be on the run in Africa. The government obviously panicked during the months of August and September until the news of the captains' deaths arrived to reassure everyone.

Over these two months, during which there might have been a rebel French army ransacking British or even German colonies, the government was undergoing a trial of its military justice:

the revision of the Dreyfus trial in the military court of Rennes. Even as he believed his son to be party to a military rebellion in Africa, Jules Chanoine had to testify under oath that Dreyfus was indeed guilty. The release of the news of the killing of Klobb was perceived widely on the right as an underhand manoeuvre against the army by the Dreyfusards in government. Questioned in parliament over this situation the minister had to answer as best he could pointed questions such as the 'interpellation' of Viscount de Montfort, a single and complex question which sought to bring down the government on 19 October 1899:

> I have the honour of asking to query in parliament the government in order to determine the responsibilities of Monsieur the minister of colonies as to why he hurried, before he was even fully informed of the events of Soudan and in particular of the Voulet–Chanoine mission, to spread in the public domain by means of the press alarming news based on inexact and incomplete information, creating thus a deep emotion which was then unfairly used against some officers of the army while causing the deepest anxieties to several honourable families.[35]

To this question the officials prepared a number of answers summarizing the government's stance. First the fact that the responsibility had been concentrated was a way of

> avoiding considering other officers as the accomplice of their chiefs; on communicating the news, the government had been forced to do so by a leak in the newspaper *La Liberté* on 28 August. The government then chose to favour absolute sincerity in the communication of whatever news [we had] received. This sincerity was manifest in the integral publication [in *Le Figaro*] of the report Granderye and, if not integral, as complete as their rather confused content allowed, of the telegrams of Lieutenant Pallier.[36]

News coverage of the Voulet–Chanoine affair lasted a long time. This was partly because information was not forthcoming in sequence. Gaps and delays between various telegrams and letters confused matters. Voulet's correspondence from April did not arrive until July, August, and September, well after his death. The parliamentary debates kept it alive and the enquiry sustained interest. In this sense it mimicked the Dreyfus affair which had, among other things, trained journalists to doubt any official version of events and led them to imagine conspiracies where they could not find evidence.[37]

With the army unwilling to budge and the government keen to bury once and for all the divisive trial, the Dreyfus affair ended in a compromise. Thanks to Jules Chanoine and most military officials, Dreyfus was found guilty in Rennes despite mounting evidence to the contrary. The new minister of war sought to appease the armed forces with this verdict but also to prepare for a discrete rehabilitation of the innocent man. Thus the trial ended with the very odd verdict of guilty of treason but with unprecedented attenuating circumstances.[38]

The Dreyfus camp was divided between his personal partisans and the partisans of his cause. The former were open to a deal with the government; the latter, around Clemenceau, would not accept anything less than a complete and instant rehabilitation. They wanted the army to recognize its crime while the family around Reinach wanted to save a man. Captain Dreyfus himself was at the end of his mental and moral resources. His health was at stake and when the government which included radicals and socialists, all Dreyfusards, offered a presidential pardon with the promise of a later review, Dreyfus accepted the iniquitous judgement. The compromise was seen by the minister of war as a way of appeasing both the military and the Dreyfusards. By the time of the verdict Voulet and Chanoine were known to be dead. The Soudanese danger was over. With the Dreyfus trial so potentially damaging to the army having ended in this rather humiliating manner recently it was obvious to all that neither the army nor the government wanted to open a long and soul-destroying enquiry into the events of Soudan. The government could ill afford another direct confrontation with the armed forces. Indeed the government found a political solution by relieving the army of its government of the colony, abolishing Soudan altogether in October 1899 and carving up its territory between other existing colonies despite the colonialists' lobby.[39] Soon afterwards a new colonial army was established on 7 July 1900, which officialized but also regulated the existence of this specific force.[40]

None of this solved the Voulet–Chanoine case which still rattled around in parliament and in the radical press. To silence these voices, the minister of colonies ordered reluctantly a full enquiry in April 1900. Its brief was meant to be broad, leading to:

> a full and faithful reconstitution of the regrettable events that took place during the mission and 2. the determination of the part, merits and responsibility of each member of the mission. At the end of the report some firm and individual proposals.[41]

The government general of Occidental French Africa appointed Commandant Laborie to enquire into the events, confront the survivors, and on the basis of evidence provide a full report. The report had two purposes. One was to enable the administration to know what to do with the survivors and the second was to appease political pressure from Paris by resting on the theory that Voulet had acted while insane. It is clear from the archives that the two aims were regarded as equally important. Tellingly only extracts of the report survive in the individual files of the survivors.

Laborie was a trusted medical officer who shared his name with Dreyfus' barrister. He was given full powers to investigate to the minutest details the events leading to the death of Klobb. Yet despite his medical qualifications his reports were remarkably devoid of any medical evidence.[42] In considering the various individuals involved, Laborie's report did not produce any mitigating circumstances. In itself this investigation was to supersede three shorter investigations: one led by Lamy on his arrival in Zinder and those reports sent from Say or Dahomey. The aims of the investigation were to assess comprehensively the role and criminal liability of each and every member of the expedition, white and black, regular and auxiliary. Laborie was given access to the soldiers and interviewed those he could find. He took time to interview each officer in detail. Pallier who had returned to Saint Louis was kept there despite a deadly yellow fever epidemic, to which he succumbed on 15 August 1900.[43] Some argued that by keeping him in Saint Louis the government had silenced a man who could have dissented from the version of events given by his fellow officers. There is no archival evidence of this allegation.

This enquiry was based on all oral evidence available. Like Lamy on his arrival in Zinder, Laborie refused to take on trust the agreed version concocted by the mission's survivors and later defended by Joalland. Lamy suspected that Joalland and Pallier knew something of the ambush against Klobb. By 12 July, at the latest, Henric, Laury, and Tourot had known of Klobb's imminent arrival. Without actual proof of his suspicion, Lamy was certain that the NCOs were aware of Voulet's plan to kill Klobb. Lamy even regarded Dr Henric as a likely accomplice.[44] Lamy's anger with Joalland for leaving without him and in haste was compounded by his suspicion that Joalland had also taken two central witnesses of the killing.

Commandant Lamy is very critical of the attitude of the Europeans of the mission who, either by a feeling of discipline or by fear of scandal, have seemed to be too closely bound to their chief. He deplores very vividly that Lieutenant Meynier, the only European survivor of the drama of 14 July, and Sergeant Souley Taraore, who seems to have been the main instigator of the plot against Voulet and Chanoine, should have gone towards Chad with Lieutenant Joalland when their testimony is essential to cast a light on these painful events.

Lamy attempted to have an instruction open at the military tribunal of Kayes on the crimes of the 14, 16, and 17 July, that is, including the killing of Voulet and Chanoine.[45] Lamy even sent, via the British Foreign Office and Nigerian outposts, a coded message which stated

Before sending the full file on this affair, Commandant Lamy asks the minister to demand the immediate return of Lieutenant Joalland and to inflict a severe punishment to this officer who seems to continue the series of scandalous acts committed by the Voulet mission since its departure from Senegal.[46]

Joalland was by then out of reach and incommunicado. Laborie later showed that no one could claim to be beyond reproach. The crimes of Voulet and Chanoine were detailed and investigated individually but the secondary officers were all found to be privy to this culture of violence. The whistle-blower, the disgraced Lieutenant Péteau, had been promoted to the rank of captain in the spring of 1900 in a vain attempt to silence him, but the report was also damning for him. He was accused of some of the earliest acts of unnecessary violence in the vicinity of Sansané Haoussa.

Captain Joalland who had taken the regular soldiers towards Lake Chad was accused of conspiring to hide his responsibility and was deemed directly responsible for the execution of the tirailleur Moussa-Kone, accused of sleeping with one of Chanoine's wives.[47]

Lieutenant Pallier, a promising officer of 29, whose papers have only recently been published by the local history society of his hometown near Limoges, had trained at the best military school. Yet he had been responsible for or accomplice to several violent episodes. In his own diary he noted the account of the slaughter of an entire village following an attack he led: 'July 2, Karankalgo, small village of 5 to 600 inhabitants surrounded with a strong defensive edge. Storming the village costs us two soldiers killed and fourteen wounded, all from the Bouba Taraore section of Captain Chanoine. All inhabitants are killed, the village is set on fire. Temperature 37 degrees, 23 minima.'[48]

Henric was accused of implicit complicity in the murder of Klobb, while Laury and the other NCOs were accused of complicity in the murder of Klobb and in numerous acts of violence. Laury's part in the execution of Corporal Tacing Taraore was likely to have sent him to court had it not been for the fact that 'it does not seem possible to send him before a court if we do not also include Lieutenant Joalland.'[49] After Lamy's death, however, considering the coverage Joalland managed to give his drive to Lake Chad and the struggle against Rabah, Joalland had to be saved from any penal pursuits; likewise Laury was also saved. The African NCOs were, on the one hand, praised for their assessment of Voulet's madness but, on the other, blamed for the murders of Voulet and Chanoine. Dembar Sar was deemed to 'have only obeyed orders he could not understand as being illegal' while Souley Taraore 'whatever he pretends most probably decided to get rid of their previous leaders but it was in a thought of self-defence and not as an act of vengeance'. Only one African NCO, Moussa Diallo, was deemed to have had any responsibility. No one came out as innocent from this report but yet no crime was deemed worthy of further prosecution.[50] Laborie was thanked and then sent back to France to a Limousin backwater to silence him.[51] The French and African survivors were then promoted and the administration ruled the matter closed.

This was to ignore the feelings of the families. During the months of June and July reports on the Voulet mission had been leaked to the press by Vigné d'Octon. Dr Voulet wrote to the vice-president of the National Assembly, Maurice Faine, to ask him to investigate on his behalf the source of the leaks. Faine described 'Dr Voulet as one of our most respectable inhabitants of the Drome department'. The minister of colonies responded bluntly: 'some grave acts have been attributed to Capitaine Voulet during his mission in the Niger region. Lieutenant-Colonel Klobb had been appointed to make an impartial enquiry about these allegations. His instructions do not imply with any certitude that Captain Voulet is guilty.'[52] This exchange contained at least one half-truth since Klobb's second set of instructions stated clearly that Voulet should be put under arrest. The presumption of innocence was unclear. In August 1899 when news of the killing of Klobb emerged, the Voulet family leaked the captain's letters, denouncing a conspiracy against him to the nationalist and anti-Dreyfusard press. The major daily nationalist, *Le Gaulois*, featured an interview with Dr Voulet which went in this direction.[53]

The killing of Klobb sent mixed signals. In the nationalist press the coverage was confused. Some nationalists, such as the Patriotic League of Déroulède and the *Figaro*, attempted to have a monument erected and national funeral held for Klobb. Eventually a pension of 6,000 francs was voted in favour of Klobb's widow and orphans.[54] Others like *Le Petit Journal* supported the Chanoine family.[55] Where all newspapers agreed was in turning their guns against the governor of Soudan, de

Trentinian. Right-wingers accused him of betraying Voulet, while the supporters of Péteau blamed him for the cover-up of Voulet's crimes.[56]

In the years that followed, both the Voulet and Chanoine families continued to lobby for the revision of their case. Dr Voulet used his local member of parliament to lobby in his favour; he later also had access to the new prime minister, Émile Combes, with whom he had been at university:

> Decided not to abandon the cause of my son who was worthy of a better fate, I would be very grateful Monsieur le président [du conseil], if you could have the conclusion of the [Laborie] enquiry communicated to us, in memory of his services to France and of the memories that bind us.[57]

None of these rather indirect connections could save his son's reputation, however. The Pallier family blamed their son's death from yellow fever on a conspiracy. Both families petitioned their local deputies and senators and some pressure was applied by them. The families were particularly incensed that the Laborie report was never published despite parliamentary lobbying in 1900:

> The still unexplained drama and badly known events of Soudan was followed with the unnecessary sacrifices, if they were not planned, of Senegal. We expected some explanation and that a light [be cast on this affair] but you do not seem to want it. The chamber being in recess no one can force you to open the files you have . . . the families and friends of the deceased of Soudan and Senegal know that we are several in parliament who are decided to obtain the truth.[58]

In the chamber of deputies accusations of murder were voiced explicitly against the government in relation to Pallier.[59] To this individual lobbying one should add the networks around

Chanoine. Jules Chanoine no longer had the power he once held, having lost much of his political kudos since his bizarre resignation over the Dreyfus affair in 1898. His former friends were weary of him. Yet he still stood on a largely honorary Comité Technique de l'Infanterie. Chanoine had friends among the officers and soon started his own enquiry, petitioning the ministers repeatedly between 1899 and 1904. Evidence from Say had been damning but evidence from Dahomey had been quite the reverse, praising Voulet and Chanoine for the efficiency of their much needed military campaign and for the clarity of their analysis of African resistance to French domination.[60]

The reports from Dahomey came late, in November 1899, too late to save Voulet but they state that the burnt villages had been set alight accidentally or by the natives themselves. Indeed there is evidence that many villages had caught fire accidentally. In March Chanoine even warned Voulet: 'be careful with these villages full of straw, with the wind that blows all the time—the fire started and we managed to limit it to 2 or 3 huts but Corporal Mousa Kouloubaly burnt himself (but not badly).'[61] Yet by the end of the mission Chanoine sent the message 'I can see Koragou burning—I think it must be your work and you cannot be far.'[62]

The officer in charge stated 'Captain Cornu and Lieutenant Viola, previously residing in the middle Niger, are praising the positive effects for the Dahomey colony of the Voulet mission on the left bank of Niger. In my opinion the word of these officers is worth at least as much as that of Péteau.'[63]

Before his informers were silenced, Jules Chanoine accumulated letters of support. The events leading to the sending of Klobb on Voulet's trail were discredited or explained as mere incidents such as those always found in times of war. The killing of Klobb itself was entirely the work of Voulet. Jules Chanoine obtained much evidence showing that his son could not have taken an active part in the ambush.

On the other hand Julien Chanoine's behaviour towards the end was so ambiguous that it could be construed as an attempt to win back the soldiers to the legitimate cause of France. Joalland, who had little love spare for Chanoine, did not exclude the possibility that he had indeed attempted to seize power from Voulet. In that interpretation of events, he was murdered by mutinous soldiers, none of whom had to face a constituted court martial. Obviously devastated by the turn of events Chanoine and Voulet's fathers launched a long campaign to see a legal case opened. In June 1903 the administration responded that its enquiry only regarded the living.

The Voulet–Chanoine affair was not going to be a replay of the Dreyfus affair. In this instance a civilian minister had been able to correct a festering situation by sending a truly republican officer to the rescue. He was then murdered. The fact that Voulet and Chanoine were also murdered offered no closure since *their* murderers were still at large. There was some poetic justice in their death and also deep irony. Jules Chanoine, who had campaigned so effectively against any revision of the Dreyfus case, never obtained from the army either the results of the promised investigation nor that his son's murderers faced trial. In increasingly desperate pleas, Chanoine tried to obtain a full enquiry; he then asked the Ministry of Justice to investigate the murder. Eventually in October 1904 he accused Sgt. Souley Taraore and fifteen native soldiers and NCOs of theft.[64] In the moments following Chanoine's death the soldiers and the women had ransacked the effects of the two officers, scattering their notes and equipment, breaking the camera and the phonograph.[65]

He queried the killing of Sibere Dialo, Sidi Berete, Mamadou Koulibali, and Moussa Dialo and directly accused Pallier and

Joalland of having colluded with Souley Taraore to 'make witnesses disappear'.

The minister of colonies decided to stop answering Chanoine's increasingly rambling letters. Yet despite their increasingly vague and paranoid tone, these letters identified the strange gaps in the inquest and these gaps remain.

The lack of a real trial for the killings of Voulet and Chanoine is a strange puzzle for the historian. Even in the midst of the repression of the Commune of Paris, in May 1871, as the French army moved in to repress the revolutionaries, two factions of the Communards faced each other. A young Communard officer, Beaufort, was summarily executed by his fellow revolutionaries. Even though all were rabble in the eyes of military justice and despite the fact that Beaufort might well have been summarily killed by the army, had he lived long enough, the French justice system set in place a full enquiry later on in 1871. Even in the midst of civil war French justice sought to ensure some rule of law. A trial subsequently took place.[66]

Nothing of the kind took place in 1900. Yet all witnesses recognized that Chanoine had not been anywhere near Klobb.[67] If he had been an accomplice his responsibility appeared limited to a passive attitude, followed, perhaps by very unenthusiastic support. Furthermore, his last words while riding towards the African soldiers had been, according to numerous witnesses 'France, France!', suggesting thus that he had no real desire to become an African warlord. To add final insult to mortal injury, Chanoine's body was, according to some sources, dismembered and cut to pieces by the women of the expedition. Yet, there is not a single shred of evidence that the Soudan military high command envisaged to sue the men that might have killed him. This is indeed very odd and Jules Chanoine challenged several administrations in vain to obtain that a full trial take place. The administration originally responded with a deafening silence, referring him back to the conclusions of Lamy's enquiry into the events or the fuller enquiry of Laborie. Neither man had it within his brief to identify who had killed Chanoine. For Voulet the story was somewhat different since the guard who shot him pleaded self-defence and, on that legitimate ground, was not made to face a trial either.

The report's conclusions were passed onto the families and year after year Chanoine exhausted every possible legal avenue to obtain from the army the sort of justice he himself had denied the Dreyfus family. Jules Chanoine and his supporters did not seem to be aware of the irony, except of course when he blamed the Dreyfusards for this situation. An officer who had been a commandant supérieur in Soudan thus claimed, 'I think it is my duty to tell you that I am protesting most energetically against the odious accusations of enemies of the army. These evil characters have based and sustained their accusations on the single evidence of a few cowardly negroes.' The same officer denied, like many others before all the evidence came to light, that 'I had Lieutenants Voulet and Chanoine as subordinates between 1895 and 1896 and I declare loudly, without even mentioning their other qualities, that their education and their good spirit made them incapable of committing the murder of which they have been accused.'[68] In October 1899 another officer attempted to dissociate Voulet from Chanoine, stating, 'I am troubled by this glorious career interrupted by this sudden bolt, by the destiny of this young captain of 27, the victim of odious calumnies and of his excessive solidarity for his unfortunate but guilty friend.'[69] Joalland himself wrote to Jules Chanoine on August 15 claiming that Julien Chanoine had been innocent of the murder of Klobb.

The paradox, of course, is that if Chanoine had not taken part actively in the ambush and murder of Klobb, he was undoubtedly responsible for many of the most violent acts of the Voulet mission. Being in charge of the warring party of the column and in particular of its cavalry, he and his men having rampaged widely around the column, he had been directly involved in most atrocities. Only in Sansané Haoussa and Birnin Konni had Voulet taken the lead in ordering the killing of women and children.

Increasingly isolated and abandoned even by members of the colonialist lobby who like Terrier were too close to the incidents for their own comfort, Jules Chanoine developed the conspiracy theory to its logical extreme. It is not surprising then that he should have claimed that

> the action of secret societies, so-called free masons who oppress and dishonour France is obvious in the preparation and execution of the catastrophe of the Chad mission. This [conspiracy] has manifested itself even further in the following years to cover its tracks and insult the memory of its victims in order to cover up the murderers even through new crimes.[70]

Ernest Judet's newspaper article in *Le Petit Journal* quoted at the onset of this chapter then developed the theory by accusing Jews and Freemasons together of having plotted the intricate web of betrayal which then led to the murder of Klobb. Indeed the journalist and others on the far right went as far as to argue that

> Voulet had to face less the natives and the climate than the *traps of the Pavillon de Flore* [Ministry of Colonies], don't we have to find that the monstrous anarchy of Soudan originates in the metropolis, in the orders and counter orders which exasperate those who have to obey them, that if guns are shot in the bush they are loaded in Paris.
>
> Alas the nefarious duel between Voulet and Klobb [was] the inevitable product of a mountain of misunderstandings and petty

squabbles and it could have occurred twenty times in similar circumstances.

Reduced to a duel in the sun, the *affaire Voulet* became another argument in the bitter rear-guard campaign of the anti-Dreyfusards against an increasingly left-wing government. Chanoine and his side argued that the 'friends of Dreyfus have provoked dreadful calamities and at the same time they have served the English and compromise for many years the future of our advance towards Chad'.[71]

In continuing the Voulet mission Joalland had expected to find his rehabilitation in victory. His gamble paid off. He used to the full the contradictory orders which intimated that even though a meeting with Lamy would be a desirable outcome, Lake Chad was the real aim of the mission. After taking over Zinder and avenging Cazemajou by pillaging the city and killing its Sultan, Joalland proceeded forth with Meynier, Klobb's second in command. The reconciliation of forces which had faced each other was a brilliant idea which enabled Joalland to re-establish some coherence to French command. His journey east showed that a lighter and well-equipped expedition was better suited to the limited resources of the country. Having left the women behind and riding camels Joalland drove forward at great speed. Yet even then the Joalland–Meynier mission, as it labelled itself, continued with many of the previous practices. On his return to Say, Joalland paid off his soldiers, dispersing the survivors of the Voulet mission, and had all the honours of a military ceremony to bid farewell to his 'faithful NCOs' (Figures 15–17).

Yet in the public eye, even though he made it to the rank of general, Joalland's career remained under the shadow of the Dankori events. After a twenty-nine-year silence, Joalland printed his youthful account while stressing that:

in writing [this book] I have only had one aim: to show that there are no secrets in the Voulet–Chanoine affair. Everything I will say is already known but I would be happy if having read my text one agreed that there is ground to file away definitively this unhappy event which even by a simple mention of its name seems to evoke mysterious circumstances...far from seeking to be polemical my dearest wish is to write the last chapter of the Dankori drama. Let's forget the first part of my book to remember only the second half.[72]

Despite his desire to be remembered for his advance on Chad and his role in the defeat of Rabah, Joalland remained tainted by association with Klobb's death. If the murder of Klobb was obviously not his deed, the crimes of Voulet have often been closely associated with him. Joalland like most other military writers eventually inflated Voulet's responsibility to include every event of the mission, even those over which he had no control. Ultimately Klobb's death served as the key for everything that had taken place prior to it. The massacres of Birnin Konni and the myriad villages ransacked before and after were effectively silenced by the colonial administration. To dwell too long on them would have had potentially grave consequences.

It is perhaps worth asking how many real lies were told. For there were lies. Some were blatant lies of omission; others were distortions of events which can only be regarded as criminal. That Joalland lied in his account to the colonial administration and in his published work is a matter of historical record and has been noted by military officials and historians alike. That a liar was rewarded despite his crimes is also a fact. The most important lie was the one that distorted the murder of a French national into a disciplinary offence.

Pallier managed to bring back the bulk of the mission to French Soudan. On arrival he was sent to the capital of French

Occidental Africa, St Louis du Senegal. Yellow fever soon took him away, adding a new layer of conspiracy theory. Dr Henric was sent back from St Louis on medical grounds. With him travelled a journalist from the Havas news agency who filed his telegram report on arrival. The Havas agency was the one that had the most developed range of overseas correspondents in the empire and the yellow fever epidemic gave one of them the opportunity to travel with Henric. As is customary, agency despatches remained to the point in order to allow journalists to spin the news; yet in this case it gave some dramatic colour to the details it transmitted:

> Whatever is said the death of Voulet is certain. He was buried by Sergeant Bouthel. As to Chanoine he could not be buried, the women of the tirailleurs tore his body to pieces and scattered his remains. After 2nd act of the drama Chanoine had said to his tirailleurs, we will go a long way to build an empire, you will keep your women but you will stay with me in a region I will designate. Tirailleurs and women avenged themselves [for] being away from their homes despite promises made to their chief to remain under his domination.[73]

On arrival Henric locked himself for a few days in a hotel room in Marseille to avoid the crowd of journalists but his version of events was already out. In reports allegedly from Henric's lips, at least one of the three graves in Soudan was empty. If the graves of Voulet and Chanoine later became a curiosity, only Klobb's grave deserved an archival file.[74]

The irony of the Voulet–Chanoine disaster is of course that it was not perceived to be one by their successors. Governor William Ponty who took charge of the region six years later deplored the scale of the devastation or the fact that the mission had contributed to the famine, but he also rejoiced at the full-scale pacification and the fact that Voulet's memory was enough to encourage local chieftains to collaborate.[75] Even reports from Say were mostly concerned with the future yield of the tax regime than with the killing of slaves. The successors of Voulet were the numerous columns heading towards the more turbulent new colony of Chad which, one after the other, continued to drain the region of scarce resources and people. If Voulet had destroyed much, the more 'regular' operations that followed continued his work and the 'ligne Tchad', the relay service of warring units heading east through the Nigerien lands, contributed to the famine of 1901–3.

Regarding the survivors the Governor General of Occidental Africa eventually decided to consider the individual cases according to 'a principle in the circumstances that we had to avoid any kind of new publicity'. In a report to yet another minister of colonies, Gaston Doumergue, in September 1902, the governor general stated his decisions. The only man to be punished officially, probably because he continued to speak in 1900 even after his promotion, was Captain Péteau. The 'blame' in his file damaged his career prospects. The conclusions of Laborie had been harsh and were picked out in the conclusions of the governor general: 'I regard Lt Péteau not worthy from beginning to end. This officer denounced not for the sake of the service but to serve himself and after committed reprehensible acts resembling the ones for which he reproached his leaders.'[76] The only punishment addressed to Joalland was minimal: 'no measures in his favour'. The same lack of support would apply to the newly promoted Lieutenant Tourot, Adjudant Bouthel, and Sergeant Major Laury. Henric was to be promoted to Médecin Major second class, to 'give satisfaction to his repeated wish that his name be cleared of the accusation of complicity in Klobb's murder stated by Lieutenant Péteau.'[77] The punishments were indeed a very light touch: Péteau, Tourot, Bouthel, Laury, and Henric were promoted.

Joalland had already been promoted during the mission and could not get any higher at this stage of his career. He later became a general, as did Meynier. Meynier returned to France in November 1900. Henric retired on health grounds. Bouthel was rushed back in 1901. Joalland revived the support networks that previously had promoted Voulet so efficiently—it is not surprising that he should win the Société de Géographie's gold medal for his 'explorations' on his return in 1902. Voulet's memory had been erased but his role was taken up by others who adhered to his ideals and who were not adverse to his methods and ideas.

7

FROM THE *HEART OF DARKNESS* TO TWENTY-FIRST-CENTURY GUILT

> A while back, facing the statue of Archinard, during the speeches, a Mousso [a white man's black mistress] was watching. She was draped in orange gauze as pale as the clouds at sunset over the river Niger, she was a statue, too, who seemed to be there in answer to the other, to evoke an old Soudan made of struggles and of flesh.[1]

Writing in 1934 on the occasion of the fiftieth anniversary of the French arrival on the river Niger, a commemoration which had brought back to Soudan the survivors of the conquest, de Trentinian, Gouraud, Gaden, Quinquandon, and Peltier 'whose youth was galloping next to our door to escort our symbolic convoy', the humanist colonial administrator Robert Delavignette nailed down the contrast between old and new, between colonial administrators and conquerors.[2] Archinard had his statue in Bamako—but it is that other statue, the living one of the abandoned African lover that matters here. The memory of the colonial encounter was one inscribed on more than one body.[3]

Having driven across the desert in a pioneering automobile rally, Octave Meynier was also at the rendezvous of nostalgic colonials.[4] Recent history was everywhere and most street names of the new African cities like Bamako or Niamey bore the names of young men who had died a mere twenty years earlier. Yet there were some lacunas as the journalist Albert Londres noted in his deeply ironic style:

> Going across the cities, I read the street names. Gallieni Street, Archinard Street, Binger Street . . . Here is the street of Lieutenant Boiteux. This lieutenant entered Timbuctu before Bonnier and Joffre. He was massacred. So was Bonnier.
>
> Bonnier Street. . . .
>
> Voulet and Chanoine gave France the Mosse . . . with fifty men they sent off the three thousand cavalrymen of the Morho-Naba [*sic*]; they took Ouagadougou. On learning this and probably a few other small things, the government sent Lieutenant-Colonel Klobb to take their place. They killed him. No *Voulet–Chanoine* Street.

He then added a reference to the common legend of Soudan:

> Chanoine, it is said, is still roaming the outer reaches of Sahel, dressed as a Tuareg!
>
> Old past![5]

The colonial past was commemorated with extreme speed—within a year of his death Cazemajou had a fort, that of Zinder, named after him; N'Djamena in Chad was also known as Fort Lamy to recall the name of the hero. No such luck for Voulet or Chanoine. Yet by being unrecalled officially their memory lived on in strange ways. Chanoine's ghostly legend of living as a Tuareg became part of the colonial folklore. This memory is now the most challenging inheritance of the colonial conquest—unlike the past it is also the most changeable.

This is not to say that living memory is the only one that remains. Colonial nostalgic memory still has some life in it. On 2 October 2006 a strange ceremony took place in Brazzaville, capital of the Republic of Congo. The coffins of Savorgnan de Brazza and four members of his family, recently exhumed from the family graves in Algiers, were escorted by the Congolese army to their new resting place in the city that bears their name. The Congolese president, Sassou N'Guesso, representatives from Gabon where Brazza founded Franceville, the republic of Centrafrique, and the then French minister of foreign affairs, Philippe Douste-Blazy, led the procession. The colonial conqueror Brazza now has his white marble, air-conditioned memorial and his eight-metre-high statue at the heart of a fountain. That such a monument should have been erected in the heart of a city where basic sanitation remains an aspiration for most of the inhabitants shocked many Congolese and surprised the French media.[6] For ten billion CFA francs (approx. fifteen million euros) the Congolese government assumed the colonial inheritance with a kind of self-confidence that had not been seen for a long time, least of all in the ex-colonies themselves. Reclaiming the empire builder, a freemason with utopian views who is alleged to have been unique in building a colonial territory without actual violence, seemed to indicate that, in some respects, the colonial past could be reclaimed for Africans. Yet this commemoration strikes a surprising note in the current climate and France, absorbed by its internal debates and European partnership, seems less present in Africa than it was during Savorgnan de Brazza's time. Indeed, throughout Africa, from Cote d'Ivoire to Algeria the governments in place, often facing considerable structural or political difficulties, tend to cast blame on their colonial past: President Gbagbo in the Ivory Coast routinely condemns the French colonial past for the woes of his country divided by civil war; in Algeria the government alternates between conciliation and denunciation. Recently French colonization, which lasted 132 years in that country, was compared to the Nazi rule of central Europe.

There are still a few symbolic marks glorifying the empire in French society but they have been neglected.[7] There are the visible remnants of the triumphal exhibition of 1931 located at the Porte Dorée.[8] The showcase 'permanent museum of the colonies' has proved as transient as the colonies themselves. Having changed names many times since being founded by Marshall Lyautey, the Art Deco masterpiece bearing the names of nearly all the pioneers and adventurers who added a significant piece of land to the patchwork is now, in bitter irony, the Museum of Immigration. Few symbols could be more explicit. Yet the new museum will not be allowed to smooth out the carved commemoration of the likes of Savorgnan de Brazza. Among the names, from Jacques Cartier to Lyautey himself, one seeks in vain for Voulet and Chanoine; yet by any standards, they too did their bit for the nation.

Characteristically the collections of the museum, primarily the *art nègre* in favour amongst avant-garde circles since the late nineteenth century, have been moved to a new symbolic '*grand projet*': the museum of the Quai Branli, museum of 'arts premiers', and legacy project of President Jacques Chirac.[9] The avowed universalism of this art project contrasts with the coarse exploitative imagery of the Musée Permanent des Colonies.

The colonies are nevertheless more than ever part of French contemporary life and in the make-up of the population. Indeed much of the new attention paid to colonial history has come from what the French critically call communitarian pressure groups. Yet the other side of Voulet–Chanoine—the *Heart of Darkness* and its avatar *Apocalypse Now*—is of course what these men have done to the people of Africa or Vietnam in the process of becoming mad or bad. Logically, since the 1970s, the Voulet–Chanoine affair has raised the more considerable matter of what violence lay at the heart of Pax Gallica in Africa. The denunciation of the crimes of the expedition took it as exemplary of French rule and not as an exception. Since the late 1990s the empire has been at the heart of debates on guilt and reparations, symbolic or material. In this context the story has acquired new currency. The French slave trade and its disguised form of indentured service have come to the attention of the media as well as pressure groups which represent French people both of the Carribean islands and of African descent.[10]

France recently began confronting its colonial past, often as a result of concerted campaigns by pressure groups. Among the many atrocities of the 'black book' of colonialism, the Voulet–Chanoine story has a unique place, probably exaggerated and now mythical.[11]

In France itself a number of organizations of immigrants coming from the ex-colonies have taken to heart to recall publicly the colonial past as an unambiguously shameful one. The political forces of the French West Indian and Indian Ocean departments, Guadeloupe, Martinique, and Reunion have also campaigned for a public acknowledgement of guilt regarding the slave trade and subsequent mistreatment and segregation of generations of Afro-French citizens. In France and in its ex-colonies, it seems that the day of reckoning has at last arrived. The French debate on its colonial past is still in its infancy but it has moved on rapidly over the past twenty years.[12] In many of these debates the military has played a crucial role. Veteran associations have taken up the cause for the African world war veterans who have never received a full pension. As the last survivors of the tirailleurs Sénégalais who fought for the French die, the French government is called upon to provide support for their village and families. A 'case mémoriale' for the last African soldier of the First World War was enhanced with the electrification of tirailleur Ndiaye's village and a tarmac road financed by French veterans, cement manufacturers, and the French and Senegalese states.[13] The Senegal government instituted a day of national commemoration on 23 May and the colonial monument to the tirailleurs was placed back in the square opposite the railway station in Dakar.[14] Ironically, the day before the French ambassador was due to reward his past services with a medal, Ndiaye died.

The celebration of Savorgna de Brazza's work in Africa could be read in similar ways. To the outcries of immigrant groups denouncing past crimes and seeking moral and material compensations, governments answer by the evocation of a fictitious golden age. The colonial past is not allowed to rest because its fundamental issues are those of today: inequality, insecurity, and servitude; the antonyms of the French motto of liberty, equality, and fraternity.

In that context what remains of the Voulet–Chanoine expedition are two interconnected yet separate debates. The first one reflects the reception and interpretations of the central plot of Joseph Conrad's the *Heart of Darkness*, which was later transposed to Vietnam by Francis Ford Coppola's film *Apocalypse Now*. In Conrad's novella, the stories are intricately written like a novel within a novel. The narrator tells the story of Marlow and his adventure along the Congo on the bloody trail of a mysterious man, Kurtz. The story is famously told second hand since the narrator is telling what he heard Marlow tell him. Begun in the night on board a barge sailing the Thames estuary it takes the reader to the dark waters of the Congo. Conrad made the point of stressing the parallels between the Congo and the Thames where the first Roman ships sailed upriver in the face of barbarity. The ship of civilization quickly hits the sands when Marlow starts describing this 'great man' who managed so efficiently to extract the wealth of Africa at immense human cost. The story is allusive and perhaps even racist—in his delirium and final illness Kurtz famously utters, 'the horror, the horror', which has stood ever since as the most profound attempt to come to terms with forms of violence that have become almost unutterable. The tale had been long in the making. It was based on Conrad's own experience in Congo and on his diaries written a decade earlier. Much rewritten, the novella was completed in 1898 and was originally published in *Blackwood's Magazine* in April 1899, precisely when Klobb was sent on the trail of Voulet and Chanoine—in search of his own Kurtz.[15]

Since a famous lecture and article by the Nigerian author Chinua Achebe,[16] the Conrad industry has been divided for the past thirty years as to whether Conrad had written a racist fantasy which contributed further to the association of evil and Africa.[17] It may be so but Conrad was not writing alone and his tale of corruption was not an unfamiliar one.

Paul Vigné d'Octon, the French member of parliament who brought up the Voulet–Chanoine affair over and over again during the parliamentarian debates, had previously written a short book, *Chair Noire*, which portrayed the gradual moral collapse and rising sensuality of a French official.[18] In this clearly autobiographical novel Vigné denounced the weakening of civilized bonds in the face of absolute cultural isolation.[19] Rather than a plea for moral relativism, Vigné d'Octon wished to highlight the risk that colonialism posed for both the colonized, brutalized and raped, and the colonizers, lost to greed.

Beyond the human characters, the hero and the malignant force of the novel is Africa and the greed it generates. Its climate and strange lore permeate throughout and white men seem to wither in its fetid atmosphere consumed by lust. Gradually, their behaviour shifts and is increasingly consistent with their perception of Africa and Africans and increasingly opposed to the cultural norms of their own homeland. In some strange way these men come to inhabit a netherworld of their own making which is primarily a paranoid fantasy of *their* Africa. Their overpowerful mastery of weapons incommensurably superior to those of the Africans (or Vietnamese) is contrasted to their loss of control over their instincts and desires. In a striking prefiguring of Sigmund Freud's *Civilization and its Discontents*, written after the First World War and which emphasized the death wish as the mirror of the sexual drive, Conrad and many observers of his day reflected on this loss of inhibitions as a threat to Western values. Georges Clemenceau, a notorious anticolonial agitator, thus denounced, 'A man is alive still, a companion of Stanley [Jameson] who was found out to have bought a girl of twelve to see her eaten in front of him.'[20] What was shocking to Clemenceau was less the act of African cannibalism than the alleged sexual gratification the white man got out of it.[21] French commentators were swift to denounce the violence of Stanley's campaigns and in particular his 'cynical' campaign to liberate Emin Pasha in Sudan. In the idealistic words of Monteil: 'An explorer is a pioneer of civilization and if some violence can be excused, when they are caused by events, it is not the same when it is planned in order to obtain the spoliation of the weakest.'[22] By these lofty standards most colonial ventures were condemnable. Yet some violence became excusable according to the circumstances.

The threat that runs throughout the *Heart of Darkness* is beyond the loss of social and cultural control, the ironic self-denial of Kurtz's ideals. What Africa represented here was the fragility of civilization and its climate seemed to nurture a 'barbarization process' as sudden and fast as the civilizing one is slow and incremental. Africa and the exploitation of Africa, the mixture of extremes of capitalism, absolute power, and 'primitive life', were solvents of extreme potency.

Since 1899, the *Heart of Darkness* has remained a key cultural prism used to read the crimes of Western men in tropical and equatorial settings and, more broadly, all unacceptable Western violence in foreign wars. In this narrative the folly of war becomes that of white men who lose their moral and ethical bearings. In Soudan, like in Congo, like later in Vietnam, the story of the *Heart of Darkness* which is also that of Voulet seems to shift the blame from the individuals to the conflicts in which they become 'mad' and bad. The breakdown of communication lines between Kurtz and his administration, like the breakdown of communication between Voulet and his backers in Paris, leads to their growing isolation and incontrollable drift from their original remit.

Furthermore the climate and the local people seem to be conspiring to undermine 'normal' Westerners whose main sin is to be what Westerners should be: enterprising and ambitious. Yet in the colonial context both these qualities turn into fatal flaws as the adventurers fall prey to hubris and over-reach themselves dramatically. Insidiously the immoral universe they inhabit gradually imposes its own rules of naked power that are incompatible with a return to Western bourgeois normality. Towards the end of the novella Kurtz may be willing to go back but only because he is gravely ill. Marlow visiting Kurtz's fiancée lies to her and pretends that he recalled her name on his deathbed. Her house stands in stark contrast to the huts in the jungle her lover ruled from.

By 12 July 1899, Voulet and Chanoine knew themselves to be unable to go back; like Joalland later, their only way back was to go further into the continent.

Their actions can only be judged according to moral norms they had ceased to recognize, to moral norms they held in contempt and which they opposed to their ideals of action. In the case of Voulet and Chanoine each new execution seemed to distance them further from the disciplined moral universe of the military. While always enacted according to their reading of the disciplinary codes, their violence increasingly disconnected them from the spirit of these codes which advocated restraint. In Conrad as in Voulet and Chanoine's story, the account that the white survivors gave, always at the exclusion of any African version of the events, highlighted the growing insanity of the events and of their response to these events. Like cogs in ineluctable machineries these men become mere pawns in a game played by pagan gods. Evil seems to inhabit the narratives which are saturated with metaphors of heat, darkness, and light.

This moral portrait made sense of some rather more pragmatic colonial policies which were, indeed, based on what the French thought of as African mores. Much of this violence was thus the product of a self-conscious but voluntarily inexact mimicry of African warlords' practices. To use Homi Bhabha's understanding of the term, mimicry indicates here a desire to be camouflaged amongst local practices—claiming at once that one seeks to change and reform African warfare while imitating its most salient features.[23] Thus Voulet and Chanoine talked of an African viewpoint on war and developed strategies deemed to fit with African political understandings. They used war drums and *griots*; they used slavery and pillage, but they also intended to justify these acts in the language of humanity and civilization. They claimed that their violence was a violence against violence; their African warfare an end to African warfare. They intended to project back a hundredfold harder the enmity they sensed around them.

Some of their thinking was predicated on their understanding of kingship in Western Africa. Yet a major flaw of their mimicry was that the mission was essentially predatory and offered no prospect of any durable settlement. Local leaders saw no point in settling with warlords who were so transient and likely to be incapable of providing assistance in future conflicts.[24] Voulet and Chanoine only took from Samory the most excessive forms of his violence. Samory negotiated often and settled many of his scores by bartering power and military roles in his state in exchange for submission. From this mimicking of African lordship, they retained only the most brutal practices and none of the key social or religious interactions that meant that Samory could be perceived as a legitimate ruler or even a liberator. Voulet and Chanoine could only ask for unconditional surrender without any offer of a payback. Much of this violence would later be negated by the evidence of 'pacification' and colonial order. It would not become history and only the recollection of daring and war against the odds would remain in the colonial propaganda.

Only when it failed, as it did in 1899, would the possibility that this 'madness' or 'evil' might turn one against one's own friends or comrades. Of all their violent acts, the killing of Klobb became the tragedy that mattered. In the *Heart of Darkness* like in Soudan, the conflict between white men became the revealing moment of horror, regardless of what these mad or bad people might have done in Soudan, Congo, or Vietnam to the indigenous people.

What had struck their contemporaries in the 'drama of Dankori' was this internecine violence and the irruption of insanity in the ranks of the colonial enterprise. The insanity led to the development, limited in effect by censorship, of military psychiatry. After the Voulet–Chanoine incident, Dr Marie of the Asylums of the Seine attempted to write on madness in the

Foreign Legion; Drs Catrin and Cavasse studied separately the dangers of insanity in the army in general and the colonial army in particular, where, the argument went, atavistic degeneracy would emerge in its most acute form.[25] According to Catrin, military life necessarily worsened lesser symptoms and revealed new ones in degenerates. The military code and its inflexible understanding of property and discipline tipped these men into crime and led to their punishment despite their diminished responsibility. The colonial situation, according to Cavasse, further exacerbated these matters. On the ground, however, any case of mental illness was dealt with by speedy repatriation so that at that stage there was no data available of insanity in West Africa.[26] The Voulet–Chanoine case (by 1900 it was readily accepted that a psychiatric diagnostic could explain everything in the scandal) was seen as revelatory of the madness of youth. Crime and madness were so closely associated that a medical diagnosis seemed to explain most crimes.[27]

Since 1870 and the case of the notorious serial killer Troppmann, who murdered a whole family for financial gain, criminal insanity had been associated with excessive ambition, and new invented categories of madness offered a convenient label for criminals whose excesses were undiagnozeable: 'reasonable insanity'.[28] This diagnostic was also associated by right-wing writers with events that followed in 1870–1. The civil war of the Paris Commune was blamed on collective madness. In 1871, the insanity of the siege, *obsidional* fever, had allegedly pushed the Communards to debauchery and excess, desecration of holy sites and murder. Yet the real violence had not been theirs. The Communards had been ineffectual defenders of Paris and in May 1871 it was the French army that committed the appalling purge of the 'bloody week' during which over 15,000 men and women were killed in the streets of Paris. Among the Communards were found soldiers who had chosen the party of insanity.

A young officer, Louis Rossel, was tried for mutiny and his defiant words echoed closely those of Voulet on 14 July 1899 when he announced that he would shoot anyone coming within firing distance.[29]

In the international press coverage of the Voulet case, there remained the suspicion that the insanity of Voulet and Chanoine was nothing of the kind and that their excesses were those of civilization itself. The theme has stuck and in a crucial moment of *Apocalypse Now*, in a scene shot in the Kurtz palace, the camera lavishes a few moments on his books. He only had a few, and the only title that can be read is *The Golden Bough*, by James George Frazer, a 'study in Magic and Religion' published in 1922 which set out to explain the violence at the heart of ancient myths. In Coppola's reading of Conrad, this dimension explains how a man like Kurtz, the paragon of American values, could have become such a monster in the jungle.

In an equally undifferentiated Africa, probably not so far from Zinder, Jules Verne placed the action of his last novel, *The Strange Affair of the Mission Barsac* (which was finished by his son Michel upon Jules' death in 1905 but only published in July 1914). It was meant to be the last novel of the immensely popular series of *Voyages Extraordinaires* which included *20,000 Leagues under the Sea, Around the World in Eighty Days, Travel to the Interior of the Earth*, and other classic novels.[30] It is a strange novel of two parts. In the first part the mission Barsac travels to Soudan in order to find out whether the natives may be granted full French citizenship. The mission is joined by a young woman, Jane Buxton, and her nephew. Ms Buxton is seeking the grave of her brother, a disgraced British officer whose mission resembles in every way that of Voulet. Convinced of his innocence she seeks his grave in French-controlled Soudan. Early in the novel it becomes clear that Barsac's idealism will not triumph and that the Soudanese will not become French citizens but also that an insidious power is at work to slow the mission down and even attempt to kill them.

This evil force is none other than a savage and drunk Englishman, the disgraced half-brother of Jane Buxton, Harry Killer. Harry Killer is the organizer and ruler of a privateering colonial kingdom called Blackland which figures on no existing map. This city is a mysterious oasis arising from the desert thanks to the works of a classic deluded mad scientist. Unlike some of his other novels the master and the scientist are not one but two characters exploiting each other. The scientist devises fantastical machinery which turns the desert into a lush colonial landscape with its capital, Blackland, guarded by aeroplanes and ultramodern weaponry. Harry Killer is merely the facilitator and military leader of this fantasy world. Through extensive slave-trading and the bloody ransacking of the Niger region he finances the relentless development of this private kingdom.

In order to keep his kingdom hidden he kidnaps the Barsac mission only to discover that his hated half-sister is part of the group. To cut a long story short the members of the mission manage to escape. Eventually a rescue mission looking for missing personalities kidnapped a year earlier discovers this monstrous society run for profit and crime. The prisoners then manage to turn the scientist against the adventurer until Blackland literally implodes. If Jules and Michel Verne exploited elements of the Voulet story they gave it more than one twist.

The villains in this plot are no longer French but British as are some of the heroes too; the colonial crimes are not the product of official colonialism but of piracy. Yet, between the lines, a number of anticolonial themes emerge which, if we agree with Antoine Tshitongu Kongolo, denounce Westerners meddling in African societies. With the mixture of high-tech interference and slavery, Blackland combines the old and the new.

To see a parallel with the Voulet–Chanoine affair makes most sense if one considers the colonial project as a whole—Voulet and Chanoine had little modern technology at their disposal beyond an unused ice-making machine, a phonograph, a camera, a gun, and rapid fire rifles—the machines were moving east well behind them, while de Trentinian dreamed of steam engines, a modern press to print the ethnographic books written by his officers, and automobile buses to link the Soudan to the modern world.[31] Yet Voulet and Chanoine's expedition, traditional as it may have looked, brought with it the promises of this violent colonial modernity built by forced labour with income generated by new taxes and war spoils.

Voulet and Chanoine were travelling in a different Africa from Conrad's, where trees were scarce and where the drums did not roll endlessly behind a canopy of rainforest bushes. They were in the Sahel; yet they referred to it as an Africa of equal darkness. Gradually, in their letters back home as well as in the survivors account, a certain form of magic realism seemed to seize the mission. They did not have books that dealt with magic. They had books on medicine, and Dr Broca's craniological guidance which enabled them to decide the intelligence of people by considering the angle of their forehead and the angle of their nose in relation to their eyes and ears.[32] They had joke books to keep them amused by the fireside—the absurd jokes of Alphonse Allais—they had treatises which would enable them to explain back to the geographical societies all the benefits one could extract from this new land. They had all this, but they did not have anything like the *Golden Bough* or similar books about magic. Yet it is they who brought out the magic. In this land where words were meant to become things—where a whim could be materialized, a desire made flesh, a grand plan come true—others apart from the white men seem to have had that power. Thus premonitions abounded: both

Joalland and Meynier described soldiers having premonitory dreams.[33]

In Joalland's terms, an old hag, la Sarranouia, was waging her witchcraft against the invaders and sent a letter of insults to Voulet.[34] On 16 April 1899, the French marched on Sarranouia's village of Lougou. After two assaults, ten casualties, and the expenditure of 7,000 bullets, Lougou fell to Joalland and Voulet. la Sarranouia, defeated but not killed, faded from history. Yet as a character she did not disappear entirely. Her successor queens have ruled to this day, their genealogy refers to la Sarranouia of 1899 as la Sarranouia Mongo. From Lougou the mission trailed through a deserted area, losing men to heat exhaustion, until a providential rainfall saved the mission.[35]

The Nigerien novelist Mamani made la Sarranouia the symbol of Nigerien resistance to the French, attributing to her magic the final crisis of the Voulet–Chanoine mission:

> After a night of fierce fighting, Voulet and his men occupied the royal city—yet the Sarranouia did not surrender—she hid in the bush and chose to attack the victors—strongly impressed by the fierce determination of the queen and terrorized by her legend as a terrible witch, a large part of the tirailleurs abandoned the Frenchman—It is thus a demoralized army that continued its journey only to break apart a few days later in a fratricidal conflict between French officers . . . African chroniclers attributed this tragic end to the evil powers of the Sarranouia.[36]

This legendary reading of the end of the Voulet mission fulfilled a number of purposes for modern Nigerien nationalists.[37] It insisted on the eventual supremacy of traditional African lore and resistance and on the flakiness of the African collaborationists to the colonial enterprise. The mass desertions mentioned by Mamani did not take place; also there was a gap of some three months between the attack of la Sarranouia's fortified village and the Klobb–Voulet conflict. Yet this story has become a nationalistic theme which gives continuity to Nigerien opposition to the excessive French presence in their politics today. It is true that none of the lands Voulet conquered were ever totally 'dominated'; in the Mosse as well as in Niger the people revolted when colonial pressure became unbearable or outrageously arbitrary. During the First World War, at times of droughts or when a saviour emerged that promised to push the invaders whence they came, resistance flared up and was soon repressed. The story of the mission itself was one of sustained and often desperate resistance, but after the conquest this did not amount to a structured and ultimately victorious resistance such as that of the Vietnamese against the French or even that of the Algerian nationalism. The myths had to be rekindled gently in a fiction abounding in stereotypes. Voulet is thus made into a 'fat bellied and hairy like a mule' pervert while la Sarranouia appears as a terrible and beautiful warrior queen, as sexy and fantastical as the French might have invented her in 1899.[38] As the late Edward Said noted, counter-Orientalism remains true to Orientalism and it still uses French fantasies.

A few years later the novel was turned into a film by the Tiauritanion film director Med Hondo. Although he was not allowed to film it in Niger, probably for fear of alienating the French, the film brought to the world's screens (mostly arts cinema) this character of the Voulet–Chanoine drama. She appeared again, transfigured as a young woman, who could serve both the causes of anticolonialism and women's rights. Since then she has featured in children storybooks such as Halima Handane and Isabelle Colin's *La Sarranouia : La reine magicienne du Niger*,[39] dance festivals, and shows, and more recently but revealingly there has been a proposal to list the Sarranouia's village, battle site, and cemetery on the UNESCO list of endangered heritage sites of world importance.[40]

Magic continued with the more happily blessed Joalland. Joalland's words sufficed, according to him, to convert a disarrayed cluster of pillagers into an orderly fighting machine again. After Klobb's death, Joalland addressed his soldiers thus:

> I explained to these simple minds the events that had taken place. I spoke of France, of sacrifice and of the idea of duty. By this open grave I admonished them: 'Always be good and loyal servants! Soudan is France and France is where our flag flies. The Colonel was meant to take it to Chad, it is our task now.' I had managed to touch the hearts of these good people.[41]

And so it was. Words alone made order possible. The further pillaging of Zinder in revenge for the unhappy expedition of the Cazamejou the previous year was the subtext. When Joalland and his men entered Zinder they let themselves enjoy the spoils of their conquest, distributing the Sultan's wealth and cloth among the tirailleurs.

The real conjuring trick was that Joalland managed his reconversion so well. His reluctant narrative and the story of Voulet–Chanoine only re-emerged in the late 1920s and especially in 1930. Why 1930? Things were changing then in the French empire. The glorious days of the conquest seemed a long way away. The great colonial exhibition was held the following year and the Mosse people were represented by a missionary bishop and some carpet weavers.[42] In Vincennes the frozen representative people of Soudan stood not far from a miniature representation of the temple of Ankhor Vat.[43] For the visitors the scenes of Soudan were presented in their glorious simplicity but there was a sense that this world was fast changing and that military rule was now a bad memory.

As the conquest of Chad became a central part of the *beau geste* and romantic legend of French colonialism the story of Voulet and Chanoine remained a fly in the ointment.[44] The additional legend of their survival was also gaining currency. Joalland himself was in danger of being remembered as a footnote rather than a main protagonist and there is clearly a self-aggrandizing purpose to Joalland's writings. At least for posterity he sought to erase Voulet.

Yet Voulet might not be dead. The recollection of his soldiers as seen in Chapter 5 was that he and Chanoine were alive. For a few months after the murders the authorities gave credence to this hypothesis.[45] Among French officers in Soudan this story had gained ground and Voulet was even alleged to have become a chief among the Tuareg. The Tuareg, the blue men of the Sahara, presented an ideal escape for Voulet and Chanoine, wearing a blue fabric over their face, migratory and racially diverse with white as well as dark skins; the two men might have disappeared among them and the French authorities would never have known. Some even added that they played a part during the Great War. Joalland, who was by 1930 at the end of his career and a general, aimed to silence the persistent rumours which suggested that Chanoine and Voulet had walked free and had been protected by the administration while ruling their own statelets among the Tuareg. The rumour was sufficiently strong for an Orientalist novelist, Franz Toussaint, to pick it up in a successful novel, *Moi le Mort*, published in 1930.[46] In this novel a mysterious inscription makes it back to Paris testifying that one of the gallant colonial officers of the conquest of Sahara, Gertal, has not died ignominiously as his friend Braine had claimed. A romantic young woman who had known the lost soldier then launches a trans-Sahara air-born rescue mission. As in Verne's novel, airplane technology is used to cross otherwise inhospitable colonial expanses of desert. On arrival the adventurers discover that the officer has not died but is the manic ruler of a local kingdom, exhibiting its violence in now familiar ways with displays of heads on sticks and corpses in the sun. Somewhat implausibly the young woman discovers that this incomprehensible insanity originated in betrayal and that her fiancé, Braine, is in fact a serial murderer. A few years earlier he had betrayed Gertal due to jealousy exacerbated by Soudanitis. Gertal abandoned in battle had then been left for dead because of Braine's cowardice. Toussaint ends the novel in a conventional manner by a twist to the sentimental plot where the anti-hero, bloody native tyrant, and ex-French soldier suddenly gets the girl and, reverting to his former gentlemanly behaviour, decides to return to civilization. The final scene sees Gertal who had trampled the French flag a few pages earlier come to his senses and raise the national emblem over his fort. Braine then meets an end suitable for his crime. Of course a few questions remain unanswered among which the most flagrant is the absence of any retribution for Gertal's crimes against the natives.

The book was widely received as a postscript to the Voulet–Chanoine affair. Even though the plot was the sort of sentimental narrative of early cinema (and Toussaint had written a few Orientalist film scripts) Toussaint had some credibility as a witness. He was born in 1879 into a military family, and undertook military service in Soudan in 1900 immediately after the Voulet–Chanoine events. Furthermore, unlike other commentators on the affair, he was a very gifted linguist and a reputed Orientalist whose other work included many translations from the Arabic.

In the 1930s the rumour of Voulet and Chanoine's survival continued unabated, leading some witnesses to explain how the body of Voulet had been disinterred even if the bones of Chanoine had never been found.[47] However implausible this story is, it fitted with every account written or published after

14 July 1899. If Voulet had indeed 'receded' into being a black chief as his peers claimed, is it not logical that he should become one of them? It would certainly close the story in some poetic manner, yet again blaming Africa for what happened to Africa.

It is through creative writing that the story re-emerged in the 1970s, especially after a lurid novel, *Le Grand Capitaine*, glorified and gave a tragic hue to the adventure of Voulet and Chanoine. An academic thesis by Muriel Mathieu covered in detail the context of the events as part of the conquest epic and in Joalland's terms.[48] Other accounts such as Jean-Claude Simoen's novelized version of the event stressed the ambiguities of Voulet's end.[49] The novel of Jean-François Alata, on the other hand, presented two young officers revolted by colonial practices who were less a reflection of Voulet and Chanoine than a complete whitewashing.[50] More recently the story has become a navel-gazing locus for a debate on colonial guilt—a *devoir de mémoire* moment. Its best illustrations have been, in 2004, the film of Serge Moati, *Capitaine des ténêbres*, and Manuel Gasquet's *Blancs de mémoire*, broadcast in 2006 on the Franco-German channel Arte. The producers of the documentary also developed a detailed pedagogical brief to be used in schools across France to teach anticolonial history, going against the grain of the rapidly aborted French law which invited teachers to give students a view of the beneficial aspects of French colonialism. Article 4 of the law of 23 February 2005 was so controversial the Conseil Constitutionnel undermined it and it was finally abrogated by presidential decree on 16 February 2006 despite right-wing parliamentary opposition.[51] Yet like much of the debates on guilt, one cannot help thinking of Hannah Arendt's verdict that 'where all are guilty no one is; confessions of collective guilt are the best possible safeguard against the discovery of culprits.'[52]

Meanwhile, the controversial memory of the affair has become a minor asset for tourism in the region. It features on the website of the Niger office of tourism, and Voulet and Chanoine's graves are given as a destination, recalling the early tourism of the area.[53] As early as 1909, Roserot de Melin travelling with the mission Tilho noted that since their refurbishment by the administrator of Tessaoua, the graves had become a site of pilgrimage for the travellers on the road to Chad (see Figure 18).[54] The mixture of magic and memory did not stop here. The trace of Voulet's mission became a road that bordered the new colonies of Soudan/Niger and Nigeria. When Voulet moved on from Lougou he chose to rewrite international law and border tracing. Even though it took another four years for this line to become the actual border, subsequent French missions had to take the Voulet itinerary with the authorization of the British authorities in Nigeria.[55] It is no small irony that the French administration should have reaped the burnt inheritance of the mission.

Since then the Voulet–Chanoine itinerary has become almost exactly the notorious national road 1 of Niger. The building of this road was in itself a furthering of the violence of the Voulet mission as more lives were lost in forced labour. The ghosts of the colonial past literally haunt this major artery of Niger.[56] Rambling spirits, dislodged by the straight road, are said to provoke fear, accidents, and deaths. Arising from war it has become one of the most dangerous roads of Africa.

8

CONCLUSION: TRAUMATIZED PERPETRATORS?

> Far, far away in Hausa Soudan near a pond and under a great Tamarin tree, two inseparable tombs . . . two names . . . no title . . . to remind the traveller that one ought to pity those who loved glory so much that it drove them to insanity and, alas, to the most abominable of crimes.[1]
>
> Should we lay the blame only at Voulet's door? I say frankly no! For long months his health had declined and the executions and exaggerated measures of repression he undertook are witness to this condition. How could we explain otherwise the difference in his attitude from what we know of how he was while in Maori territory and what he became after the capture of Konni? Was it not the result of the disease contracted in Mosse territory? How could this poor boy who had been such an admirable officer, who had been the Voulet of the Humbert Column, the Voulet of the Mosse, become an assassin if it were not for a disease?[2]

Joalland took a view commonly shared by his comrades, blaming the second in command for much of the preparation of the crime and even for most of the atrocities along the way. Chanoine had it within *his* nature to act as a brute, Voulet was betrayed by nature and illness drove him to the unnerved state of a feeble sufferer of neurasthenia, sometimes unable to move forward, sometimes paralysed by his own acts of transgression. In the era of decadent aesthetics he fitted another trope of banal brutality brought about by circumstances. In the terminology of psychiatry at that time, he showed the symptoms of traumatic neurosis. In this final chapter the madness of Voulet will be reassessed—not on clinical ground—there is no trace of it left in the archives—but as a means of exploring the meanings Western societies give to the violence that takes place, away from our shores but always in our name.

In attempting to come to terms with the crimes of the past and their frequent renewal in the present—the ever more acutely felt presence of genocidal massacres, for instance—historians have turned to the psychological in order to understand the triggers of extreme violence. Among the terms that have acquired an uneasy currency is that of trauma. Ever since the Vietnam War the concept of trauma has been claimed by veterans associations and their physicians, until the turning point of 1980 when post-traumatic stress disorder (PTSD) entered the American psychiatric classification of recognized mental illnesses.[3] This classification has since ensured that access to psychiatric help be available to all witnesses or protagonists in traumatic situations. In courts, PTSD has become a category of psychiatric damage for which compensation can be obtained. The narratives of trauma have become much more than autobiographical stories; they have served to denounce abandonment, social betrayal, and systemic inhumanity.

Certainly the trauma narratives have tended to be sketched in terms of victimhood. But the historiography has been enthralled by the relatively simple explanatory power of events on people. In the words of self-help books 'an experience can be described as traumatic when a person's ability to cope has been completely overwhelmed by a terrible event'; these books then define this traumatic event as having been a 'threat to this person's or other people's physical integrity', leading to 'intense fear, helplessness or horror'.[4] While there is certain circularity in the argument, since a trauma is the product of a traumatic event which itself is an incident likely to cause physical trauma (in the first accepted meaning of the term which meant damage), this populist interpretation fits well with much of the historiography. A trauma can be either physical or moral or both in origin, and is known to happen suddenly to previously overconfident individuals who thought themselves immune to psychic damage.[5] In this interpretation war is necessarily traumatic, at least in its combat phases, and the trauma is necessarily of a psychological nature. The fear of a threat to one's integrity would not be distinguishable from the act of inflicting this violence on others. Historians such as George Mosse have used this model to engage with a concept of brutalization already latent in the philosopher Hannah Arendt's views on the rise of totalitarian violence. The brutalization, or gradual inuring to the pain of others, would thus contain within itself a form of victimhood, a brutality against oneself: the killing of a civilized self.

The diagnosis of PTSD revisited the idea of trauma, or traumatic neurosis as it was known in the work of Charcot in France in the 1890s, and in that of Janet, Freud, and Ferenczi thereafter. Traumatic neurosis has had a chequered and interrupted history. Originally associated with the accidents of modern life—in particular train accidents—trauma became more closely associated with hysteria in France, where the psychiatry and psychology of hysteria was giving credence to these ideas of the self. While often understood as a product of heredity, insanity was also explained as a response to environmental physical aggression, or trauma. As shown in Chapter 2, the concept of insanity in some contexts presented itself as a handy blanket excuse for forms of violence exerted in the colonial sphere. The military and journalists were equally adept at using these terms.[6] Joalland excusing Voulet could find common ground with Vigné d'Octon accusing Voulet. Of course one emphasized his vulnerability to disease and climate, possibly African poison, while the other emphasized the criminal dimensions of his behaviour; yet both agreed, in the end, on his diminished responsibility. Whereas Vigné tended to find a predisposition to violence in the character or mental abilities of Voulet and Chanoine, Joalland argued that only Chanoine had mental deficiencies which led him to becoming a Sadist. Voulet, on the other hand, was a victim of his environment.

The causes might be different in the sense that Joalland would argue the forces of climate, warfare, and fever while Vigné d'Octon would add to these the military system and the officers' ambition and their mental make-up.[7] Yet within this pattern of explaining the experience of insanity, the act of inflicting could also be considered traumatic. In this sense both the military colleagues and their denunciators would concur in making Voulet as much a victim as a perpetrator, a traumatized perpetrator.

In this sense the Voulet–Chanoine situation emerges as a forerunner of the 'atrocity-producing situation' which has been used to explain extreme acts of violence that took place during the Vietnam War, in particular the My Lai massacre of 16 March 1968.[8] As for Vietnam the concept of the self-traumatized perpetrator could help appease a divisive political debate and ultimately exonerate the perpetrators–victims.[9]

This drive into horror is one narrated with great aplomb and depth by Joseph Conrad in *Heart of Darkness*. As Ronald Paulson has shown there is a void at the heart of that most puzzling of novellas. Never is it clearly said what Kurtz does in Congo and his final words, 'the horror, the horror', could refer indifferently to the crimes he has committed himself or to the fear he has been living with over the years.[10] This character is thus a figure of fear and a fearful man. Voulet and Chanoine, but perhaps more Voulet than Chanoine, also seem to have become fearsome and fearful at the same time. Under a veneer of self-control they distanced themselves from their subordinates and ruled with a brutality that seemed 'excessive' in the sense that it made even the rapport between officers difficult. Both were accused of cowardice by their comrades and in their surviving correspondence to each other they showed acute risk awareness in relation to illness and battle danger.

Even if one accepts the fraught explanatory pattern of a traumatized perpetrator, it is unclear what moral conclusions can be gained from it. It is unsettling to think that if everyone is a victim then no one is. For Vigné d'Octon and his associates, Voulet and Chanoine revealed the evil (in French *le mal* has the dual meaning of illness and evil) within the military colonial project and they may have become, temporarily at least, evil themselves. They considered that what they eventually lost was a sense of agency as civilized and decent men. They were no longer men in their own right but rather delirious characters whose criminal responsibility would be limited in French courts.[11]

The key difference between their insanity and that of a famous manic murderer like Troppmann whose ambition led him to become a cause célèbre of 1870 would be that it had come about as a result of their career ambitions in the service of a national policy.[12] The other survivors never claimed to have been traumatized by what they had been complicit with. The only bitter grievances came from Dr Henric, who felt neglected from the awards and promotion that eventually greeted the other survivors. That the military and the anti-militarist agreed leads to an uneasy conclusion, namely that some psychological common ground existed, identifying trauma as a self-descriptive category but that historians since have mistaken for an analytical one.

In a meaningful sense trauma explains neither Voulet's or Chanoine's behaviour nor the multitude of less sustained but occasionally equally acute acts of brutality that took place in Africa during the period.

To describe Voulet as insane portrayed a conveniently irresponsible individual or perhaps, in the most extreme pages of Vigné, system. But that lack of responsibility also portrayed the brutality as uniquely unaccountable even in a criminal court. In this story Voulet and Chanoine were heroes and they could as easily have become villains because of the circumstances; they had been literate and educated and yet they had been 'ensavaged' by Africa. Yet if one excludes this convenient description, one is faced with the realization that the events of 1898–1900 took place at a particular moment in Western history during which violence became part of a coherent tapestry of causalities in which individual agency and criminal responsibility could be so interwoven with circumstances as to disappear.

Yet, as this book aimed to show, Voulet and Chanoine practised warfare in a manner customary to them and many of their colleagues. Some colonizers did not use brutality to the same extent, though the possibility remained, even in the peaceful conquest of Savorgnan de Brazza. By 1898 the military leadership in Soudan was split between modernizers like de Trentinian, who aimed to establish a coherent and legalistic rule, and more violent colleagues who judged 'pacification' incomplete. In a sense Voulet represented a faction who saw little gain in the routine tedium of administrating the empire but the conquest as an ongoing confrontation between colonizers and barbarians. They interpreted their own action as violence and understood that violence as part of an economy of power. In the words of Hannah Arendt they made a crucial mistake in confusing violence and power: 'violence can always destroy power; out of the barrel of a gun grows the most effective command, resulting in the most instant and perfect obedience—what cannot grow out of it is power'.[13]

Nevertheless, despite the systematic and, in their eyes, rational use of violence, Voulet and Chanoine's subordinates, who also practised the same war techniques and adhered to the same aims, could explain away 'the excess' in the language of the psychiatrist. Some thirty years earlier in the 1870s such a language was unnecessary to explain the excess of violence that terminated the Communard insurrection. Of course the Communards were portrayed as criminally insane but the extreme repression during which prisoners were decimated or executed randomly was never psychologized.

The period during which the Voulet–Chanoine affair came to light has been described by the French historian Pierre Nora as the 'psychological turn' and this turn was undoubtedly a tool to make sense of violence. Yet explaining away extreme violence was also potentially a formidably liberating tool for the violence.

Trauma is also a concept deeply steeped in a discourse of revelation and memory. In this sense a scandal was the narration that evoked and solved symbolically, for the French at least, the traumatic situation. Beyond the actual damage inflicted, trauma is also elicited to describe an affection of memory. In the Freudian and Janet terminology of neurosis, a trauma is often at the heart of what cannot be told and which eventually develops into physical and mental symptoms. A case may be made as Chapter 4 argues for the Hauka cult to tie in with such a definition of trauma.

The Voulet–Chanoine scandal was set within another scandal—that of the Dreyfus affair—which had revealed the tensions and hidden hatred in French society. The African brutality story played a small role and merely added to a negative image of the French military. In the atmosphere of civil war that engulfed France, the story of Voulet and Chanoine had to compete for headline space with the anarchists' events and the threat of military coup raised by the ultra-nationalists.

In 1900, one could draw a multitude of conclusions from the Voulet–Chanoine affair. Some of them were of limited relevance and related to the practice of war in Africa; others were of a moral kind. The conclusions of the enquiry into the Voulet–Chanoine failure were based primarily on the reasons why the mission had gone astray. It postulated that there was another, better, way of waging war in Africa. It deplored the logistical errors of the mission and the staffing of the mission. While the superior officers blamed Voulet and Chanoine for their behaviour, they primarily lay blame at the door of their Parisian political backers.

In France, bafflement over the affair revealed that most assumed that the mission's aims and most of its means were within the range of acceptable practices. In any war, similar 'errors' will be decoded as misapplied norms and misunderstood rules of engagement. The pacifists on the other hand had an easy task denouncing the essential evil residing at the heart of any form of violence, be it in self-defence or for aggrandizement purposes.

What the Voulet–Chanoine moment captured was a threshold, a moment when a certain kind of war became unacceptable for those sponsoring it and for the tax-paying public funding it, what the anthropologist Fassin and the historian Bourdelais have named a construct of the intolerable.[14] This threshold corresponded to a first age of globalization when the media acquired unprecedented freedom and when news and capital travelled freely across the world.

A number of questions arise. What were the boundaries of war and were these boundaries shifting so swiftly that the men engaged in fighting could only operate outside of them? What makes violence finally unacceptable? And what role do these moments of excess play in our representation of warfare? True, historians are not philosophers and one may contest the legitimacy of the storyteller; yet the primary conclusions of the affair have been explored by competent authorities then and more recently. In the long run, what matters is that a number of Voulets and Chanoines roam an increasingly divided and fractious world and that the heart of darkness of 1900 remains that of 2010. The crossing of thresholds is something we all experience in our lifetime; a moment comes when what was acceptable is no longer acceptable. More troubling are those thresholds that one crosses walking backwards—when the politically available and acceptable overturns ethical stances once regarded as carved in stone. In our time the use of sporting euphemisms such as *waterboarding* has made anodyne and ultimately almost an acceptable tool of counter-terrorism what is effectively water torture. Through language a process and policies have brought back techniques of violence which previously had been regarded as unacceptable. The fact that they were unacceptable did not make them impossible but they belonged to the realm of criminal activities. That they had been in continuous use is possible—that they are now regarded as banal is shocking.

The violence of Voulet and Chanoine took place at a threshold moment for many reasons. One may be that for the first time since the French Revolution and 1848 at the time of the abolition of slavery in French colonies, human rights had once more become central to the political debates.[15] True, these rights were those of Frenchmen rather than of Voulet's female captives and the victim was a Jewish French officer rather than the massacred people of Birnin Konni. Yet these debates which echoed so feebly in the colonies nevertheless meant that when Voulet and Chanoine's mission became newsworthy questions were raised and a scandal erupted. Without Dreyfus it is likely that the scandal would have been even more completely buried; it is unlikely that Klobb would have been sent on their track. In an era when the terms humanitarian and humanitarianism resounded with fresh meanings some means had become unacceptable, whatever the ends.

Ironically perhaps, but certainly logically, humanitarianism was a word that recurred frequently under the pen of Voulet. Even as the villages were burning and his troops ransacked the land for slaves and food, he would note that his war was a humanitarian one. What did he mean by this and why use this language? One explanation for this strange insistence on ideal standards was that by 1899 they had become pervasive. The words originated from the cult of humanity and the idealistic philosophy of Auguste Comte but they had been contested throughout the nineteenth century. Balzac in his novel *Les employés* used it as a synonym for the imbecile cult of humanity, gradually arising from its relative obscurity; the idea of humanitarianism slowly achieved an almost universal positive meaning.[16] Ironically the term had been mainly used in war situations ever since the Red Cross was founded followed by full-scale development in 1870–1. The concept then was very specifically framed as an effort to minimize the sufferings of civilian and military victims of war. Gradually, though, the focus began to change and more concern was devoted to the rights of civilians. In this sense the international agreements were simply new codes of law for old practices since even before the creation of the Geneva conventions, rules of engagement such as the *droit des gens*, the rights of civilized people, that informally set what was acceptable behaviour apart from barbarous acts of war. In the 1890s the term began to acquire new and broader meanings.

What historians and sociologists have called 'the invention of the social' was taking place throughout Europe and this 'invention' was taking on political forms which used the language of compassion.[17] Essentially the idea of the invention of the social was that philanthropic developments and mass mobilization had an effect on the manner in which people understood the social bind and the role of the state and charities. From purely religious obligations charitable deeds shifted to become acts of social redistribution, rights rather than obligations. Simultaneously other concepts such as unemployment emerged, while large trade unions and socialist parties started to present alternative models of social organization centred on social rights. In this sense developing humanitarian policies became more inclusive of peacetime needs of the poor, as well as necessary terms in the political language.[18] In France the notions were entangled in civil war. The Commune of Paris in 1871 was led in the name of 'the social' which, while largely undefined, summarized the revolutionary aspiration of impoverished radical republicans. The brutal military repression of 1871 left deep scars when some 15,000 Parisians were executed on orders from the conservatives. Many others were deported to New Caledonia only to be repatriated on humanitarian grounds ten years later.

In that time things had moved on and the French Republic increasingly relied on its radical past to ensure its existence. The humanitarian language had become a part of the rhetoric of social compassion. A prime minister of 1895, Léon Bourgeois, made solidarity the motto of the Radical party which ruled most of France's coalition governments.[19] To the left, French socialists were on the threshold of obtaining a political position in government, with their first minister appointed in June 1899, while the same military officers who had so enthusiastically executed suspected socialists by firing squad in 1871 remained in control of the army. The enemies of yesterday collaborated in power sharing in a tense relationship that recalled the possibility of civil war. Yet, some things had changed and even though the army occasionally committed atrocities when it was used as a police force, the language of humanitarianism was gaining ground.

What did it mean in practice? There perhaps is the most important question and it remains valid to this day. What can humanitarianism, with its social and brotherly love aspirations, really mean on the ground? What does such a vague term cover? France by 1899, despite its political left and new CGT trade union, remained a deeply unequal society dragging behind its neighbours in terms of social security, pension funds, and medical cover. The social tensions between the anticlerical left and the Catholic right were often played up by politicians to mask the fact that the French state remained reluctant to intervene in social matters. More often than not humanitarianism served as a fig leaf to cover the politicians' reluctance to engage the state clearly in new social territories.

For the military the rules had not changed much since the second empire. The army codes and military law of 1857 were more protective of effects and items of clothing than people.[20] Rather than invite individual agency, the code enforced the duty to obey orders blindly and to aim for the abolition of the will. As a result the French army was not an enthusiastic endorser of international laws and in 1870 the French had largely ignored the terms of the Geneva Convention they had signed four years earlier. These rules of war as set up in Geneva were building on the tradition of *droit des gens*,[21] and on gentlemanly conventions of the past.[22] Enshrined in a declaration of principle which is still with us today it set the boundaries of what was acceptable violence in very narrow terms. The soldiers alone were meant to fight and civilians were supposed to be kept aside, like spectators. It has of course not escaped anyone's notice that ever since 1864 civilians have become ever more enmeshed in war and that much violence has been directed at them in order to break the resistance of opposing armies. Yet as an ideal the Geneva Convention set a law under which terms one could, in theory at the time, end up in court. In 1898–9 such a court was merely a dream for some Genevan lawyers. Since 1864, however, the international agreements had piled up and in 1899 the first international peace conference concluded in The Hague with new conventions on war which specifically banned pillage, confiscation, and random killings. Under its terms most acts of war led by Voulet and Chanoine were illegal. The new agreement followed previous ones in claiming that it served 'the interest of humanity and the ever increasing requirements of civilization'.[23] But, as in previous agreements, the principles applied to civilized nations only.[24] Besides, the limited precedents of the American Civil War had only sent a few men to court for their crimes.

No one on the winning side faced a legal challenge. If Voulet knew anything of the law of war this knowledge was limited to the forewarning he sent to Klobb, announcing to him that his intention was not to submit to him and that any further advance would lead to a confrontation. The laws of war did not apply to Africans. Even though there was already a range of forbidden weapons identified since the St Petersburg convention of 1868, their use was not an issue when it came to African conquest. The treatment of prisoners was also irrelevant. Since Voulet's enemies were the local people his war was on them and no law of war would hinder his progress. Yet, somehow, his war became unacceptable. Some of his methods such as the burning of villages, the use of fire in battle, the killing of all armed opponents and the rounding up of captives, and even the distribution of these slaves were not new. The French in the conquest of Algeria had used smoke to kill enemies hidden in a cave, burnt villages in reprisals, and captured and deported large groups of people. The same was true in Soudan.

Why did the colonial environment escape this prism? Crucially all international legislation and rules of engagement depended on a strict Eurocentric view of the world which recognized war purely as the conflict between organized, uniformed armies of nation-states. The armies of the chieftains of Africa were not regarded as armies strictly speaking and the African states were never recognized as real states. The terms used—tribes, bands, primitive kingdoms—ensured that in the hierarchy of civilization these were never regarded as genuinely civilized. Against the uncivilized no need to be civilized seemed to be the argument.

Even against well-recognized ancient civilizations such as the Ottoman Empire or China the representations of cruelty and barbarity freed Western powers from abiding to their own rules. True, saying so publicly could still shock, and Kaiser Wilhelm's speech to his troops departing for China to repress the Boxer Rebellion and alleviate the siege of the embassies in Beijing was to backfire. Advising his men to behave like Huns he created the negative stereotype that remained attached to German troopers during the First World War. Even without such an incendiary speech the practices of war against the Chinese and the strident denunciation of the Ottoman Bashi Bouzouks in Bulgaria demonstrated that Europeans adopted singularly relative applications of universal principles.

This contradiction or tension in views of civilization was particularly strong in France, which, more than any other European nation, has defined civilization as the core of their values, imagining their own ideals to be universal ones. When America declared the rights of man for its own people, the French convention of 1789 claimed universal rights applicable everywhere. In colonial practice the principles of the republican ideals were routinely contradicted, the contradiction being disguised by evolutionist perspectives, the slow assimilation of native people, and conflicting interpretation of the 'colonial mission'. These tensions have remained and when the ex-colonized led by President Bourguiba of Tunisia created the Francophonie political and cultural network, they attempted to distinguish the universal from the contingent, the worthwhile inheritance from the useless one. Burkina Faso, Mali, and Niger all have French as their national language and as the economical means of ensuring a lingua Franca for extremely diverse linguistic groups (for whom pluri-linguism is also the rule). Colonialism was never entirely cynical but its most cynical applications remained shocking to the French metropolitan audience. Yet a measure of proportionality seemed to apply. Voulet shocked his colleagues by the intemperance of his language towards them and by his brutality which did not seem to be proportionate or variable. Even if French officers tended to be absolutely convinced of their own racial superiority, they shared some concern for their own troops and a paternalistic sense of their duties. Voulet's lack of compassion towards his porters, the local villagers, or even his own soldiers shocked even in the new colony. The rumour of his excesses was amplified by the bad impression colleagues had of him.

When Voulet and Chanoine found themselves unable to justify the means by the end, when their ruthlessness failed to deliver, and when the mission became increasingly bogged down and crawling, Voulet lost the ability to justify his methods by any standard of efficiency. If his violence could have been justified as an efficient tool of war, its excesses were utterly shocking when considered as methods of government. The expediency which had ruled the conquest moment of the empire was no longer tolerable when empires began to affirm themselves in comparison with others. The scandal of the Free State of Congo, the private property of King Leopold of Belgium, was not a scandal of conquest but of systematic excess and overexploitation. If war escaped much scrutiny, governing a conquered land did not.[25] In Soudan conquest and government became almost synonymous. The colony coalesced so quickly that within a year of first sighting by a French soldier, a camp, an administration, and a tax were established. The path that Voulet took probably represented nothing more than a military advance in his view but his superiors expected it to become a road linking the new provinces to the old ones. Voulet was aware that his warring would make coming back by the same road a difficult enterprise; he had not mastered the consequences of his action.

Nevertheless he was not the loose 'cannon' he was later portrayed to be. One of the many bitter ironies of the Voulet–Chanoine affair was that it was the failure of the politics of accountability. Throughout the campaign Voulet remained accountable in the most literal manner. He kept regular books which balanced and clearly delivered results for each franc spent. The financial constraints under which he laboured were the product of a strong democratic state holding its warriors to account but only in a fashion. His books recorded bullets and expenses, incomes and outcomes. Ultimately, had Voulet made it to Chad and had he survived the war against Rabah there is no doubt that he would yet again have delivered the goods he had been commissioned to retrieve for the empire. His war was cheap relative to the land it acquired for the empire. His detractors complained that each conquest called for further 'pacification' and that his methods in the Mosse planted the seeds of rebellion and resistance. Furthermore the rapid expansion of the Soudan stretched a declining budget beyond its limits. In the eyes of French parliamentarians, each new conquest further undermined the viability of the empire from a taxation point of view. In the budget committee of 1899 which considered past expenditure as well as the spending programme for that year, Gaston Doumergue, later minister of colonies, argued:

> We must dispel this error that seems to have inspired our colonial administration for far too long, that military expenditures are special and consequently that they should be charged to the metropolitan budget. They are, it is said, expenses of sovereignty! Nothing could be further from the truth. To see them like this is to alter the nature of our occupation and our relation to the colonial people.[26]

Consequently the colonial military budget was slashed and the armed forces were recalled or dismissed. Yet, the military would argue, Voulet had 'delivered' the Mosse to the empire at little cost even if ruling that new region was to become a heavy burden for a fragile colonial budget.

France at the end of the nineteenth century was a society immersed in its accounts books. Some very public ones were found to be failing and the great Panama scandal made politicians and journalists especially interested in the traditional collusion between businessmen and statesmen. The 1891 scandal revealed a web of bribery and corruption reaching the highest spheres of the French state which had enabled the draining of vast sums towards the Panama Canal project which had gone bankrupt in 1889. This bankruptcy involved hundreds of thousands of small subscribers. The subsequent scandal smeared French politicians with accusations of corruption by Jewish businessmen Cornelius Herz and Jacques Reinach. More than the reality of the corruption, the rumours undermined many on the centre left like Georges Clemenceau who later became heralds of political transparency during the Dreyfus affair. Accountability was at the heart of 1890s French politics. Yet this culture of accountability had always been a Damocles' sword for the military. They knew that the real cost of war always exceeded their budget and that only if they went above and beyond what they were required to deliver, in terms of glory, land, and subjugated people, would they be forgiven. Like any political system dominated by accountants (and readers may relate to current circumstances if they wish) the accounting creates its own perverse effects—the most damaging of which is probably that people cannot be accounted for as precisely as bullets and that, on the balance sheet, bullets become more visible—one might say more important—than the targets they hit.

Wars in democracies have this double exigency of being financially accountable and morally respectable. Yet they often can be neither. Utopians like the Italian nationalist leader Giuseppe Mazzini deduced from this paradox that national democracies would naturally tend to be pacifist and that war would recede among the cruelties of the distant past. The conquest of Africa, that of the Philippines by the USA, and all the imperial wars waged since by the greatest democracies of the world have amply demonstrated how democracies can survive their own contradictions.

In order to do so, however, their rules of transparency are fulfilled in one fashion while their practices are occulted. War remains a dirty business and conquest is usually the most violent form. At a time of massive technological discrepancies the efficiency of the conquerors could take chilling dimensions and be more evocative of a slaughterhouse than of a traditional struggle.[27] Yet as Jennifer Karn Alexander has recently reminded, there are no intrinsic moral values associated with efficiency and efficiency through force has ranked equal to more liberal forms of effective rule.[28]

The military has known their masters well and how to play this win or lose all game whereby the results have enabled a cover-up of whatever violence was felt had to be exercised. The military's attempt to hide the reality of their actions has been part of this democratic paradox which put in play parallel sets of accounting systems which could not relate to each other in the assessment of war. Although democracies became the greatest imperial drivers ever witnessed by the end of the nineteenth century the wish to accumulate land and people cheaply had to be fulfilled without the disturbance of unsightly violence.

One may ask then why should violence be so disturbing? Philosophers and historians have argued that violence did indeed become less appealing to the ruling classes who favoured more diffused and more efficient forms of violence. Michel Foucault, Michael Ignatieff, and scores of others have noted that public executions receded from the public gaze when the death penalty came under threat, that prisons replaced the gallows when the need to punish more widely and more frequently became imperative.[29] Violence in police records everywhere has grown almost relentlessly in the long term since records began in the early nineteenth century, but these records also reflect a growing intolerance of violence, included new forms of violence and improved recording processes. Violence in war followed a similar pattern. The crimes and horrors of the past were extreme and the few soldiers' voices we have, such as Sergeant Bourgogne's diary from the Napoleonic war show this well.[30] Yet, somehow, these matters remained internal military business. The visibility of violence was limited by the absence of independent media on the one hand and by a different sensibility to brutality. One might draw comforting conclusions from this yet this is not my object. Extreme violence might have become abject, disgusting and revolting, fascinating all the same but surely one should ask what role do moments of abject violence play in democracies?

As mentioned earlier in this conclusion even the most violent outbursts such as that of My Lai reveal less than they obscure.[31] The Voulet–Chanoine story was so singular in its conclusion, the confrontation between French officers, that the final episode of 14 July 1899 effectively hid the original scandal of rampant violence in colonial warfare.

In none of the texts does one find any open contestation of what went on after Say. The whistle-blower, Péteau, had been responsible for similar reprisals which involved the slaughter of whole villages; if anything he had been involved at a time when these acts were still infrequent. In their defence the officers spoke of disgust and uneasiness; some claimed that events happened when they were not there, that the orders had been given by the translators rather than by the officers. Eventually they fell back on the universal defence used in other similar circumstances: we were only obeying orders. Pallier responded violently to Péteau in those terms:

> Officers were kept aside and were the victims of petty vexations and their silent disapproval of some acts justified [Voulet and Chanoine's] suspicion, the absolute lack of trust and respect was beyond bounds. Perhaps in exposing this situation I will be blamed for not leaving the mission—to this I will answer that Lieutenant Péteau who left was accused, in odiously false reports, of being a coward and rebellious, furthermore military discipline does not allow one to leave unpleasant chiefs who might even be repulsive. And finally I would ask if despite these sad circumstances our duty was not to consider only the aim and to participate, regardless, in the accomplishment of a task we felt to be of considerable importance for France.[32]

The officer who commanded in My Lai, Lieutenant Calley, could have used very similar language. This is what the psychologists Kelman and Hamilton have called crimes of obedience, primarily in reference to the notorious murders of My Lai during the Vietnam War. Then a squad had torched and systematically destroyed a suspected village, on the basis of ambiguously phrased superior orders. The officer in charge was tried and pardoned before making a political career from the incident. In Kelman and Hamilton's psychological model, the legitimacy of hierarchies and authority creates situations of non-choice. The fear of punishment for disobedience, punishable by death in the 1890s French context in time of war, 'is more likely to influence behaviour because it reinforces the already strong push towards obedience built into the structure of the authority situation'.[33]

Parallels could be made with atrocities committed by the armed forces of authoritarian regimes during the 1930s and 1940s or since; yet the parallel with My Lai is perhaps more pertinent in the sense that Voulet and Chanoine belonged to an army established along legal principles in a liberal society which put the balance of powers, and therefore mitigating the principle of authority, at the heart of its social and individual power relations.

Ever since the experiments of the 1950s psychologists have shown that individual behaviour tends to follow assumed patterns and norms with obedience to group rule above and beyond any ethical qualms. In this context Voulet and Chanoine had reinforced their authority very consistently after the departure from Dakar. They created a power pyramid (see Chapter 5). This structure was based on obedience. In case of conflict they possessed the right to issue a letter of dismissal which would be damaging enough to break a promising career. In the military records it is made abundantly clear that the whistle-blower was the first guilty party of whatever crimes he denounced. Bypassing hierarchical routes Péteau was explicitly indulging in subversive disobedience; doing so through the press having avoided any censorship or authorization was akin to full-scale betrayal.

Joalland, Pallier, Henric, and the NCOs decided to obey and they clearly believed this obedience to be the only honourable avenue open to them. Their claims that they either ignored or merely witnessed violent acts are explicitly demonstrated to be false by the African witnesses and the Laborie report; some had been with Voulet before and knew his methods well. Their obedience was framed in terms of loyalty and a shared common interest in the success of the mission which would reward all participants with career advancement and fame. This colonial work involved a large degree of venture association, as shown in Chapter 4. The returns on their sufferings could only be obtained on completion of the mission. Anything that stood in the way was merely distracting from the ultimate objective, the secret orders in the hands of the commander in chief. Voulet and Chanoine alone knew what the remit of the mission was and in which terms it was phrased. It allowed them to command with an unusual degree of authority over officers who were only marginally younger or less experienced than themselves. This culture of obedience was one of the most important outcomes of military training and drilling. The training of soldiers followed close drilling and the mission took time to form its troops according to Western battle order and group cohesion exercises such as marching and simultaneous manoeuvring. The results were said to be wondrous and the Senegalese tirailleurs acquired a mythical reputation for obedience: 'Service' is a magical word for the Senegalese; it represents duty for them.[34] This disciplining machinery was also a formidable silencing operation and the military believed that they could address most moral issues within the army itself. The scandal almost never happened on this scale.

Had Klobb not been killed it is likely that he would have managed to minimise the scandal as he intended. Voulet and Chanoine might have been punished but probably not all that severely. In the archives only a handful of cryptic documents on various unspeakable acts would have gone unnoticed and the great legend of the conquest of Chad would have been untarnished. If in the *Heart of Darkness* Kurtz had managed to remain 'admirable', his efficiency and energy would have been regarded by all as a model, though perhaps in the same undesirable way as unattainable role models can be. One can feel a similar note of admiration when a report drawn from Laborie's conclusion summarized: 'Voulet was a cannon ball shot across the Niger towards Chad who burns everything on its way. He was as brutal and probably as unconscious [as a bullet].' Voulet and Chanoine had been weapons who had not been controlled and managed by their superiors but they remained formidable conquerors. Even thirty years after Voulet's death his comrades still sought to retrieve what had been 'good' from the 'bad'.[35] Chanoine had no such luck. Compared with conquistadores like Cortes, Voulet showed that these moral judgements could not be so easily separated. The tension of the *Heart of Darkness* was between two white men facing each other and through this confrontation alone the truth could come out. Similarly in the Voulet–Chanoine affair, the Africans themselves were so disenfranchised in every conceivable manner that only through the killing of Klobb would the story come to light. Yet in its excess it became a monstrous curiosity rather than a revelatory moment.

True, Voulet and Chanoine were operating in excessive ways for almost every aspect of their mission but they were not new agents in Soudan: they had a past and it was known. They combined excesses, they did not invent them. The reports from

Dahomey make clear what might have happened to them had they accepted the arrival of Klobb:

Klobb answered to him that one should take into account the exaggerating and general *malicious* nature of the blacks [*canaillerie*] but that there were two facts absolutely beyond doubts: the massacre of women and children in Sausané Haoussa and the murder of a tirailleur by Captain Voulet. Not wishing to dwell on these facts, the number of two showed that these atrocities were not 'numerous' in Soudan.

Defending the Dahomey staff, the officer decided to minimize the events and deny that many had taken place.[36] The exceptionally well-documented cases were simply mentioned anecdotally. In a different political climate, that of the neighbouring colony of Dahomey, it is likely that nothing would have come out. Even though Kirtachi had been torched, 'the fire so easily blamed on the mission was only the result of the natives' carelessness.' It is also plausible that Voulet might have got away in Soudan had he managed better his contacts with the rear or begun his exactions further east. Depending on his contacts at the rear many were happy to bury the 'problem' quite literally:

We are not seeking to create any problem and the following fact will show this to you—leaving your camp the column left in a small ravine nearby a pile of corpses of porters which should have been buried.

The officer of Say was then happy to oblige and erase this embarrassing trace of the mission's presence.[37]

In this sense a crisis like the Voulet–Chanoine scandal remained just that: an instance of abuse, a moment of excess rather than an open window on common practices. It focused the debate but in doing so, it also grotesquely deformed the terms of the debate. Similarly the incidents of war that occasionally hit our radar today are taken out of context and seem to reveal little else than a shocking abnormality. Abu Graib prison comes to mind. The incidents and the trial that ensued were limited to those individuals whose naivety had led them to assume that they were covered by a system. The licence they had to commit crimes, others had as well; torture and violence were part of the training and admitted policy. But, and it is a crucial but, all this remained an implicit rule of engagement and never an explicit principle of warfare. Voulet and Chanoine likewise confused practices and policies and very probably failed to understand until the end why Klobb had been sent after them. Voulet seems to have assumed, together with Chanoine, that this was a Soudan military plot to relieve him of his prestigious mission in favour of a man of competing ambition. When he read Klobb's papers Voulet realized the criminal nature of the charges against him and allegedly said to Chanoine, 'you are even more heavily charged than any of us'.[38]

Until that moment he had shown no self-consciousness of his crimes—only an exacerbated awareness of his privileged position and of the enmities his fame and sudden rise had created. Looking back to Paris and to his back-stabbing colleagues he did not seem to see that his acts of conquest could be read as the antithesis of a civilizing mission. Some might regard this as evidence of psychosis. Yet it is not only mad men that commit crimes in times of war. Their diaries and private papers as well as their correspondence reveal their real obsession: delivering results with the means at their disposal while accounting for every item and sums put in their hands. They claimed to be the masters of their men and of their own destiny; yet, in their routine violence which they mistook for power and their deluded ambitions which they called glory, Voulet and Chanoine embodied the ordinary cruelty of the servants of the modern state. It is that cruelty, perhaps not generally or consistently applied but almost always hidden when it took place sufficiently far away, that exposed the vacuity of altruistic colonial ideals and ensured that 'facing such facts, the word civilization becomes the bloodiest of ironies.'[39]

ENDNOTES

The endnotes include references to the files relevant to the Voulet–Chanoine affair. The main files are to be found in the Archives Nationales Section d'Outre Mer (AOM) in France. I have cross-referenced these official documents with information contained in the Archives des Missionaires d'Afrique (AGMAfr), or White Fathers, which was the only religious society present in the region east of Senegal at the time; and to documents kept in the Archives Nationales du Sénégal (ANS) and in the Archives de l'Afrique Occidentale Française (AAOF) in Dakar. References to French military archives are referred to as SHAT (service historique de l'armée de terre).

Note

H. A. S. Johnston, *The Fulani Empire of Sokoto* (Oxford University Press, 1967), 1.

Chapter 1 Dying for French Soudan

1. French Soudan was a distinct territory from what is now called Sudan (which was then known as British Sudan). It covered the territories of Burkina Faso, Niger, and Mali. At the onset of the story none of these territories were yet fully controlled by the French armies and many wars were fought in the 1890s in order to control them. See for instance Lieutenant Gatelet, *Histoire de la conquête du Soudan Français: 1878–1899* (Berger Levrault, 1901). These territories changed identity several times over their short colonial history and the current borders were settled relatively late in the day. Daniel Miles McFarland, *Historical Dictionary of Upper Volta (Haute Volta)* (Scarecrow Press, 1978); Michael Crowder, *West Africa under Colonial Rule* (Hutchinson, 1968), 93–109.
2. Charles Paul Louis Chanoine, normally known as Julien Chanoine was born in 1870 in Paris. Paul Gustave Lucien Voulet was born in 1866.
3. Arsène Klobb, *Dernier carnet de route au Soudan Français* (Flammarion, 1905); rpt. in *idem* and Lt. Octave Meynier, *A' la recherche de Voulet, sur les traces sanglantes de la mission Afrique Centrale* (Cosmopole, 2001), 26.
4. Klobb, 8 July 1899, *Dernier Carnet de route*, 186.

5. AOM, Mission 110, Official telegram, GGA of AOF to General de Trentinian, 16 April 1899.
6. AOM, Mission 110, 'rapport Pallier', 15 August 1899. The figure often given for the Birnin Konni massacre is 10,000; Pallier estimated the killing at 1,000 out of a population of 7 or 8,000.
7. AOM, Mission 49, Klobb to Binger, 11 June 1899.
8. The presidency under the Third Republic had gradually lost its real importance and the president was fast becoming a figurehead while the main responsibility of government was taken over by the prime minister, confusingly also named president of the council of ministers. Gen. Jules Chanoine, *Documents pour servir à l'histoire de l'Afrique occidentale française de 1895 à 1899, correspondance du capitaine Chanoine pendant l'expédition du Mossi et du Gourounsi, correspondance de la mission Afrique centrale* (n.p., 1901), 15.
9. The story of the colonial lobby is well known and clearly identified. It combined business interests, politicians associated with colonial interests, officers, and diplomats. It grew to become one of the largest interest groups in the French parliament. Charles Robert Ageron, *France coloniale ou parti colonial?* (Armand Colin, 1970); Michael Persell, *The French Colonial Lobby: 1885–1938* (Stanford University Press, 1983); Hubert Bonin, Catherine Hodeir, and Jean-François Klein, *L'Esprit économique imperial: 1830–1970* (SFHOM, 2008); C. M. Andrew and A. S. Kanya-Forstner, 'The French "Colonial Party": Its Composition, Aims and Influence, 1885–1914', *Historical Journal* 14:1 (Mar. 1971), 99–128.
10. This story fits with the conquest of Chad: Pierre Gentil, *La Conquête du Tchad: 1894–1916*, 2 vols (SHAT, 1971).
11. Chanoine, *Documents pour servir à l'histoire*, 269–72. AOM, Mission 11, Instruction to Captain Voulet.
12. Chanoine, *Documents pour servir à l'histoire*, 177.
13. See Albert Lorofi, *La Vie Quotidienne des officiers de l'Infanterie de Marine pendant la conquête de la colonie du Soudan Français* (L'Harmattan, 2008).
14. Gen. Paul Joalland, *Le Drame de Dankori: Mission Voulet-Chanoine; mission Joalland-Meynier* (Argo, 1930), 10.
15. The earlier drafts of the instructions were much clearer in that particular direction. AOM, Afrique III, 37, 32, draft orders approved by Delcassé.
16. AOM, FM SG, Afrique III, 33, mission Marchand in Fachoda.
17. The mapping and conquest of Africa went together. See Thomas Bassett, 'Cartography and Empire Building in Nineteenth-Century West Africa', *Geographical Review* 84:3 (1994), 316–35.
18. The speech of Jules Ferry is regarded as the most blatant and open definition of colonialism, and is widely available. See for instance Alice L.

Conklin, 'Colonialism and Human Rights, a Contradiction in Terms? The Case of France and West Africa, 1895–1914', *American Historical Review* 103:2 (Apr. 1998), 419–42; *idem*, *A Mission to Civilize: The Republican Idea of Empire in France and West Africa, 1895–1930* (Stanford University Press, 1997); James Jerome Cooke, *New French Imperialism, 1880–1910: The Third Republic and Colonial Expansion* (David and Charles, 1973); Thomas Francis Power, *Jules Ferry and the Renaissance of French Imperialism* (Octagon Books, 1944). For the full text see http://www.assemblee-nationale.fr/histoire/Ferry1885.asp

19. On Rabah or Rabih see Richard Gray, *A History of Southern Sudan, 1839–1898* (Oxford University Press, 1961). Ironically Burnu ended up as a German colonial territory of Northern Kamerun.
20. See for instance the *Bristol Mercury and Daily Post*, 2 December 1898. Joseph Amergboh, *Rabah, conquérant des pays tchadiens* (Les nouvelles éditions africaines, 1976); a German witness, von Oppenheim, wrote a contemporary biography of Rabah, *Le Domaine tchadien de Rabah* (L'Harmattan, 2003).
21. David Robinson, *The Holy War of Umar Tal* (Oxford University Press, 1985); Émile Ducoudray and Ibrahima Baba Kaké, *El Hadj Umar, le prophète armé* (Les nouvelles éditions africaines, 1975).
22. Yves Person, *Samori: la Renaissance de l'empire Mandingue* (ABC, 1976); Michal Tymowski, *L'Armée et la formation des états en Afrique occidentale au XIXe siècle—essai de comparaison, l'état de Samori et le Kenedougou* (Wydawnicta Uniwersytetu Warszawkiego, 1987).
23. Henri Gouraud (1867–1946) was one of the rising stars of the French colonial adventures.
24. James J. Cooke, 'Anglo-French Diplomacy and the Contraband Arms Trade in Colonial Africa, 1894–1897', *African Studies Review* 17:1 (1974), 27–41.
25. Tymowski, *L'Armée et la formation*, 162–3.
26. Roberta Ann Dunbar, 'Slavery and the Evolution of Nineteenth Century Damagaran', in Suzanne Miers and Igor Kopytoff (eds), *Slavery in Africa* (University of Wisconsin Press, 1977), 155–78.
27. Finn Fuglestad, *A History of Niger, 1850–1960* (Cambridge University Press, 1983), 54–5; AOM, H mission 110, Cazemajou; AAOF 1 G222 Mission Cazemajou in Haut Soudan.
28. Elikia M'Bokolo, *Resistances et Messianismes, histoire generale de l'Afrique* (Agence de Coopération, 1990), 41–2. Rabah's empire spread from Darfur to Chad in 1887 and to Bornu south of Lake Chad in 1895. Its capital was Dikwa.
29. See Archives Nationales, fonds privés, 66 AP 2–4 Expédition Afrique Centrale ; Also SHAT, 1 K168.

30. Lt-Col. Parfait-Louis Monteil, *De Saint Louis à Tripoli par le lac Tchad voyage au travers du Soudan et du Sahara pendant les années 1890-1-2* (Félix Alcan, 1894).
31. AAOF 1G221, Voulet referred to the machine gun owned by Donald Stewart of the Nigerian forces whom met on the newly established border.
32. Chanoine, *Documents pour servir à l'histoire*, 162.
33. From the enquiry led by Laborie it became clear that Voulet had not been explicitly authorized to hire 450 irregular soldiers. AOM, Mission 11, 15 December 1900.
34. AOM, Afrique III, 37, Letter to Minister of Colonies, January 1899.
35. Chanoine, *Documents pour servir à l'histoire*, 206.
36. Joalland, *Drame de Dankori*, 35–7.
37. After a century of good crops and good rainfalls, the Niger region began its century-long period of drought and poor crops. Stephen Baier, *An Economic History of Central Niger* (Clarendon Press, 1980), 30–4. Major droughts were recorded in North Africa at the same period; Idrissa Kimba, *Guerres et Sociétés: les populations du 'Niger Occidental au XIXe siècle et leurs réactions face à la colonisation* (Études Nigériennes, 1981), 56.
38. Monteil, *De Saint Louis à Tripoli par le lac Tchad voyage*, 8; H. A. S. Johnson, *The Fulani Empire of Sokoto* (Oxford University Press, 1967).
39. AOM, Afrique III, Voulet to Minister, Report from Tibiri, 1 March 1899, 11.
40. Lt-Col. Parfait-Louis Monteil, *Les Conventions Franco-Anglaises des 14 juin 1898 et 21 mars 1899* (Plon Nourrit, 1899), 12.
41. AAOF, 'Rapport politique' from Say, Captain Granderye, 1 March 1899.
42. AOM, Mission 110, exchange of letters with Delaunay, 31 January 1899.
43. Chanoine, *Documents pour servir à l'histoire*, 206.
44. AOM, Afrique III, 38, 9, 'rapport' from chef de bataillon Crave. The exact figure of the number of victims was contested and then revised downwards.
45. AOM, Mission 110, Letter from Delaunay to Voulet, 1 February, 1899.
46. AOM, Afrique III 38, 1, 'rapport' from capitaine Granderye commandant le convoi de ravitaillement de la région Nord Est, 15 Febuary 1899.
47. AOM, Afrique III, 38, 75 bis, 'rapport' from Say, December 1899.
48. AOM, Mission 110, 'Rapport politique' from Say, March 1899.
49. AOM, Afrique III, 37b, 112, Captain Voulet, Tibiri, 1 March 1899.
50. The Dosso area was a contested border between the two colonies of Dahomey and Soudan. The captain in post in Dahomey, Captain Cornu, was in open conflict with the residents of Say. AAOF, 11 G 1, rapports politiques de Say, 16 August 1899.

51. This theme forms the basis of nationalist novels which will be discussed in Ch. 7; see Abdoul-Aziz Issa Daouda, *La Double Tentation du roman nigérien* (L'Harmattan, 2006).
52. Joalland, *Drame de Dankori*, 50.
53. Chanoine to Robert de Caix, 9 April 1899; Chanoine, *Documents pour servir à l'histoire*, 292–3.
54. AOM, Mission 110, Voulet papers, Chanoine to Voulet 26, April 1899.
55. Gen. Octave Meynier, *Mission Joalland Meynier,* Collection les grandes missions coloniales (Algiers, 1947).
56. Joalland, *Drame de Dankori*, 68.
57. AOM, Afrique III, 37 bis, Letter to minister of colonies, 25 May 1899.
58. Joalland, *Drame de Dankori*, 58.
59. On a measured assessment of the role of slavery in these predatory regimes see Andrew Hubbell, 'A View of the Slave Trade from the Margin: Souroudougou in the Late Nineteenth-Century Slave Trade of the Niger Bend', *Journal of African History* 42:1 (2001), 25–47, esp. 28–9.
60. Parfait-Louis Monteil, *Vade Mecum de l'officier d'infanterie de marine* (L. Baudoin et Cie, 1884), 166–9.
61. Joalland, *Drame de Dankori*, 77.
62. Evidence of rape is difficult to obtain; yet, it is mentioned explicitly in AOM, Mission 110, 'Rapport politique' from Say, March 1899.
63. Colonel Klobb–Lieutenant Meynier, *A' la recherche de Voulet*, 93.
64. Joalland, *Drame de Dankori*, 74.
65. The archives are not supporting Joalland entirely since there is no mention of beheading in Voulet's private papers. AOM, Mission 110, Voulet, private paper note to Mayori Hakkou, 3 July 1899.
66. AOM, Afrique III, 38, 'rapport' from Commandant Lamy, 25 December 1899.
67. These documents did not exist and much of this testimony is highly suspect.
68. AOM, Mission 110, Rapport Tourot, Mafoita, Nefouta 18 July 1899.
69. This version published by Joalland can be found in identical terms in the reports written in August 1899. AOM, Mission 110, 'Rapport' Joalland, Mafoita, 25 July 1899.
70. It is a little unclear who initiated this comparison between Voulet and Samory Touré. Samory was regarded (and still is) as a military genius, and the greatest man of war since Umar Tall; see Ch. 3.
71. Joalland, *Drame de Dankori*, 95.
72. AOM, Mission 110, 'Rapport' Tourot, Mafoita, Nefouta 18 July 1899
73. AOM, Mission 110, 'Rapport' Joalland on the circumstances of the death of Lieutenant-Colonel Klobb, 15 August 1899.
74. AAOF, 11 G 1, 'Rapport' Granderye.

75. Albert Londres, *Terre d'ébène* (Le Serpent à Plumes, [1929] 1998), 68.
76. AMA, Jean-Marie Hébert, *Ma drôle de guerre*, manuscript, N103. The veteran was interviewed in Deodogou in 1937.
77. Joalland, *Drame de Dankori*, 100.
78. AOM, Afrique III, 38, 15. Note ministère des affaires étrangères, 26 August 1899.
79. AOM, Afrique III, 38, 52 note on the measures taken since 14 July.
80. AOM, Afrique III, 38, 53, note dated 10 October 1899.
81. Robert Maestri, *Commandant Lamy, un officier francais aux colonies* (Maisonneuve et Larose, 2000), 230.
82. The next sultan of Zinder was deposed allegedly for plotting against the French. In fact it corresponded to a time when French administrators had decided to rule directly and do away with traditional chiefs. See AAOF, 11 G5, *Complot du Sultan de Zinder*, 1906.
83. AOM, Afrique III, 38, 66–68, reports from Pallier to Kayes received between 14 and 16 October. Arriving in a confused order the Pallier reports puzzled the officials who were thus told of Pallier's return before they were informed of the division of his forces.
84. Commandant Reibell, *Le Commandant Lamy d'après sa correspondance et ses souvenirs de campagne, 1858–1900* (Hachette, 1903), 548.
85. Chanoine, *Documents pour servir à l'histoire*, 287.
86. Auguste Terrier, 'La Mission Joalland-Meynier', *Journal des Voyages* (14 July 1901), 102–3.
87. Sven Lindqvist, *Exterminate all the Brutes* (Granta, 1992), 163–70.
88. Revealingly, this museum is now becoming a museum of immigration in 2007. See Robert Aldrich, *Vestiges of the Colonial Empire in France* (Palgrave, 2005), 35–48.
89. The classic text, *Drame de Dankori*, came out belatedly from the artillery officer Joalland, who took over the mission. Although written in 1901, Joalland did not release the book until 1930, at a time when the events received renewed attention in the context of growing opposition to the harsh rules of colonial administration.
90. Myron J. Echenberg, 'Jihad and State-Building in Late Nineteenth Century Upper Volta: The Rise and Fall of the Marka State of Al-Kari of Boussé', *Canadian Journal of African Studies* 3:3 (1969), 531–61.
91. Jeanne Kambou-Ferrand, *Peuples Voltaïques et conquête coloniale, 1885–1914* (L'Harmattan, 1993), 156–7.
92. Colonel Baratier, *Épopées Africaines* (Perrin, 1913); Lieutenant Gatelet, *Histoire de la conquête du Soudan Français, 1878–1899* (Berger Levrault, 1901).

Chapter 2 Civilization and Africa

1. Jean-Pierre Biondi, *Les Anti-colonialistes: 1881–1962* (Robert Laffont, 1993), 27; Thomas Francis Power, *Jules Ferry and the Renaissance of French Imperialism* (Octagon Books, 1944).
2. Georges Clemenceau's answer is a classic text which can be found studied in French schools: http://www.monde-diplomatique.fr/2001/11/A/15802.
3. Warwick Anderson, 'The Trespass Speaks: White Masculinity and Colonial Breakdown', *American Historical Review* 102:5 (1997), 1343–70.
4. C. Forth, '*La civilization* and its Discontents: Modernity, Manhood and the Body in the Early Third Republic', in C. Forth and B. Taithe (eds), *French Masculinities* (Palgrave, 2007), 85–102.
5. See for instance Jean-Martin Charcot, *Leçons du mardi à la salpêtrière: policliniques, 1887–1888*, notes de cours de MM. Blin (Charcot [fils] et Colin, Bureaux du progrès médical, 1887), 311–29.
6. Robert A. Nye, *The Origins of Crowd Psychology: Gustave Le Bon and the Crisis of Mass Democracy* (Sage Publications, 1975); William D. Irvine, *The Boulanger Affair Reconsidered* (Oxford University Press, 1989); James Harding, *The Astonishing Adventure of General Boulanger* (W. H. Allen, 1971); Michael Burns, *Rural Society and French Politics: Boulangism and the Dreyfus Affair 1886–1* (Princeton University Press, 1984); James R. Lehning, *To be a Citizen* (Cornell University Press, 2001).
7. Gustave Le Bon, *The Crowd: A Study of the Popular Mind* (Macmillan, [1895] 1896), 118.
8. For a full discussion of the war against Paris see Robert Tombs, *The War against Paris* (Cambridge University Press, 1981); *idem*, *The Commune of Paris* (Longman, 1999); and Bertrand Taithe, *Defeated Flesh* (Manchester University Press, 1999).
9. Joshua Cole, *The Power of Large Numbers* (Cornell University Press, 2000).
10. Africanitis was the headline of the *Pall Mall Gazette* of 2 September 1899 devoted to the Voulet–Chanoine affair.
11. A 'cercle' was an administrative and spatial unit used by the French military administration to rule colonial territories.
12. Raymonde Bonnetain, *Une Française au Soudan, sur la route de Tombouctou, du Sénégal au Niger* (Paris, 1894), 160.
13. Jean Rode was in fact a civilian administrator, Eugène Bouton, as revealed by Vigné d'Octon in the parliamentary debate of 30 November 1900 on the Voulet–Chanoine affair. His article had been published in the autumn of 1899: 'Un regard sur le Soudan', *La Revue Blanche* 20 (1899), 321–30.
14. Urbain Gohier, Preface to Paul Vigné d'Octon, *La Gloire du Sabre*, 4th edn (Flammarion, 1900), vii.

15. Urbain Gohier (1862–1951) was an exceptionally powerful and prolific polemicist whose extreme views were condemned when he published *L'Armée contre la Nation* (La revue Blanche, 1898). His radical anti-Semitism did not prevent him from supporting Dreyfus but he later developed increasingly authoritarian views which led him to support Vichy in the Second World War. Henry Mark Narducci, 'The French Officer Corps and the Social Role of the Army, 1890–1908', Wayne State University, 1981, 14–21.
16. F. Buret and M. A. Legrand, *Les Troupes coloniales: Maladies du soldat aux pays chauds* (J. B. Baillière et fils, 1897); Louis Huot and Paul Voivenel, *Le Cafard* (Grasset, 1918); M. A. Legrand, *L'Hygiène des troupes européennes* (Charles Lavauzelle, 1893).
17. Some doctors that have treated post-traumatic stress disorder now consider nostalgia to be a form of PTSD; see Louis Crocq, *Les Traumatismes psychiques de guerre* (Odile Jacob, 1999), 36 (this is a rather ahistorical extrapolation). Bill Bynum defined it as a discarded diagnosis, 'Nostalgia', *Lancet* 358:9299 (22 Dec. 2001), 2176; George Rosen, 'Nostalgia: A Forgotten Psychological Disorder', *Clio Medica* 10 (1975), 29–52; Von Klaus Brunnet, *Nostalgie in der Geschichte des Medizin* (Tritsch, 1984). The topic had also long been a favourite of doctoral theses, often endlessly plagiarized from one another. See Denis Guerbois, *Essai sur la nostalgie* (1803); E. A. Gaillard, *Considérations sur la nostalgie* (1804); P. M. Lourde Seilliès, *Considérations générales sur la nostalgie* (Montpellier, 1804); C. Castelnau, *Considérations sur la nostalgie* (Paris, 1806); Lachard, *Dissertation sur la Nostalgie* (Paris, 1808); A. F. A. Thenin, *Essai sur la nostalgie* (Paris, 1810); I. N. C. A. Florence, *Dissertation sur la nostalgie* (Montpellier, 1814), F. Boudet, *Dissertation médicale sur la nostalgie* (Montpellier, 1814); J. L. A. Pauquet, *Dissertation sur la nostalgie* (Paris, 1815); L. Ducrost de Longerie, *Dissertation sur la nostalgie* (Paris, 1815); M. Reynal, *Dissertation sur la nostalgie* (Paris, 1819); J. Huysp Buisson, *Considérations sur la nostalgie* (1818); Rémi Victor Allard, *Dissertation sur la nostalgie* (Didot Jeune, 1820); J. J. A. Martin, *Dissertation sur la nostalgie* (1820); J. P. Mezin Durantin, *Essai sur la nostalgie* (Montpellier, 1820); J. B. Bureau-Rabinière, *Dissertation sur la nostalgie* (Strasbourg, 1823); Joseph Vincent Huet Bienville, *Dissertation sur la nostalgie* (Paris, 1821); François Jacquier, *Dissertation sur la nostalgie* (Paris, 1821); Jules Yvonneau, *Considérations médico-philosophiques sur la nostalgie* (Paris, 1821); J. A. Edmond Puel, *De la Nostalgie* (Paris, 1822); Joseph Casimir Blain, *Essai sur la nostalgie* (Montpellier, 1825); J. B. H. Masson, *De la Nostalgie considérée comme cause de plusieurs maladies* (Paris, 1825); V. M. Besse, *De la Nostalgie* (Paris, 1828); J. J. L. A. Jalabert, *Essai sur la nostalgie* (Montpellier, 1827); Pierre Moreaud,

Considérations sur la nostalgie (Paris, 1829); J. H. M. Duret, *Essai sur la nostalgie* (Paris, 1830); Louis Jean Barnetche, *Essai sur la nostagie* (Montpellier, 1831); Jose Felicieno de Catilho Beneto, *Dissertation sur la nostalgie* (Paris, 1831); G. L. V. Pillement, *Essai sur la nostalgie* (Paris, 1831); Pierre Urbain Briet, *Essai sur la nostalgie* (Paris, 1832); Téophile François Collin, *Considérations sur la nostalgie* (Paris, 1832); Charles Fraisse, *De la Nostalgie* (Didot, 1833); Auguste Lachaume, *Essai sur la nostalgie* (Montpellier 1833); Bertrand Clamel, *Dissertation sur la nostalgie* (Paris, 1836); Eugène Poisson, *Dissertation sur la nostalgie* (Paris, 1836); François Joseph Lacordaire, *Essai sur la nostalgie* (Montpellier, 1837); L. V. Analoni, *De la nostalgie ou de la maladie du pays* (Paris, 1837); Jacques Antoine Ciccarelli, *Coup d'oeil sur les passions en général suivi de quelques proposition sur la nostalgie* (Montpellier, 1837); J. P. L. Paulinier, *Sur la Nostalgie* (Montpellier, 1837); Pierre Camille Bouviet, *De la Nostalgie ou mal du pays* (Montpellier, 1837); Hippolyte Mitre, *Essai sur la nostalgie* (Montpellier, 1840); Alexandre Mutel, *De la Nostalgie* (Montpellier, 1849); Louis Tailhade, *Quelques considérations sur la nostalgie* (Montpellier: Ricard, 1850); J. R. Parron, *Essai sur la nostalgie* (Montpellier, 1851); Claudius Caine, *Essai sur la nostalgie* (Paris, 1852); Oscar Devic, *La Nostalgie ou mal du pays* (Montpellier, 1855); Emmanuel Eugène Blache, *Dissertation sur la nostalgie* (Strasbourg, 1860); Auguste Benoist de la Grandière, *De la Nostalgie ou mal du pays* (Paris, 1873); Charles François Geit, *Quelques considérations sur la nature de la nostalgie, ses causes et son traitement* (Montpellier, 1874). See also Lisa O'Sullivan, *Dying for Home*, Doctoral Dissertation, University of London, 2006; Michael S. Roth, 'Dying of the Past: Medical Studies of Nostalgia in Nineteenth Century France', *History and Memory* 3 (1991), 5–29; and Eugène Fritsch, *La Nostalgie du soldat* (Jouaust, 1876), 4–6.

18. G. Reynaud, *Hygiène coloniale, II. Hygiène des colons* (J. B. Baillière, 1903), 12.
19. Fritsch, *La Nostalgie du soldat*, 6–12.
20. See La Grandière, *De la Nostalgie*, 3.
21. Gustave Martin, 'L'Influence du climat tropical sur le psychique de l'européen', in *Les Grandes Endémies tropicales, études de pathogénie et de prophylaxie* (Vigot, 1932), 101–15.
22. Danuta Mendelson, *The Interface of Medicine and Law: The History of the Liability for Negligently Caused Psychiatric Injury (Nervous Shock)* (Ashgate, 1998).
23. O. Saint Vel, *Hygiène des européens dans les climats tropicaux* (Edmond Delahaye, 1872), 39.
24. Martin, 'L'Influence du climat tropical', 114.

25. E. Garnier, *Hygiène de l'européen à la Guyane française*, Thèse, Montpellier, 1880, 33.
26. On overwork and neurasthenia see: George M. Beard, *A Practical Treatise on Nervous Exhaustion (Neurasthenia)*, 4th edn (E. B. Treat, 1894); C. H. F. Routh, *On Overwork and Premature Mental Decay*, 4th edn (Baillière, Tindall and Cox, 1886), 19; Anderson, 'The Trespass Speaks'; Anna Crozier, 'Sensationalising Africa: British Medical Impressions of Sub-Saharan Africa, 1890–1939', *Journal of Imperial and Commonwealth History* 35:3 (2007) 393–415; Marijke Hijswijt-Hofstra and Roy Porter (eds), *Cultures of Neurasthenia from Beard to the First World War* (Rodopi, 2001).
27. Animals found it equally difficult to thrive in the sun; see L. Petit, 'Contribution à l'étude de l'agriculture de la zoobactérie, de l'hygiène et de la pathologie vétérinaire au Soudan Français (Haut Sénégal et Haut Niger)', unpublished manuscript, book III, p. 95. AOM, Soudan, II, 2.
28. 'De la médecine tropicale à la santé au pluriel', in Anne-Marie Moulin (ed.), *Médecines et santé—Medical Practices and Health* (ORSTOM, 1996), 7–27, esp. 11; David Arnold (ed.), *Warm Climates and the Emergence of Tropical Medicine* (Rodopi, 1996).
29. Maryinez Lyons, *The Colonial Disease: A History of Sleeping Sickness in Northern Zaire, 1900–1940* (Cambridge University Press, 1992).
30. Although these might present an additional risk of lead poisoning. L. J. B. Bérenger Féraud, *Traité clinique des maladies des européens au Sénégal*, vol. 2 (Delahaye, 1878), 471.
31. AOM, Mission 11, invoices maison Conza.
32. AAOF, 1G234 Mission Afrique Centrale.
33. AOM, Mission 11, invoices maison Conza. Alcoholism was routinely denounced in France and 1900 seems to have been a peak in alcohol consumption. Patricia E. Prestwich, *Drink and the Politics of Social Reform: Antialcoholism in France since 1870* (Society for the Promotion of Science and Scholarship, 1988); Didier Nourrisson, *Le Buveur du XIXe siècle* (Albin Michel, 1990).
34. Some regions seem to have been more dangerous, however; Ch. E. Charlopin, *Considération sur la dysenterie des pays chauds* (1868); E. Pichez, *De la Dysenterie endémique en Cochinchine* (1870).
35. *L'Algérie, guide de l'émigrant par un colon* (Agence territorial Algérienne, 1881), 45.
36. Lion Murard and Patrice Zilberman, *L'Hygiène dans la république* (Fayard, 1997).
37. Alexandre Layet, *La Santé des européens entre les tropiques, leçons d'hygiène et de médecine sanitaire coloniale* (Felix Alcan, 1906).

38. Yvonne Turin, *Affrontements culturels dans l'Algérie coloniale, écoles, médecine, religion, 1830–1880* (François Maspéro, 1971). Medical advice was in any case resisted, p. 335. A classic text was that of Charles Scovell Grant whose *Petit Guide Pratique de l'Ouest Africain* (C. Doin, 1893) had recently been translated from English into French.
39. Parfait-Louis Monteil, *Vade Mecum de l'officier d'infanterie de marine* (L. Baudoin et Cie, 1884), 176–7.
40. Edouard Guillaumet, *Tableaux Soudanais* (Flammarion, 1899), 154–5. It is still unclear what the disease was. It might have been a result of quinine poisoning or a final stage of malaria.
41. Albert Lorofi, *La Vie quotidienne des officiers de l'infanterie de marine pendant la conquête de la colonie du Soudan français: 1890–1900* (L'Harmattan, 2008), 36–42; Philip D. Curtin, *Death by Migration: Europe's Encounter with the Tropical World in the Nineteenth Century* (Cambridge University Press, 1989).
42. O. Saint-Vel, *Hygiène des européens dans les climats tropicaux, des créoles et des races colorées dans les pays tempérés* (Delahaye, 1872), 9–18.
43. A. Jousset, *Traité de l'acclimatement et de l'acclimatation* (Octave Doin, 1884).
44. Saint Vel, *Hygiène des européens*, 99. Adell Patton, *Physicians, Colonial Racism and Diaspora in West Africa* (University Press of Florida, 1996).
45. There is a considerable literature devoted to this subject; see for instance David Arnold, *Imperial Medicine and Indigenous Societies* (Manchester University Press, 1988); also Andre Cunningham and Bridie Andrews (eds), *Western Medicine as Contested Knowledge* (Manchester University Press, 1997); S. J. Kuntiz, *Disease and Social Diversity: The European Impact on the Health of Non-Europeans* (Cambridge University Press, 1994); David Arnold, *Colonizing the Body* (University of California Press, 1993); Jean-Claude Bado, *Médecine coloniale et grandes endémies en Afrique* (Karthala, 1996).
46. See A. Benoist de la Grandière, *Souvenirs de Campagne: Les Ports d'Extrême Orient* (Société Française d'histoire d'Outre Mer, L'Harmattan, [1869] 1994), 188. La Grandière only managed to serve for two years abroad before being pensioned off.
47. For a good biographical notice see Louis Dulieu, *La Médecine à Montpellier*, Tom IV, vol 2 (Les Presses Universelles, 1990), 780–3.
48. Jean-Baptiste Fonssagrives, *Traité d'hygiène Navale ou de l'influence es conditions physiques et morales dans lesquelles l'homme de mer est appelé à vivre* (J. B. Baillière, 1856).
49. See G. Treille, *Note sur l'hygiène au Sénégal*, (Masson, 1892) *& Principes d'Hygiène coloniale* (Carré, 1899); Dr A. Quennec, *Guide médical*

à l'usage des explorateurs (L. Murer, 1897); Juste Navarre, *Manuel d'Hygiène colonial* (Doin, 1895); A. Nicolas, *Manuel d'hygiène coloniale* (Chaillez, 1894).

50. William B. Cohen, *The French Encounter with Africans, White Responses to Blacks, 1530–1880* (Indiana University Press, 1980), 125. Owen White, *Children of the French Empire: Miscegenation and Colonial Society in French West Africa, 1895–1960* (Oxford University Press, 1999).
51. Paul Vigné d'Octon, *Chair noire, préface de Léon Cladel* (Alphonse Lemerre, 1889), 211.
52. Paul Vigné d'Octon, *La Vie et l'amour: les doctrines freudiennes et la psychanalyse* (Edition de l'Idée Libre, 1934).
53. Paul Vigné d'Octon's *La Vérité sur les origines de l'homme* (Edition de l'Idée Libre, 1931) was one of the more popular science books Vigné wrote in the 1930s. These books were aimed at a left-wing readership sympathetic to his ideas but seeking some conveniently digested state of the art.
54. See the privately printed biography of Vigné d'Octon written by his second wife and widow, Hélia Vigné d'Octon, *La Vie et l'oeuvre de Paul Vigné d'Octon* (imp de Causse, sd. *c*.1950), 53.
55. On Charcot see Mark Micale, *Approaching Hysteria, Disease and Its Interpretation* (Princeton University Press, 1995).
56. Medical practitioners were then uncommonly associated with political life and the first thirty years of the new Republic were the apex of medical presence in French parliament. See Jack D. Ellis, *The Physician-Legislators of France* (Cambridge University Press, 1990).
57. Vigné d'Octon, *La Vie et l'oeuvre*, 35.
58. Vigné d'Octon, *La Gloire du Sabre*, 177.
59. The debate existed in most colonial empires. Often opposing metropolitan and colonial medical staff, it reflected directly the tensions between sceptical and enthusiastic views of the empire. See David N. Livingstone, 'Tropical Climate and Moral Hygiene: The Anatomy of a Victorian Debate', *British Journal for the History of Science* 32:1 (1999), 93–110.
60. The debate on 'popular' imperialism has long been discussed by historians, in particular because it is a debate on the support for often unpalatable practices. The current French consensus is that the French public was often largely indifferent or ignorant of colonial events and that anticolonial feelings dominated. Revisionist accounts are now challenging this perspective which might have been partially inspired by a desire to excuse the French public. Henri Brunschwig, *Mythes et réalités de l'impérialisme francais, 1871–1914* (Armand Colin, 1960); Raoul Girardet, *L'Idée coloniale en France de 1871 a 1962* (La Table Ronde, 1972); Jean-Pierre Biondi, *Les Anticolonialistes: 1881–1962* (Robert Laffont, 1993); Pascal Blanchard

and Armelle Chatelier, *Images et colonies* (Syros, 1993). Also see the classic study of British imperial propaganda: John M. Mackenzie, *Propaganda and Empire* (Manchester University Press, 1986).

61. Georges Clemenceau, *Le Grand Pan* (Imprimerie Nationale, 1995).
62. Robert Charles Ageron, *L'Anticolonialisme en France de 1871 à 1914* (Presses Universitaires de France, 1973).
63. Nicolas Bancel, Pascal Blanchard, and Françoise Vergès, *La République coloniale* (Pluriel, 2003), 74–6.
64. Blanchard and Chatelier, *Images et colonies*.
65. Préface de Mr Le Vicomte Melchior de Vogue of the French Academy, in Lt Col. Parfait-Louis Monteil, *De Saint Louis á Tripoli par le lac Tchad voyage au travers du Soudan et du Sahara pendant les années 1890-1-2* (Felix Alcan, 1894), p. v.
66. See for instance the highly popular Colonel Baratier, *Épopées africaines* (Perrin, 1913).
67. See among others Tony Chafer and Amanda Sackur (eds), *Promoting the Colonial Idea: Propaganda and Visions of Empire in France* (Palgrave, 2002); David Slavin, *Colonial Cinema and Imperial France* (Johns Hopkins University Press, 2001).
68. Julia Clancy-Smith, *Rebel and Saint: Muslim Notables, Populist Protest, Colonial Encounters* (University of California Press, 1994).
69. See AOM Alg GGA 3X1 Rinn papers. The anxiety was particularly strong after the mass uprising of 1871 led by El-Mokrani. Colonel Robin, *L'Insurrection de la Grande Kabylie en 1871* (Henry Charles Lavauzelle, 1900); Martin Lings, *A Sufi Saint of the Twentieth Century: Shwikh Ahmad Al'Alaw¯I* (Cambridge Univeristy Press, 1993).
70. Raphael Danziger, *Abd Al-Qadir and the Algerian Resistance to the French* (Holmes and Meier, 1977).
71. Monteil, *Vade Mecum*, 247–8.
72. AOM, FM, Soudan I, 11bis, de Trentinian to the commandant de poste of Niger-Volta, 24 Dec. 1898.
73. Vigné, *La Vie et l'amour*, 44.
74. That Madagascar was a dangerous destination was well known since at least the 1880s; yet the military ignored all advice in the conquest. Henry Girard, *Essai de topographie médicale de Sainte-Marie de Madagascar*, Thèse, Montpellier, Cabirou Frères, 1887.
75. Buret and Legrand, *Les Troupes coloniales*, 12.
76. Bérenger Féraud, *Traité clinique des maladies*, 338.
77. A. R. H. Brochet, *Souvenirs médicaux d'une campagne au Gabon* (Montpellier, 1887), 48.
78. AOM, Mission 110, Voulet papers, Chanoine to Voulet 7 July 1899.
79. AOM, Mission 110, 150, Henric to Pallier, 19 July 1899.

Chapter 3 Privateering for France

1. Paul Leroy-Beaulieu, *Le Sahara, Le Soudan et les Chemins de Fer Transsahariens* (Guillaumin, 1904), p. ix.
2. Ibid. 356–7.
3. AOM, FM, Mission 49, Wages of Capitaine Pallier. Dr Henric was on the same salary.
4. AAOF, 15 G 97, Affaires diverses. The wages of the governor of Soudan, for comparison, were 26,586 francs with a discretionary allowance of 12,000.
5. Odylle Roynette, *Bon pour le service: l'expérience de la caserne en France a la fin du XiXe siècle* (Belin, 2000), 9.
6. André Bach, *L'Armée de Dreyfus: Une histoire politique de l'armée française de Charles X à l'Affaire* (Tallandier, 2004), 114–21, 129–32.
7. David Prochaska, *Making Algeria French: Colonialism in Bône, 1870–1920* (Cambridge University Press, 1990); Kenneth J. Perkins, *Qaids, Captains and Colons: French Military Administration in the Colonial Maghrib, 1844–1934* (Africana Publishing, 1981); Mahfoud Bennoune, *The Making of Contemporary Algeria, 1830–1987: Colonial Upheavals and Post Independence Development* (Cambridge University Press, 1988); Charles André Julien, *Histoire de l'Algérie Contemporaine*, vol. 1 (Presses Universitaires de France, 1986), 441–3. Colonel Robin, *L'Insurrection de la Grande Kabylie en 1871* (Henri Charles Lavauzelle, 1900). See the harrowing portrayal given by Mahfoud Bennoune, 'Origins of the Algerian Proletariat', *MERIP Reports* (1981), 5–13, although to talk of peasant revolt in 1871 as Bennoune does is to superimpose a neo-Marxist viewpoint on an aristocratic and religious-led insurrection (10). Also Eric R. Wolf, *Peasant Wars of the Twentieth Century* (Faber and Faber, 1973), 218–24.
8. Alice Bullard, *Exile to Paradise: Savagery and Civilisation in Paris and the South Pacific* (Stanford University Press, 2000).
9. See Richard L. Roberts, *Warriors, Merchants and Slaves: The State and the Economy in the Middle Niger Valley, 1700–1914* (Stanford University Press, 1987).
10. Eugène Fromentin, *Un Été dans le Sahara* [1856] and *Une Année dans le Sahel* [1858] (Plon, 1912); Peter Dunwoodie, *Writing French Algeria* (Clarendon Press, 1998).
11. John H. Zarabell, 'Framing French Algeria: Colonialism, Travel and the Representation of Landscape', Ph.D. dissertation, University of California, 2000.
12. General Reibell, *Carnet de Route de la Mission Saharienne Foureau Lamy* (Plon, 1931).

13. Daniel Grévoz, *Les Méharistes français à la conquête du Sahara* (L'Harmattan, 1994).
14. Parfait-Louis Monteil, *Vade Mecum de l'officier d'infanterie de marine* (L. Baudoin et Cie, 1884), 162.
15. François Zucarelli, 'La Vie politique des quatres communes du Sénégal de 1872 à 1914', *Éthiopiques* 12 [online] ⟨http://www.refer.sn/ethiopiques/article.php3?id_article=546& artsuite=1⟩ accessed October 2008; Mamadou Diouf, *Histoire du Sénégal* (Maisonneuve et Larose, 2001), 138–56; H. O. Idowu, 'The Establishment of Elective Institutions in Senegal, 1869–1880', *Journal of African History* 9:2 (1968), 261–77; Allan Christelow, 'The Muslim Judge and Municipal Politics in Colonial Algeria and Senegal', *Comparative Studies in Society and History* 24:1 (Jan. 1982), 3–24.
16. David Robinson, *La Guerre Sainte d'Al Hajj Umar: Le Soudan occidental au milieu du xix siècle* (Karthala, 1988).
17. Gen. Jules Chanoine, *Documents pour servir à l'histoire de l'Afrique occidentale française de 1895 a 1899, correspondance du capitaine Chanoine pendant l'expédition du Mossi et du Gourouni, correspondance de la mission Afrique centrale* (n.p. 1901), 253.
18. Joe Lunn, '"Les Races guerrières": Racial Preconceptions in the French Military about West African Soldiers during the First World War', *Journal of Contemporary History* 34:4 (1999), 517–36.
19. Henri Brunschwig, *Noirs et Blancs dans l'Afrique Noire Française ou comment le colonisé devint colonisateur, 1870–1914* (Flammarion, 1974).
20. The military were crucial in the production of earliest forms of ethnological knowledge in these regions. They studied and added to precursor traveller narratives which were often quite dated by the end of the nineteenth century. For instance Barth was a necessary source but was often contradicted by the changes that had taken place since then. See Helen Tilley and Robert J. Gordon, *Ordering Africa, Anthropology, European Imperialism and the Politics of Knowledge* (Manchester University Press, 2007); Emmanuelle Sibeud, *Une Science impériale pour l'Afrique? La construction des savoirs africanistes en France, 1878–1930* (EHESS, 2002), 26–9.
21. These categories were also applied by the highest levels of government in Soudan; see *Notices Générale sur le Soudan* (Kayes, 1897–8), AAOF, 1 G195, part I, Ethnology.
22. Monteil, *Vade Mecum*, 260–1.
23. This is a particularly important issue in ethnically divided countries such as Rwanda and Burundi but these broad categories have also been critical in other parts of Africa and North Africa. For a French perspective on

this issue see Jean-Loup Amselle and Elikia M'Bokolo (eds), *Au Coeur de l'ethnie: Ethnies, tribalisme et État en Afrique* (La Découverte, 2005).

24. Lieutenant Gatelet, *Histoire de la conquête du Soudan Français, 1878–1899* (Berger Levrault, 1901), 2–10; Lunn, '"Les Races guerrières"'; Myron Echenberg, *Colonial Conscripts: The Tirailleurs Sénégalais in French West Africa, 1857–1960* (Heinemann, 1991); Charles Mangin, *La Force noire* (Hachette, 1910); Eric Deroo and Antoine Champeaux, *La Force noire: Gloire et infortunes d'une légende coloniale* (Taillandier, 2006); Nicole M. Zehfuss, 'From Stereotype to Individual: World War I Experience with Tirailleurs Sénégalais', *French Colonial History* 6 (2005), 137–58, esp. 140–1.
25. Emily Lynn Osborne, 'Circle of Iron: African Colonial Employees and the Interpretation of Colonial Rule in French West Africa', *Journal of African History* 44 (2003), 29–50; the power and cunning of the translator is a favoured subject in the work of the Malian author Hampâté Bâ. See for instance *L'Étrange destin de Wangrin* (10/18, 1993). Also see AAOF 11G1 on the suspicion arising from the role of translators and political agents.
26. William B. Cohen, *The French Encounter with Africans, White Response to Blacks, 1530–1880* (Indiana University Press, 1980); Richard Fogarty and Michael Osborne, 'Constructions and Functions of Race in French Military Medicine, 1830–1920', in Sue Peabody and Tyler Stovall (eds), *The Color of Liberty, Histories of Race in France* (Duke University Press, 2003), 206–36.
27. In this instance at least we have definite evidence that racial scientific theories were known and adopted within the ranks of the army—the recent revisionism which casts a doubt on the circulation of racial ideas does not apply here. See Peter Mandler, 'The Problem with Cultural History', *Cultural and Social History* 1:1 (2004), 94–117.
28. Full citizenship was disputed; see Catherine Coquery-Vidrovitch, 'Nationalité et citoyenneté en Afrique occidentale française: Originaires et citoyens dans le Sénégal colonial', *Journal of African History* 42:2 (2001), 285–305.
29. The theme has been explored for a long time by historians. The issue is obviously of contemporary relevance too. Raymond Betts, *Assimilation and Association in French Colonial Theory* (Columbia University Press, 1961).
30. See for instance 'L'expansion Française vers le Tchad', *Questions Diplomatiques et Coloniales* (15 Dec. 1899), 469–72.
31. AOM, FM, Soudan I, 11 bis.
32. Mahir Saul and Patrick Royer, *West African Challenge to Empire: Culture and History in the Volta-Bani Anticolonial War* (Ohio University

Press, 2001), 176–7; Myron J. Echenberg, 'Late Nineteenth-Century Military Technology in Upper Volta', *Journal of African History* 12:2 (1971), 241–54. African war technology was particularly lacking the means of producing efficient gunpowder.

33. When Chanoine encountered some of Samory's *sofas* in Gurunsi they had some modern rifles and their cavalry had Winchester rifles. AAOF, 1 G 221.
34. Bonnier was briefly the acting governor before the arrival of the civilian Grodet in 1893. AOM, FM, SG, Soudan; AAOF, 1 G 132; 15 G 231 'Rapport' Joffre.
35. Thomas A. Hale, *Scribe, Griot and Novelist: Narrative Interpreters of the Songhay Empire* (University of Florida Press, 1990), 30–45.
36. Jean-Pierre Olivier de Sardan, *Concepts et conceptions Songhay-Zarma* (Nubia, 1982), 224–30. Hale does not find this distinction so prominent in today's Niger.
37. Yves Person, *Samori: la renaissance de l'empire Mandingue* (ABC, 1976); Michal Tymowski, *L'Armée et la formation des états en Afrique occidentale au XIXe siècle—essai de comparaison, l'état de Samori et le Kenedougou* (Wydawnicta Uniwersytetu Warszawkiego, 1987).
38. Chanoine, *Documents pour servir à l'histoire*, 14.
39. Jeanne-Marie Kambou-Ferrand, *Peuples Voltaïques et conquête coloniale, 1885–1914* (L'Harmattan, 1993), 156–7.
40. Ibid. 353–80; Samuel Salo, 'Le Moog-Naaba Wogbo de Ouagadougou (1850–1904)', in Yenouyaba Georges Madiega and Oumarou Naro (eds), *Burkina Faso, cent ans d'histoire, 1895–1995* (Kathala, 2003), 631–57.
41. AAOF 1G221, Mission Voulet–Chanoine in the Mosse, 1896–7.
42. The full complex story is explained in Myron J. Echenberg, 'Jihad and State-Building in Late Nineteenth Century Upper Volta: The Rise and Fall of the Marka State of Al- Kari of Boussé', *Canadian Journal of African Studies/Revue Canadienne des Études Africaines* 3:3 (1969), 531–61, esp. 559.
43. Thomas M. Painter, 'From Warriors to Migrants: Critical Perspectives on Early Migrations among the Zarma of Niger', *Africa: Journal of the International African Institute* 58:1 (1988), 87–100, esp. 90.
44. AAOF 2 G 1/11 Rapport périodiques du Soudan, rapport politique March 1899. The French colonial administrator or 'Resident' of Ouagadougou complained that the Mosse was not 'pacified' at all.
45. Kambou-Ferrand, *Peuples Voltaïques et conquête coloniale*, 384–5.
46. J.-P. Olivier de Sardan, *Les Sociétés Songhay-Zarma (Niger-Mali): Chefs, guerriers, esclaves, paysans* (Khartala, 1984), 152–5.
47. AOM, Missions 10, 29 March 1897.

48. Person, *Samori*, TIII, 1812; Kambou-Ferrand, *Peuples Voltaïques et conquête coloniale*, 144–5.
49. AAOF, 15 G 97 'Rapport' from Chaudié, 16 Dec. 1897. Jean-Baptiste Chaudié was the first governor General of French West Africa from 1895 until 1900.
50. Chanoine, *Documents pour servir à l'histoire*, 54 (author's emphasis).
51. AOM, Missions 10, Journal de marche, Lt. Chanoine, May 1897.
52. Chanoine, *Documents pour servir à l'histoire*, 41.
53. James J. Cooke, 'Anglo-French Diplomacy and the Contraband Arms Trade in Colonial Africa, 1894–1897', *African Studies Review* 17:1 (1974), 27–41.
54. Julien Chanoine, 'Mission Voulet–Chanoine, itinéraire du capitaine Chanoine', *Bulletin de la Société de Géographie* 20 (1899), 221–79, n. 1.
55. *A' Travers le Monde* (1898), 21–3; *Le Tour du Monde* (14 Aug. 1897).
56. Chanoine, *Documents pour servir à l'histoire*; Gatelet, *Histoire de la conquête*, 346–66; Lt Col Parfait-Louis Monteil, *Les Conventions Franco-Anglaises des 14 juin 1898 et 21 mars 1899* (Plon Nourrit, 1899), 12.
57. AAOF 2 G 1/11, 'Rapports périodiques du Soudan', 31 Dec. 1899.
58. See 'Mission Voulet–Chanoine', *Bulletin de la Société de Géographie de Lille*, XXXI, 1899, 357–68.
59. AOM, FM/Missions/10.
60. Pierre Guillem, *L'Expansion, 1881–1898* (Imprimerie Nationale, 1985), 109.
61. Catherine Coquery-Vidrovitch, *Brazza et la prise de possession du Congo* (Mouton, 1963); Henri Brunschwig, *Brazza Explorateur* (Mouton, 1972).
62. *Questions Coloniales et Diplomatiques*, 15 May 1899, 77.
63. Jacques Frémeaux, 'L'Armée coloniale et la république (1830–1962)', in Olivier Forcade, Éric Duhamel, and Philippe Vial (eds), *Militaires en République, 1870–1962, les officiers, le pouvoir et la vie publique en France* (Publications de la Sorbonne, 1999), 101–9, esp. 105. On Destenave's attack on the Sanusiyya see Jean-Louis Triaud, *Tchad 1900–1902, une guerre franco-lybienne oubliée?* (L'Harmattan, 1988).
64. AAOF 1 D 199, Deuxième affaire de Sargadié.
65. M. L. D'Aufreville, 'La Renaissance coloniale de la France', *Revue Politique et Parlementaire* 19 (1899), 332–50.
66. The British press certainly perceived it to be so; see *The Times*, 18 Oct. 1897, 7; also Edmund Morel, 'The French in Western and Central Africa', *Journal of the Royal African Society* 1:2 (1902), 192–207.
67. Henry Alis, *Nos Africains, la mission Crampel, la mission Dybowsk* (Bibliothèque nationale, 1894), 160; C. M. Andrew and A. S.

Kanya-Forstner, 'The French "Colonial Party": Its Composition, Aims and Influence, 1885–1914', *Historical Journal* 14:1 (Mar. 1971), 99–128, esp. 103; 'Compagnies de Colonisation', *Questions Diplomatiques et Coloniales* (1 Oct. 1899), 171.

68. Paul Webster, *Fachoda: la bataille pour le Nil* (Edition du Félin, 2001), 134.
69. Discussed further in Chs. 6 and 8; see Adam Hochschild, *King Leopold's Ghosts*, 2nd edn (Pan Books, [1998], 2007), epilogue. On a Belgian rehabilitation see Michel Dumoulin, *Léopold III de la Controverse à l'histoire* (Complexe, 2001).
70. See for instance, Baron Hulot, 'Rapport', *Bulletin de la société de Géographie* 1 (1900), 197–206.
71. Gen. Octave Meynier, *Mission Joalland-Meynier* (Collection les grandes missions coloniales, 1947), 16.
72. Chanoine, *Documents pour servir à l'histoire*, 177.
73. Ibid. 302.
74. AOM, Mission 11, received 11 December 1899.
75. Dr Charles Colin, *Le Soudan occidental* (Berger Levrault, 1883), 3.
76. Colonel Gouraud, *Zinder, Tchad, Souvenirs d'un Africain* (Plon, 1944), 128.
77. D'Aufreville, 'La Renaissance', 347–9.
78. Allen Isaacman and Richard Roberts (eds), *Cotton, Colonialism and Social History in Sub-Saharan Africa* (Heinemann, 1995), see in particular the articles by Richard Roberts, 'The Coercion of Free Markets: Cotton, Peasants and the Colonial State in the French Soudan, 1924–1932', 221–46, and Thomas J. Bassett, 'The Uncaptured Corvee: Cotton in Cote d'Ivoire, 1912–1946', 247–67. These early aspirations to cotton self-sufficiency were voiced as soon as the colonies were established but developed over thirty years until the French launched the Office du Niger in 1932, which developed large-scale irrigated cotton production.
79. Jean-Pierre Biondi, *Les Anti-colonialistes: 1881–1962* (Robert Laffont, 1993), 35–6. Communards were divided on the matter; some like Louise Michel refused to be associated with the 'pacification of New Caledonia'. Bullard, *Exile to Paradise*.
80. AAOF, 15 G 15, *arrêtés et directives du Lieutenant Gouverneur Général du Soudan*.
81. Gatelet, *Histoire de la conquête*, 494–501.
82. AOM Mission 11, GGA to minister of colonies, 12 July 1898.
83. AOM, Afrique III, 38, 75 bis, De Trentinian, 'Rapport' from Kayes, 7 October 1899.
84. AOM, Mission 11, 1 July 1898; the minister at the time was the anglophobic Hanoteau.

85. AOM, Mission 11, Commission de la Cour des Comptes, 7 January 1902.
86. AOM, Mission 11, 5 November 1901.
87. General Joalland, *Le Drame de Dankori: mission Voulet–Chanoine, Missiona Joalland-Meynier* (Argo, 1930), 13–14.
88. AOM, Mission 11, 1 July 1898, *Minister of colonies to Minister of war.*
89. AAOF, 1 G234, Telegram, 20 September 1898, Bamako.
90. AAOF, 1 G234, Mission Afrique centrale, Timbuktu, 27 October 1898.
91. AOM, Afrique III, 78, letter of 25 January; telegram of 3 February 1899.
92. AOM, Mission 110, Chanoine to Terrier, 9 February 1899.
93. AOM, Afrique III, 39, Mission Bretonnet, 7–84.
94. Letter to his father 9 February 1899. Chanoine, *Documents pour servir à l'histoire*, 218.
95. Andrew Hubbell, 'A View of the Slave Trade from the Margin: Souroudougou in the Late Nineteenth-Century Slave Trade of the Niger Bend', *Journal of African History* 42:1 (2001), 25–47, esp. 46.
96. Much was made of Chanoine's use of criminally convicted tirailleurs; one of them, Boa Diakité, who had been an NCO, had been released at Chanoine's demand. In fact these tirailleurs had only been convicted for petty theft at the end of the previous engagement. AOM, Afrique III, 38, rapport Lamy, 9.
97. Echenberg, *Colonial Conscripts.*
98. Chanoine, *Documents pour servir à l'histoire*, 12.
99. AOM, Soudan II/2, 'Rapport' on the Soudan, February 1894.
100. French colonial administration later remained a lean operation often relying on ad hoc measures to enact its grand plans. See William B. Cohen, *Rulers of Empire, The French Colonial Service in Africa* (Hoover Institution Press, 1971).
101. AOM, Afrique III, 39, 74, Gambingui, 9 October 1899.
102. *Questions Coloniales et Diplomatiques*, 1 April 1899, 387.
103. J. F. V. Keiger, 'Omdurman, Fashoda and Franco-British Relations', in Edward M. Spiers (ed.), *Sudan: The Conquest Reappraised* (Frank Cass, 1998), 162–76.
104. André Lebon, *La politique de la France en Afrique, 1896–98, Mission Marchand, Niger, Madagascar* (Plon, 1901).
105. See E. D. Morel, 'The French in Western and Central Africa', *Journal of the Royal African Society* 1:2 (1902), 192–207; Ian Brownlie, *African Boundaries* (C. Hurst, 1979).
106. Delcassé began his approaches quite early nevertheless. See *The Times*, 24 March 1899.
107. Roger Glenn Brown, *Fashoda Reconsidered: The Impact of Domestic Politics on French Policy in Africa, 1893–1898* (Johns Hopkins University

Press, 1970); Marc Michel, *La Mission Marchand, 1895–1899* (Mouton, 1972); Gabriel Hanotaux, *Le Partage de l'Afrique: Fachoda* (Flammarion, 1909); Guy de la Batut, *Fachoda ou le renversement des alliances* (Gallimard, 1932); Webster, *Fachoda*.

108. Henri Brunschwig, 'Anglophobia and French African Policy', in P. Gifford and W. Roger Louis, *France and Africa* (Yale University Press, 1971).

Chapter 4 Officers and Gentlemen?

1. Colonel Baratier, *Epopées Africaines* (Perrin, 1913), 17. Albert Baratier (1864–1917) had been with Marchand in Fashoda and had been part of many campaigns against Samory.
2. Robert Aldrich, 'Colonial Man', in C. Forth and B. Taithe (eds), *French Masculinities* (Palgrave, 2007), 123–40.
3. Jacques Migozzi and Philippe Le Guern (eds), *Production(s) du Populaire* (Presses Universitaires de Limoges, 2004); Jean-Pierre Bacot, *La Presse illustrée au XiXe siècle* (Presses Universitaires de Limoges, 2005), 98–9, 150–1; David Spurr, *The Rhetoric of Empire: Colonial Discourse in Journalism* (Duke University Press, 1993).
4. Tamar Garb, *Figures of Modernity: Figure and Flesh in Fin-de-siècle France* (Thames and Hudson, 1998); C. E. Forth and A. Carden-Coyne, *Cultures of the Abdomen* (Palgrave, 2005); Forth and Taithe, *French Masculinities*.
5. Lyautey published a number of important books such as *Le Rôle social de l'officier* (Perrin, 1892), originally published in *La revue des Deux Mondes* in 1891, and *Le Rôle colonial de l'armée* (Armand Colin, 1900). Not a Soudanese officer himself he was a disciple of Gallieni. See Pascal Venier, *Lyautey avant Lyautey* (L'Harmattan, 2000). He is still a figure of considerable importance and hagiographies have followed each other in quick succession. See Arnaud Tessier, *Lyautey, le ciel et les sables sont grands* (Perrin, 2006).
6. Hydaspes [check], *The Truth about the Indian Army and Its Officers with Reference to The French Local Army of Algeria* (Simpkin, Marshall, 1861).
7. L. E. Mangin, *Le Général Mangin* (Lanore, 1986); Arthur Conte, *Joffre* (Perrin, 1998).
8. Commandant Gallieni, *Deux Campagnes au Soudan Français, 1886–1888* (Hachette, 1891).
9. Marc Michel, *Gallieni* (Fayard, 1989). James Sibree, 'General Gallieni's "Neuf Ans à Madagascar": An Example of French Colonization', *Journal of the Royal African Society* 8:31 (1909), 259–73; Stephen Ellis, 'The Political Elite of Imerina and the Revolt of the Menalamba: The Creation of

a Colonial Myth in Madagascar, 1895–1898', *Journal of African History* 21:2 (1980), 219–34.

10. Préface de Mr Le Vicomte Melchior de Vogüé of the French Academy, in Lt Col. Parfait-Louis Monteil, *De Saint Louis à Tripoli par le lac Tchad voyage au travers du Soudan et du Sahara pendant les années 1890-1-2* (Félix Alcan, 1894), p. vi.
11. In Frederick Cooper's terms, power was 'arterial' rather than capillary, meaning by that the French could only reach key centres rather than cover the colony with a fine web of controls. Frederick Cooper, 'Conflict and Connection: Rethinking Colonial African History', *American Historical Review* 99:5 (Dec. 1994), 1516–45.
12. While the figure of 311 is probably very accurate, the figure of 4,105,027 indigenous people is likely to be wildly inaccurate and probably underestimated. It gives an idea of the limited French presence. AAOF, 22 G19, Recensement général de l'AOF.
13. Organized rebellions among tirailleurs were not infrequent despite what military propagandists like to say. The killing of officers was very rare but acts of disobedience, assault, and desertions were common especially in isolated posts. In May 1899 for instance the resident Prins in Baguini, Chari, had to run for his life because of a rebellion. AOM, Afrique III, 39, 40.
14. AOM Afrique III, 37, 29, Voulet letter to minister, 9 July 1898.
15. AOM, Afrique III, 37, Voulet to Minister, Report from Tibiri, 1 March 1899, 10.
16. Jules Chanoine, *Documents pour servir à l'histoire de l'Afrique occidentale française de 1895 à 1899, correspondance du capitaine Chanoine pendant l'expédition du Mossi et du Gourounsi, correspondance de la mission Afrique centrale* (n.p., 1901), 8.
17. AOM, Mission 110, note de service, Voulet, 19 April 1899.
18. AOM, Mission 110, Rapport Tourot, Nafouta, 18 July 1899.
19. See for instance the chapter devoted to Sgt Moriba Keita in Baratier, *Épopées*. For a broader picture see R. Aldrich, *Colonialism and Homosexuality* (Routledge, 2003).
20. The surviving evidence is obviously more discreet on the matter but the archives contain a few letters which cast a faint light on the domestic arrangement of the Voulet mission. AOM, Mission 110, Rapport Joalland, Mafoita, 25 July 1899.
21. AOM, Mission 110, Letter to Pallier from Captain Angeli in Dosso, February 1899.
22. AOM, Mission 49, 350 Conclusions rapport Laborie.
23. AOM, Mission 49, 352, Conclusions rapport Laborie.

24. AOM, Mission 49, St Louis, Rapport des conclusions Laborie, GGA to Minister, 4 October 1901.
25. The relationship between empire and sexuality is one increasingly being well explored. See for instance: Susan Pedersen, 'National Bodies, Unspeakable Acts: The Sexual Politics of Colonial Policy-making', *Journal of Modern History* 63:4 (Dec. 1991), 647–80; Anne McClintock, *Imperial Leather, Race Gender and Sexuality in the Colonial Context* (Routledge, 1995), esp. Ch. 6; Ann Laura Stoler, *Carnal Knowledge and Imperial Power* (University of California Press, 2002).
26. AOM, Mission 110, Rapport Joalland, Mafoita, 25 July 1899.
27. Gen. Paul Joalland, *Le Drame de Dankori: Mission Voulet-Chanoine; mission Joalland-Meynier* (Argo, 1930), 76.
28. Parfait-Louis Monteil, *Vade Mecum de l'officier d'infanterie de marine* (L. Baudoin et Cie, 1884), 304–5.
29. AOM, Afrique III, 35, telegram from Porto Novo, 20 August 1899, Fonssagrive to minister.
30. AAOF, 1G161, *Mission Monteil*, 1893.
31. Odille Roynette, *Bon pour le service: l'expérience de la caserne en France à la fin du XiXe siècle* (Belin, 2000), 343–9.
32. Henry Mark Narducci, 'The French Officer Corps and the Social Role of the Army, 1890–1908', Wayne State University, 1981, 121, 165–216.
33. The evidence from subsequent years shows that French occupation was resisted very actively around Say. Captain Angéli was defeated in September 1899 while attempting to conquer the village of Sargadjé. AAOF, 11 G1, affaire Angéli.
34. This military law was available to all regular soldiers as part of their *livret*, a document which detailed their career so far, the goods entrusted to them by the administration, and the laws applying to them. *Livret du Soldat—modèle 1897 No 30, annexe du décret du 14 janvier 1889 modifié par la note ministérielle du 9 novembre 1890* (Imprimerie Nationale, 1897).
35. Jean-Marie Lundy, 'Mémoire de criminologie appliqué à l'expertise médicale, Le traitement pénal dans l'armée Française sous la troisième république', Université René Descartes, Droit Médical, 1987, 9–17. *L'Intransigeant* was created in 1880 by the maverick left-winger Rochefort, an ex-Communard; it later became a staunchly anti-Semitic and increasingly nationalistic newspaper during the Dreyfus affair.
36. 'Mission Voulet-Chanoine, de Dienné à Sansané-Haoussa', *Bulletin de la Société de Géographie* 20 (1899), 221–35, 79–84.
37. AOM, Mission 110, 'Rapport' Pallier, 15 August 1899.
38. Ibid.

39. Sgt. Ernest Bolis, *Mes Campagnes en Afrique et en Asie, 1889–1899; légion étrangère infanterie de Marine* (Claude Gassmann, 2001), 5–7, 32–3.
40. Ibid. 46.
41. L. H. Gann and Peter Duigan, *The Rules of German Africa, 1884–1914* (Stanford University Press, 1977); Denis Laumann, 'A Historiography of German Togoland, or the Rise and Fall of a "Model Colony" ', *History in Africa* 30 (2003), 195–211; Kenneth Mackenzie, 'Some British Reactions to German Colonial Methods, 1885–1907', *Historical Journal* 17:1 (1974), 165–75.
42. AOM, Soudan II, 2, 'Rapport' from Ambassador Waddington, 'Rapport' from de Lamothe on the events, notes to Captain Roix.
43. *L'Illustration* 2511 (11 April 1891), 312–13.
44. AOM, Soudan II, 2, Telegram from Kayes to Bakel.
45. AOM, Soudan II, 2, Telegram from Bakel to Kayes.
46. AOM, FM, Soudan I, 11 bis, de Trentinian to the commander of Niger-Volta, 24 Dec. 1898.
47. Hannah Arendt, *The Origins of Totalitarianism* (Harvest Books, 1950), 187–91.
48. Gen. Octave Meynier, *Mission Joalland-Meynier* (Collection les grandes missions coloniales, 1947), 8–9.
49. Narducci, 'The French Officer Corps', 97–121.
50. André Mévil in *L'éclair*, 12 Sept. 1899, also *Questions Diplomatiques et Coloniales*, T8, 110.
51. Claude Digeon, *La Crise allemande de la pensée française* (PUF, 1959).
52. Jean Rouch, *La Religion et la magie Songhay* (Anthropologie Sociale, Université de Bruxelles, 1989), 72–3. Dongo was characterized by his violence, notably the killing of entire villages; thus his role was God of Thunder. On healing see 306. Also *idem*, *Les Hommes et les dieux du fleuve, essai ethnographique sur les populations songhay du moyen Niger, 1941–1983* (Artcom, 1997).
53. Chanoine, *Documents pour servir à l'histoire*, 290–1.
54. AOM, Afrique III, 37, 1. Voulet to the Minister of Colonies, Sansané Haoussa, January 1899.
55. Monteil, *Vade Mecum*, 162; Voulet had publicized his organizational skills and published an article on the best means of setting up a *colonne*. Lt Paul Voulet, 'La Jonction du Soudan et du Dahomey, 1896–7', *Revue Générale des Sciences Pures et Appliquées*, 895–6.
56. AOM, Mission 11, invoices from Librairie Paul Sevin and Flammarion, 5 July 1898 and librairie Belard.

57. AOM Afrique III, 37, 45, telegram from Jules Chanoine to his son announcing that his brother has passed the examination to St Cyr military school (the equivalent of West Point or Sandhurst).
58. William Sernam, *Les officiers français dans la nation, 1848–1914* (Aubier, 1982), 7.
59. Elikia M'Bokolo, *Resistances et Messianismes, histoire générale de l'Afrique* (Agence de Coopération, 1990), 80–90.
60. Charles Monteil, *Contes Soudanais* (Ernest Leroux, 1905). Monteil (1871–1949), an eminent anthropologist of the region, taught 'Soudanese' at the Écoles des Langues Orientales Vivantes.
61. AOM, Afrique III, Voulet to Minister, 'Rapport' from Tibiri, 1 March 1899, 10.
62. O. Meynier (ed.), *Les Carnets de route du Lieutenant Colonel Klobb* (PUB, 1 Nov. 1898), 119–20.
63. Henry Alis, *Nos Africains, la mission Crampel, la mission Dybowski* (Bibliothèque Nationale, 1894).
64. Capitaine Heumann, *Le Soudan, Gordon et le Mahdi* (Charles Lavauzelle, 1886).
65. Arsène Klobb, *Dernier carnet de route au Soudan Français* (Flammarion, 1905), appendix, 284.
66. Robert Maestri (ed.), *Commandant Lamy, un officier français aux colonies* (Maisonneuve et Larose, 2000); Commandant Reibell, *Le Commandant Lamy d'après sa correspondance et ses souvenirs de campagne, 1858–1900* (Hachette, 1903), F. Foureau, *D'Alger au Congo par le Tchad par F. Foureau* (Masson, 1902).
67. AOM, Afrique III, 37b, 98, 4 June 1899.
68. See colonial hagiographers such as the academician Henry Bordeaux, *L'Épopée noire : la France en Afrique Occidentale* (Denoël et Steele, 1936).
69. Reibell, *Le Commandant Lamy*, 570.
70. Maestri, *Commandant Lamy*, 225.
71. General Reibell, *Carnet de Route de la Mission Saharienne, Foureau Lamy* (Plon, 1931), 76–7.
72. AOM Afrique III/41 b, Mission Saharienne.

Chapter 5 Slaving and African Warfare

1. Urbain Gohier, préface to Paul Vigné d'Octon, *La Gloire du Sabre*, 4th edn (Flammarion, 1900), pp. vi–vii.
2. Charles A. M. Lavigerie, *L'Armée et la Mission de la France en Afrique* (A. Jourdan, 1875).

3. Alexis M. Gochet, *La Traite des nègres et la croisade africaine*, 2nd edn (Ch. Poussielgne, 1889); *idem, La Barbarie africaine et l'action civilisatrice des missions catholiques au Congo* (Dessain, 1889), 5–7; AGMAfr, Lavigerie, A.17 campagne anti-esclavagiste. This campaign represented an immense investment of time and effort for the final years of Lavigerie's life.
4. There is a huge historiography on this topic; see Jeff D. Bass, 'An Efficient Humanitarianism: The British Slave Trade Debates, 1791–1792', *Quarterly Journal of Speech* 75:2 (1989), 152–65; Thomas L. Haskell, 'Capitalism and the Origins of the Humanitarian Sensibility', Part 1, *American Historical Review* 90:2 (Apr. 1985), 339–61; Part 2, 90:3 (June 1985), 547–66; David Brion Davis, John Ashworth, and Thomas L. Haskell in the forum of *American Historical Review* 92:4 (Oct. 1987), 813–28.
5. Kevin Grant, *A Civilised Savagery: Britain and the New Slaveries in Africa, 1884–1926* (Routledge, 2005); Gochet, *La Traite des nègres*; Seymour Drescher, 'British Way, French Way: Opinion Building and Revolution in the Second French Slave Emancipation', *American Historical Review* 96:3 (June 1991), 709–34.
6. The key texts of the period on slave trading originated from pioneer writers such as Livingstone and Verney Lovett Cameron, and from the German explorer Gustav Nachtigal, *Sahara and Sudan*, vol III: *The Chad Basin and Bargirmi* (Hurst, 1987), Ch. 6, 'Slave Raids', 340–68, which appeared first in English in *Harper's* in 1874 and in French soon afterwards.
7. Elikia M'Bokolo, *Résistances et Messianismes, histoire générale de l'Afrique* (Agence de Coopération, 1990), 41.
8. AOM Afrique III, 37, 1. Voulet to the Minister of Colonies, Sansané Haoussa, January 1899.
9. Capitaine Heumann, *Le Soudan, Gordon et le Mahdi* (Charles Lavauzelle, 1886), 32–3, 42–66.
10. Charles A. M. Lavigerie, *L'Esclavage Africain: conférence sur l'esclavage dans le haut* Congo (Siège de la société anti-esclavagiste, 1888); R. P. Cussac, *L'Apôtre de l'Ouganda, le père Lourdel* (Grands Lacs, *c.*1920); see also the 1895 biography by Chanoine Nicq.
11. Abdul Sheriff, *Slaves, Spices and Ivory in Zanzibar* (James Currey, 1987); François Renault, *Tippo-Tip: un potentat arabe en Afrique centrale* (L'Harmattan, 1987).
12. François Renault, *Libérations d'esclaves et nouvelles servitudes* (Nouvelles éditions africaines, 1976); François Renault and Serge Daget, *Les Traites négrières en Afrique* (Karthala, 1985).
13. Gochet, *La Traite des nègres*, 51–2; Lavigerie, *L'Esclavage Africain*.
14. James R. Lehning, *To Be a Citizen: The Political Culture of the Early French Third Republic* (Ithaca: Cornell University Press, 2001); Steven C. Hause, *Hubertine Auclert: The French Suffragette* (Yale University Press,

1987); Joan Wallace Scott, *Only Paradoxes to Offer: French Feminists and the Rights of Man* (Harvard University Press, 1996), 115–16.

15. Renault and Daget, *Les Traites négrières*, 222–3.
16. On the relationship between missionaries and colonizers in the French empire see J. P. Daughton, *An Empire Divided: Religion, Republicanism and the Making of French Colonialism, 1880–1914* (Oxford University Press, 2006).
17. AGMAfr Lavigerie, A.17.178, 278–313. On Joubert see *La Vie chevaleresque de Joubert l'Africain*, institution Libre de Cambrée, B1/JBR2; AMA, C10, Dossier Joubert; Houdebine and Bounier, *Le Capitaine Joubert* (Grands Lacs, n.d.).
18. Lavigerie, *L'Armée et la Mission*, 14.
19. Gochet, *La Traite des nègres; idem, La Barbarie africaine*, 5–7.
20. Lavigerie, *L'Esclavage Africain.*
21. In this Lavigerie was not alone. See Grant, *A Civilised Savagery.*
22. Sheriff, *Slaves, Spices and Ivory in Zanzibar*; Renault, *Tippo-Tip*.
23. Gochet, *La Traite des nègres*, 51–2.
24. Vigné d'Octon penned one of the forewords to one of the leading *maitre d'armes* of the time, the adjudant Ringnet's *Épee, Fleuret, Manuel pratique du Combat suivi du code du duel*, with additional prefaces by E. D'Hauterive and Dr de Pradel (Henri Charles Lavauzelle, 1905). The book was devoted to the real fencing of dueling, suggesting that the prefacers, who had belonged to Ringnet's class, were themselves beneficiaries from this training.
25. Vigné d'Octon, *La Gloire du Sabre*, 59–60. This account is verified in the administrative records and any historical account of the early Senegalese tirailleurs.
26. AOM, Mission 11, leather folder of Chanoine's private papers, 16 March 1897, letter 5 to the resident of Ouagadougou.
27. The journals or *diaires* of the missionaries report many instances of this practice. See AGMAfr, Diaire de Ségou, 4 Septembre 1896.
28. Yet polygamists found it more difficult to obtain French citizenship despite having a right to it in Dakar and St Louis or the rights acquired by serving in the army. For Algeria, see J. Bowlan, 'Polygamists Need Not Apply: Becoming a French Citizen in Colonial Algeria, 1918–1938', *Proceedings of the Annual Meeting of the Western Society for French History*, 24 (1997), 110–19.
29. The Harem was an object of special and spurious interest; see Malek Alloula, *The Colonial Harem* (Manchester University Press, 1986).
30. AAOF 11G 5, rapport de Zinder sur les effets du Sultan. His fortune was estimated at approx. 25,000 francs, taking into account all debts and credits. The household of the Sultan was 368 strong in 1905. The deposed

Sultan was the brother of the one killed by Pallier and the harem had been constituted before 1899.

31. Gen. Paul Joalland, *Le Drame de Dankori: Mission Voulet-Chanoine; mission Joalland-Meynier* (Argo, 1930), 37.
32. Octave Meynier, *Les Conquérants du Tchad* (Flammarion, 1923), 106.
33. J. Malcolm Thompson, 'Colonial Policy and the Family Life of Black Troops in French West Africa, 1817–1904', *International Journal of African Historical Studies* 23:3 (1990), 423–53.
34. Raymonde Bonnetain, *Une Française au Soudan, sur la route de Tombouctou, du Sénégal au Niger* (Paris, 1894), 73.
35. Martin Klein, *Slavery and Colonial Rule in French West Africa* (Cambridge University Press, 1998), 16.
36. Michal Tymowski, 'Les Esclaves du commandant Quiquandon', *Cahiers d'Études Africaines* 158 (2000), 351–62.
37. Bonnetain, *Une Française au Soudan*, 73.
38. See Paul Leroy Beaulieu, *De la colonisation chez les peuples modernes* (Guillaumin, 1874), 333–4; Dan Warshaw, *Paul Leroy-Beaulieu and Established Liberalism in France* (North Illinois University Press, 1991), 99; Maurice Lazrey, *The Emergence of Class in Algeria: A Study of Colonialism and Social Political Change* (Westview Special Studies, 1976).
39. AOM, Soudan II, 2, Rapport sur le Soudan, February 1894.
40. Catherine Coquery-Vidrovitch, *L'Afrique et les Africains au XIXème Siecle* (Armand Colin, 1999), 196–7; Kevin Grant, *A Civilised Savagery: Britain and the New Slaveries in Africa, 1884–1926* (Routledge, 2005).
41. Anne Phillips, *The Enigma of Colonialism: British Policy in West Africa* (James Currey; Indiana University Press, 1989), 32.
42. Andrew Hubbell, 'A View of the Slave Trade from the Margin: Souroudougou in the Late Nineteenth-Century Slave Trade of the Niger Bend', *Journal of African History* 42:1 (2001), 25–47, esp. 46.
43. AOM, Mission 110, Memorandum, Bouthel to Voulet, 22 June 1899. Voulet approved in the margins and noted 'this proves that Bouthel thinks for himself'.
44. F. Foureau, *D'Alger au Congo par le Tchad* ([Masson, 1902] L'Harmattan, 1990), 552.
45. Ibrahim Bba Koke and Elikia M'Bokolo, *Histoire générale de l'Afrique* (ABC, 1977), 44.
46. An irony about the 'Mounts Kong' is that there is no mountain in that location. The mounts of Kong are a geographical myth of early explorers. See Thomas J. Bassett and Philip W. Porter, ' "From the Best Authorities": The Mountains of Kong in the Cartography of West Africa', *Journal of African History* 32:3 (1991), 367–413. The Kong region, however, does exist and corresponds to the north of modern Ivory Coast.

47. The campaign was very controversial due to its cost and lack of success. Monteil lost in this occasion all the credit he had earned in his travels to Chad a few years earlier. Lt Col. Parfait-Louis Monteil, *Une page d'histoire coloniale, la Colonne de Kong* (Henri Charles Lavauzelle, 1902).
48. AAM, Diaire de Ségou, 1 March 1898.
49. AOM, Mission 110, Le capitaine Dubreuil à Lieutenant Gouverneur, 22 Aug. 1899.
50. AAOF 1 G222 Mission Cazemajou dans le haut Soudan.
51. AOM, Mission 110, Rapport Pallier, 15 Aug. 1899.
52. AOM, Mission 110, Rapport politique de Say, March 1899.
53. AOM, Mission 110, Papiers Voulet, Chanoine to Voulet, 26 Apr. 1899.
54. Gen. Jules Chanoine, *Documents pour servir à l'histoire de l'Afrique occidentale française de 1895 à 1899, correspondance du capitaine Chanoine pendant l'expédition du Mossi et du Gourounsi, correspondance de la mission Afrique centrale* (n.p. 1901), 249.
55. Bello Ali, chief of Liboré to A. Salifou, 17 March 1974, quoted in Muriel Mathieu, *La Mission Afrique Centrale* (L'Harmattan, 1995), 255.
56. AOM, Mission 110, Rapport politique de Say, March 1899.
57. AOM, Afrique III, 38, 75 bis, report of Commandant Crave, December 1898.
58. AOM, Afrique III, 38, 75bis, report Granderye and Crave.
59. Censorship was normal policy for military operations. William Sernam, *Les officiers français dans la nation, 1848–1914* (Aubier, 1982), 41.
60. AAOF 11 G1, rapports politiques de Say. Delaunay sent a favourable report in January and only wrote negatively in March after his dispute with Voulet over whether Say effectively controlled both shores of the Niger.
61. Michal Tymowski, *L'Armée et la formation des états en Afrique occidentale au XIXe siècle—essai de comparaison, l'état de Samori et le Kenedougou* (Wydawnicta Uniwersytetu Warszawkiego, 1987), 78–9.
62. AOM, Mission 110, Rapport Joalland, Mafoita, 25 July 1899.
63. AOM, Mission 110, Rapport Pallier, 15 Aug. 1899.
64. AOM, Mission 110, Papiers Voulet, Chanoine to Voulet, 1 April 1899.
65. AOM, Mission 110, Rapport politique de Say, March 1899.
66. AOM, Mission 110, 'Rapport' from Lieutenant d'artillerie de Marine Salaman au Lt Gal, flotille du Niger, lettre T 106, Ségou, 8 May 1899.
67. Malin Şaul, 'Money in Colonial Transition: Cowries and Francs in West Africa', *American Ethnologist* 106 (2004), 71–84.
68. Barth quoted in H. A. S. Johnston, *The Fulani Empire of Sokoto* (Oxford University Press, 1968), 163.
69. Marion Johnson, 'The Cowrie Currencies of West Africa', Part II, *African History* 1:12 (1970), 331–53, esp. 345. Also see Jan Hogendorn and

Marion Johnson, *The Shell Money of the Slave Trade* (Cambridge University Press, 1986).

70. AOM, Mission 11, leather folder of Chanoine's private papers.
71. Bonnetain, *Une Française au Soudan*, 198–201.
72. AOM, Mission 11, leather folder of Chanoine's private papers. 4 March, 1897.
73. Klein, *Slavery and Colonial Rule*, 31. This was a contested policy; see AOM, SG, Soudan XIV and XVI 2, 6.
74. This practice was signalled in Eugène Bouton (Rodes), 'Un Regard sur le Soudan', *La Revue Blanche* 20 (1899), 321–30, esp. 329.
75. William Gervase Clarence-Smith, *Islam and the Abolition of Slavery* (Hurst, 2006), 102.
76. Denise Bouche, *Les Villages de liberté en Afrique Noire Française, 1887–1910* (Mouton, 1967).
77. They were significantly established along the main administrative thoroughfares of the colony. Other villages also existed, funded by the Société anti esclavagiste de France; Bouche, *Les Villages*, 184–6.
78. Bouche, *Les villages*, 66–78.
79. Quoted ibid. 73.
80. Ibid. 88.
81. Bouton, 'Un Regard sur le Soudan', 328.
82. AOM, SG, Soudan xiv/1.
83. Jacques Frémeaux, 'L'Armée coloniale et la république (1830–1962)', in Olivier Forcade, Éric Duhamel, and Philippe Vial (eds), *Militaires en République, 1870–1962, les officiers, le pouvoir et la vie publique en France* (Publications de la Sorbonne, 1999), 101–9, esp. 103. A. S. Kanya-Forstner, *The Conquest of Western Sudan: A Study in French Imperialism* (Cambridge University Press, 1969), 225–7, esp. 228.
84. Grodet failed to be obeyed and was contested violently. See C. W. Newbury, 'The Formation of the Government General of French West Africa', *Journal of African History* 1:1 (1960), 111–28, esp. 114. Also see Kanya-Fortsner, *The Conquest of Western Sudan*, 233–6.
85. As this chapter is being completed, a Nigerien woman, Adijatou Mani, has recently won a trial against the government of Niger for failing to abolish slavery despite its recent criminalization. Major anti-slavery organizations estimate slavery in Niger at 43,000. See http://uk.reuters.com/article/worldNews/idUKL0761264920080407, accessed 3 November 2008.
86. Phillips, *The Enigma of Colonialism*, 29–34.
87. The story has acquired a quasi-mythical status discussed in Gregory Mann, *Native Sons: West African Veterans and France in the Twentieth Century* (Duke University Press, 2006), 21–36; Richard Roberts and

Martin Klein, 'The Bambare Slave Exodus of 1905 and the Decline of Slavery in the Western Soudan', *Journal of African History* 21 (1980), 375–94.

88. AGMAfr, Diaire de Ségou, 31 May 1898; also Diaire El Golea, 24 June 1899. On the fraught relationship between colonial administration and missionaries see Joseph-Roger de Benoist, *Église et pouvoir colonial au Soudan français* (Karthala, 2000).
89. Mathieu, *La Mission Afrique Centrale*, 97.
90. AOM, Misssion 110, 69, Péteau to Voulet, 22 January 1899.
91. AOM, Mission 49, St Louis, Rapport des conclusions Laborie, GGA to Minister, 4 October 1901.
92. AGMAfr, Diaires of Ségou, 1897.
93. See Edward M. Spiers, *The Victorian Soldier in Africa* (Manchester University Press, 2004), 159–79.
94. Andrew Porter, 'Sir Roger Casement and the International Humanitarian Movement', *Journal of Imperial and Commonwealth History*, 29:2 (2001), 59–74.
95. Jean-Pierre Biondi, *Les Anticolonialistes (1881–1962)* (Robert Laffont, 1993), 70–1.
96. *L'illustration* 2959 (11 Nov. 1899), 308.
97. Potentially this is an issue that has never ceased to exercise historical debates; see A. Dirk Moses (ed.), *Empire, Colony, Genocide: Conquest, Occupation and Subaltern Resistance in World History* (Berghahn Books, 2008). For a structural explanation of extreme 'genocidal' violence see Ben Kiernan, *Blood and Soil: A World History of Genocide and Extermination from Sparta to Darfur* (Yale University Press, 2007).
98. Mahir Saul and Patrick Royer, *West African Challenge to Empire: Culture and History in the Volta-Bani Anticolonial War* (Ohio University Press, 2001), 23–9.
99. Ibid. 196–206. According to the authors, this campaign was the last to use demonstrative violence such as Voulet's.

Chapter 6 Conspiracy Theories and Scandals

1. 'Occasional Notes', *Pall Mall Gazette* (22 August 1899).
2. Odile Roynette, 'Les Conseils de guerre en temps de paix entre réforme et suppression (1898–1928)', *Vingtième Siècle. Revue d'histoire* 73 (Jan.–Mar. 2002), 51–66, esp. 52; Jean Marsil, *Réforme de la Justice militaire* (Stock, 1901).
3. The Dreyfus affaire has an immense historiography. See, for a concise introduction, Martin P. Johnson, *The Dreyfus Affair* (St Martin's Press,

1999); Eric Cahm, *The Dreyfus Affair in French Society and Politics* (Longman, 1996); Richard Griffiths, *The Use of Abuse: The Polemics of the Dreyfus Affair and Its Aftermath* (Berg, 1991).

4. George Barlow, *A History of the Dreyfus Case* (Simpkin, Marshall, Hamilton, 1899); Frederick Cornwallis Conybeare, *The Dreyfus Case* (G. Allen, 1898).
5. Émile Zola, *The Dreyfus Affair: 'J'Accuse' and Other Writings* (Yale University Press, 1996).
6. Stephen Wilson, *Ideology and Experience: Antisemitism in France at the Time of the Dreyfus Affair* (Associated University Presses, 1982).
7. Pierre Birnbaum, *Le Moment antisémite, un tour de France en 1898* (Fayard, 1998).
8. Jules Chanoine, *Examen critique et réfutation d'une relation de l'expédition de Chine en 1860 rédigée par le Lieutenant de vaisseau Pallu* (Dentu, 1864).
9. Joseph Reinach, *Histoire de l'Affaire Dreyfus*, 2 vols (Bouquins, 2006), ii. 190.
10. Ibid. i. 368–9.
11. Gen. Jules Chanoine, *Documents pour servir à l'histoire de l'Afrique occidentale française de 1895 a 1899, correspondance du capitaine Chanoine pendant l'expédition du Mossi et du Gourounsi, correspondance de la mission Afrique centrale* (n.p., 1901), 7.
12. AOM, Mission 110, Julien Chanoine, Journal de Marche.
13. AOM, Mission 11, Telegram, 13 Feb. 1899.
14. AOM, Afrique III, 37, 89, Kiladi, 2 Feb. 1899 to General de Trentinian.
15. Chanoine, *Documents pour servir à l'histoire*, 219, footnote.
16. *Le Matin*, 1 Oct. 1899.
17. AOM, Mission 110, Jules Chanoine to Col. Vinard, Lieutenant Governor, Soudan Français, 10 Sept. 1899.
18. AOM, Afrique III, Voulet to Minister, 'Rapport' from Tibiri, 1 Mar. 1899, 10.
19. *Le Petit Journal*, Friday, 6 Oct. 1899.
20. With the exception of J. P. Daughton, 'A Colonial Affair? Dreyfus and the French Empire', *Historical Reflections* 31:3 (2005), 469–83.
21. Allan Mitchell, 'The Xenophobic Style: French Counterespionage and the Emergence of the Dreyfus Affair', *Journal of Modern History* 52:3 (1980), 414–25.
22. AGMAFr, Diaire de Ouagadougou, 26 July 1901.
23. Christopher Forth, *The Dreyfus Affair and the Crisis of Victorian Manhood* (Johns Hopkins University Press, 2006).
24. Hélia Vigné d'Octon, *La Vie et l'oeuvre de Paul Vigné d'Octon* (imp de Causse, sd. *c.*1950), 46–9.

25. Jean-Pierre Biondi, *Les Anticolonialistes, 1881–1962* (Robert Laffont, 1993), 55.
26. John Hobson, *Imperialism: A Study*, 1st edn ([1902], Cosmo, 2003); V. I. Lenin, *Imperialism: The Highest Stage of Capitalism* (International Publishers, 1939). See the debates in John Cunningham Wood, 'J. A. Hobson and British Imperialism', *American Journal of Economics and Sociology* 42:4 (Oct. 1983), 483–500.
27. William D. Irvine, *Between Justice and Politics: The League des Droits de l'Homme, 1898–1945* (Stanford University Press, 2006; Jean-Pierre Machelon, *La république contre les libertés? Les restrictions aux libertés publiques de 1876 à 1914* (Presses de la fondation Nationale des Sciences Politiques, 1976), 9–13.
28. Victor Basch, *Le Deuxième procès Dreyfus, Rennes dans la Tourmente*, ed. Françoise Basch and André Hélard (Berg International, 2003).
29. Walter Benjamin certainly regarded Boulanger and other romantic figures as prototypes of fascist leaders. See *Arcades Project* (Harvard University Press, 2000).
30. Félix Rocquain, 'La Mission Marchand à l'Académie des Sciences Morales et Politiques', *Questions Coloniales et Diplomatiques* (15 May 1899), 77–87.
31. AOM, Afrique III, 37, 28, Delcassé to Minister of Colonies, July 1898.
32. Gabriel Hanotaux, *Le Partage de l'Afrique: Fachoda* (Flammarion, 1909); Guy de la Batut, *Fachoda ou le renversement des alliances* (Gallimard, 1932), 195–6; Paul Webster, *Fachoda: la bataille pour le Nil* (Edition du Félin, 2001).
33. The news of the Boer War reached Soudan in October 1899; AOM, Mission 110, 27 Oct. 1899, Angeli to Pallier.
34. Chanoine, *Documents pour servir à l'histoire*, 7.
35. AOM, Afrique III, 38, 71, Interpellation Vicomte de Montfort, 19 Oct. 1899.
36. AOM, Afrique III, 38, 74, note for the minister, 9 Nov. 1899.
37. AOM, Afrique III, 38, 132, *L'Éclair*.
38. Robert E. Kaplan, 'Making Sense of the Rennes Verdict: The Military Dimension of the Dreyfus Affair', *Journal of Contemporary History* 34:4 (1999), 499–515.
39. 'La Dislocation du Soudan français', *Questions Diplomatiques et Coloniales* (1 Oct. 189), 8:157–8; in the archives see AOM, GGA AOF/VII/4 Dislocation du Soudan.
40. *Instruction pour l'établissement de la statistique médicale des troupes coloniales stationnées aux colonies* (Imprimerie Nationale, 1902).
41. AOM, Mission 110, Minister of Colonies to GGA, April 1900.

42. This is not as surprising as it may seem since medical expertise played a very limited role in French courts at that time. Frédéric Chauvaud, *Les Experts du crime: la médecine légale en France au xixème siècle* (Aubier, 2000), 40–3.
43. AAOF H 45, Yellow Fever, 'bulletins sanitaire et avis de décès'. The epidemic was extremely serious and decimated the settler community, killing 196 white people in August alone.
44. AOM, Afrique III, 38, 2, report on the circumstances of the death of Lieutenant-Colonel Klobb.
45. Ibid.
46. AOM, Afrique III, 38bis, 96, Coded message sent by the commander of British forces in Lakaya to colonial office, passed to the French embassy.
47. AOM, Mission 110, 2, enquiry, GGA, 17 April 1900, Dakar.
48. Marc Pallier, 'Journal de route', in *Sous les Drapeaux 1870–1939, première partie 1870–1900* (Mémoire du Canton de Nieul, 2006).
49. AOM, Mission 49, St Louis, 'Rapport des conclusions Laborie', GGA to Minister, 4 Oct. 1901.
50. Ibid.
51. AOM, Mission 49, *Journal Officiel*, 1900, 2967, cols. I and II.
52. AOM, Afrique III, 37 b, 117, report of the verbal exchange between the minister and the deputy Maurice Faine on 4 July 1899.
53. This interview was then covered in all the major newspapers. See *The Times*, 28 Aug. 1899, 3.
54. *Pall Mall Gazette*, 13 Nov. 1899, 8.
55. Klobb's widow obtained that her husband should be buried in Timbuktu as instructed in his private papers. She opposed any attempt to use Klobb's memory in the political tug of war of the period. AOM, Afrique III, 38 C, Inhumation de Klobb.
56. See *Estafette*, 15 Oct. 1899; 3 Mar. 1899; 9 Nov. 1899; *Écho de Paris*, 25 Sept. 1899; 4 Oct. 1899; 21–3 Oct. 1899; *Éclair*, 12 Sept. 1899; *Intransigeant*, 14 Oct. 1900.
57. AOM, Mission 110, 22 May 1903.
58. AOM, Afrique III, 41, 178. Le Provost de Tauroy to Minister of Colonies.
59. *Journal Officiel* (1900), 2268–71.
60. AOM, Mission 110, Jules Chanoine to Vinard, 29 Sept. 1899.
61. AOM, Mission 110, Papiers Voulet, Chanoine to Voulet, 12 March 1899.
62. AOM, Mission 110, 123, Voulet papers, 30 June 1899.
63. AOM, Afrique III, 38 bis, 22 Nov. 1899. Report from Dahomey, Lieutenant Viola, and Captain Cornu.
64. AOM, Mission 110, various letters to Gallifet, Minister of War, 21 Nov. 1899; 1 Dec. 1902 to General André, Minister of War; to the Minister of Justice, 8 Feb. 1903.

65. AOM, Mission 110, 'Rapport Joalland', report on the circumstances of the Death of Lieutenant-Colonel Klobb, 15 Aug. 1899.
66. Bertrand Taithe, *Citizenship and Wars* (Routledge, 2001), 138.
67. Chanoine, *Documents pour servir à l'histoire*, 14.
68. Tane to Jules Chanoine, 30 Sept. 1899, in Chanoine, *Documents pour servir à l'histoire*, p. xlix.
69. Lieutenant Colonel Gouraud to Jules Chanoine, 19 Oct. 1899, ibid. p. li.
70. Ibid. p. lvii.
71. Ibid. lxii–lxvi.
72. General Joalland, *Le Drame de Dankori: mission Voulet–Chanoine, mission Joalland–Meynier* (Argo, 1930).
73. AOM, Afrique III, 38, 137, Agence Havas, 11 Sept. 1900.
74. AOM, Afrique III, 38c, Klobb's grave.
75. J-P. Olivier de Sardan, *Les Sociétés Songhay-Zarma: chefs, guerriers, esclaves, paysans* (Karthala, 1984), 148–53.
76. AOM, Mission 49, 149 Rapport du ministre Doumergue.
77. AOM, Mission 110, GGA AOF, to Minister of Colonies, Rapport Laborie, Sept. 1902.

Chapter 7 From the *Heart of Darkness* to Twenty-First-Century Guilt

1. Robert Delavignette, *Soudan, Paris, Bourgogne* (Bernard Grasset, 1935), 65.
2. Bernard Mouralis and Anne Piriou (dir.), with the collaboration of Romuald Fonkoua, *Robert Delavignette, savant et politique, 1897–1976* (Kartala, 2003).
3. See Gisèle Bergmann, 'Quand la chair s'y met: approche phénomènologique de la rencontre entre civilisés et non-civilisés dans la littérature coloniale, 1870–1914', Doctoral thesis, University of Bayreuth, 2000.
4. Trans-Sahara expeditions of the 1920s were filmed, in particular the propaganda *croisière Noire* of 1925. See Peter J. Bloom, *French Colonial Documentary, Mythologies of Humanitarianism* (Minnesota University Press, 2008), 65–93.
5. Albert Londres, *Terre d'ébène* ([1929] Le Serpent à Plumes, 1998), 68.
6. *Libération*, mercredi 4 Oct. 2006, Christophe Ayad and Thomas Hofnung, 'L'hommage rendu à Brazza fait débat au Congo', and Blandine Flipo, ' "n'y avait-il pas une autre urgence" les congolais protestent contre le coût exorbitant du mausolée.'
7. Robert Aldrich, *Vestiges of Empire in France* (Palgrave, 2004).
8. Dana S. Hale, *Races on Display, French Representations of Colonized Peoples, 1886–1940* (Indiana University Press, 2008), 51–3. Patricia A.

Morton, 'National and Colonial: The Musée Des Colonies at the Colonial Exposition, Paris, 1931', *Art Bulletin* 80 (1998), 357–77.

9. Peter Mark, 'The Future of African Art in Parisian Public Museums', *African Arts* 33:3 (Autumn 2000), 1–93.
10. Serge Chalon et al., *De l'Esclavage aux réparations, comité devoir de mémoire* (Karthala, 2000).
11. See Marc Ferro (ed.), *Le Livre noir du colonialisme: XVIe-XXIe siècle : de l'extermination à la repentance* (Robert Laffont, 2003).
12. Daniel Rivet, 'Le Fait colonial et nous. Histoire d'un éloignement', *Vingtième Siècle. Revue d'histoire* 33 (Jan.–Mar. 1992), 127–38.
13. http://www.culture.gouv.sn/article.php3?id_article=313; *Le Monde*, 12 Nov. 1998.
14. See http://www.tirailleursenegalais.com/
15. Jonah Raskin '*Heart of Darkness*: The Manuscript Revisions', *Review of English Studies* NS, 18:69 (Feb. 1967), 30–9; William Atkinson, 'Bound in "Blackwood's": The Imperialism of the "*Heart of Darkness*" in Its Immediate Context', *Twentieth Century Literature* 50:4 (Winter 2004), 368–93.
16. Chinua Achebe, 'An Image of Africa, Racism in Conrad's *Heart of Darkness*', in *Hopes and Impediments* (New York: Doubleday, 1989), 1–20.
17. Hunt Hawkins, 'Conrad's Critique of Imperialism in *Heart of Darkness*', *PMLA* 94:2 (Mar. 1979), 286–99.
18. Paul Vigné d'Octon, *Chair Noire* (Alphonse Lemerre, 1889). See Jennifer Yee, 'Malaria and the Femme Fatale: Sex and Death in French Colonial Africa', *Literature and Medicine*, 21:1 (2002), 201–15.
19. See Bergmann, 'Quand la Chair', 25–8.
20. Georges Clemenceau, *Le Grand Pan* (Charpentier, 1896), 20.
21. See Francis Barker, Peter Hulme, and Margaret Ivasen (eds), *Cannibalism and the Colonial World* (Cambridge University Press, 1998).
22. Lt. Col. Parfait-Louis Monteil, *De Saint Louis à Tripoli par le lac Tchad voyage au travers du Soudan et du Sahara pendant les années 1890-1-2* (Felix Alcan, 1894), 7.
23. See Homi Bhabha, 'Of Mimicry and Man', in Frederick Cooper and Ann Laura Stoler (eds), *Tensions of Empire, Colonial Cultures in a Bourgeois World* (University of California Press, 1997), 152–60.
24. See Michal Tymowski, *L'Armée et la formation des états en Afrique occidentale au XIXe siècle—essai de comparaison, l'état de Samori et le Kenedougou* (Wydawnicta Uniwersytetu Warszawkiego, 1987), to see the relationship between war, military, and state building in late African states.
25. Dr Marie, 'La folie à la légion étrangère', *Revue blanche* 26 (1902), 401–20; Dr Louis Catrin, *Aliénation mentale dans l'armée* (Rueff, 1901);

Marius Antoine Cavasse, *Les dégénérés dans l'armée coloniale*, Thèse de la faculté de médecine, Bordeaux, 1903. Also see Jean-Marie Lundy, 'Mémoire de criminologie appliqué à l'expertise médicale, Le Traitement pénal dans l'armée Française sous la troisième république', Université René Descartes, Droit Medical, (1987), 34.

26. See AOF, H 26 and Archives Nationales du Sénégal H 209.
27. Ruth Harris, *Murders and Madness: Medicine, Law and Society in the Fin-de-Siècle* (Clarendon Press, 1989).
28. Frédéric Chauvaud, *Les Experts du crime: la médecine légale en France au xixe siècle* (Aubier, 2000), 137–8.
29. See Bertrand Taithe, *Citizenships and Wars* (Routledge, 2001); Louis Nathaniel Rossel, *Mémoires et correspondance de Louis Rossel*, preface by Victor Margueritte with a biography by Isabella Rossel (P. V. Stock, 1908); Édith Thomas, *Rossel 1844–1871* (Gallimard, 1967).
30. Antoine Tshitongu Kongolo, 'L'étonnante aventure de Blackland', in Jules Verne, *L'étonnante Aventure de la Mission Barsac*, 2 vols (L'Harmattan, 2005), i.13–21.
31. AAOF, 15 G 231, 20 Aug. 1899, 'Rapport' in favour of establishing print works in Soudan, 20 August 1899.
32. The key text is the one issued by the Paris société d'Anthropologie, *Instructions pour le Sénégal par messieurs Isidore Geoffroy St Hilaire, de Castelnau et P. Broca* (Bennyer, 1860).
33. Octave Meynier, *Les conquérants du Tchad* (Flammarion, 1922), 154; General Joalland, *Le Drame de Dankori: mission Voulet–Chanoine, mission Joalland–Meynier* (Argo, 1930), 53.
34. Joalland, *Drame de Dankori*, 58.
35. Ibid. 64.
36. Abdoulaye Mamani, *Sarranouia: le drame de la reine magicienne* (L'Harmattan, 1980), 1.
37. See Antoinette Tidjani Alou, 'Sarraounia et ses intertextes: Identité, intertextualité et émergence littéraire', *Sudlang* 5 (2005), 44–70.
38. Mamani, *Sarranouia*, 9.
39. Halima Handane and Isabelle Colin, *Sarranouia: La reine magicienne du Niger* (Cavis Eden, 2004). The story, although checked for accuracy by Professor Boube Gado of the university Abdou Moumouni of Niamey, follows closely Mamani's version, including the presumed age of la Sarranouia as a young witch queen.
40. See http://whc.unesco.org/en/tentativelists/5046/. Lougou itself is now depopulated and subject to development initiatives: see http://www.tarbiyya-tatali.org/?Lougou-and-Saraouniya
41. Joalland, *Drame de Dankori*, 105.

42. AGMAfr, Voillard, 224. Mgr Thévenoud himself travelled all the way to Vincennes with White Fathers, Sisters, and young women of the *ouvroirs*. The carpets did not sell.
43. See Patricia A. Morton, *Colonial Modernities: Architecture and Representation at the 1931 Colonial Exposition, Paris* (MIT University Press, 2000).
44. The survivors like Meynier and Reibell were the most conspicuous propagandists of the colonial legend; see for instance General Reibell, *Cinq étoiles à notre firmament imperial: Sidi Brahim, Camerone, Fachoda, Prise de Samory, conquête du Tchad* (Raoul et Jean Brunon, 1943).
45. AOM, Afrique III, 38, 65. Until the reception of Pallier's full account on 14 October 1899 the doubt remained.
46. See *Intermédiaire des chercheurs et des curieux*, 15 Oct. 1933, 96, col. 717; Franz Toussaint, *Moi, le mort . . .* (Albin Michel, 1930).
47. See *Intermédiaire des chercheurs et des curieux*, 15 Oct. 1934, 97, col 108.
48. Muriel Mathieu, *La Mission Afrique Centrale* (L'Harmattan, 1995), originally a doctoral thesis of Toulouse in 1975.
49. Jean-Claude Simoen, *Les Fils de rois : le crépuscule sanglant de l'aventure africaine* (Lattès, 1996).
50. Jean-François Alata, *Les Colonnes de feu* (L'Harmattan, 1996).
51. http://lmsi.net/article.php3?id_article=365
52. Hannah Arendt, *On Violence* (Harvest Books, 1970), 65.
53. http://www.niger-tourisme.com/liste_offres_det.php?id=42& id_voy=1, seen 12 July 2007.
54. The first tourists to mention the graves include M. I. Roserot de Melin, *Dans la région du Tchad avec la mission Tilho* (*Le Tour du Monde*, 1909), 421–32, esp. 426.
55. General Gouraud, *Zinder Tchad, souvenirs d'un Africain* (Plon, 1944), 15–17.
56. Adeline Masquelier, 'Road Mythographies: Space, Mobility and the Historical Imagination in Postcolonial Niger', *American Ethnologist* 29:4 (2002), 829–56, esp. 830.

Chapter 8 Conclusion: Traumatized Perpetrators?

1. Octave Meynier, *Les Conquérants du Tchad* (Flammarion, 1922), 164.
2. General Joalland, *Le Drame de Dankori: mission Voulet–Chanoine, mission Joalland–Meynier* (Argo, 1930), 99.
3. This classification, known as DSM-III, has been the subject of numerous debates and has been roundly criticized as a political exercise; yet PTSD has now acquired almost universal currency. See A. Young, *The Harmony of Illusion: Inventing PTSD* (Princeton University Press, 1995); for a

French critical perspective see D. Fassin and Richard Rechtman, *L'Empire du traumatisme, enquète sur la condition de victime* (Flammarion, 2007), 136–9; Louis Crocq, *Les Traumatismes psychiques de guerre* (Odile Jacob, 1999), 11–30; Chris R. Brewin, *Post-Traumatic Stress Disorder: Malady or Myth?* (Yale University Press, 2003), 10–22.

4. Claudia Herbert and Ann Wetmore, *Overcoming Traumatic Stress* (Robinson, 1999), 3–4.
5. This follows the theories of Sandor Ferenczi published in 1933 and 1934; see *Le Traumatisme* (Payot, 2006), 33–9.
6. See for instance *The Times* coverage of the Klobb murder on 22, 23, and 24 August 1899.
7. Ever since the 1880s the debate between social and biological explanations for psychosis has raged even if heredity has been replaced by genetic factors. For a firmly socio-cultural revisionist approach see Warren Larkin and Anthony P. Morrison (eds), *Trauma and Psychosis: New Directions for Theory and Therapy* (Routledge, 2006).
8. Robert Lifton, *Home from the War: Learning from Vietnam Veterans* (Beacon Press, 1973); as Fassin and Rechtman analysed it following Young this explanation has led to the idea that trauma should be the normal response to abnormal situations. Also see Kendrick Oliver, 'Atrocity, Authenticity and American Exceptionalism: (Ir)rationalizing the Massacre of My Lai', *Journal of American History* 37:2 (2003), 247–68; and Kendrick Oliver, *The My Lai Massacre in American History and Memory* (Manchester University Press, 2005).
9. Data on post-traumatic stress disorder among veterans has shown that participating in atrocities led to PTSD; see Brewin, *Post-Traumatic Stress Disorder*, 49.
10. Ronald Paulson, *Sin and Evil: Moral Values in Literature* (Yale University Press, 2007), 212–13.
11. On mental illnesses and French courts see Michel Foucault, *Moi, Pierre Rivière* (Folio, 1994); Ann-Louise Shapiro, *Breaking the Codes: Female Criminality in Fin-de-siècle Paris* (Stanford University Press, 1996); R. Harris, *Murders and Madness: Medicine, Law and Society in the Fin-de-Siècle* (Oxford University Press, 1989); R. Nye, *Crime, Madness and Politics in Modern France: The Medical Concept of National Decline* (Princeton University Press, 1984).
12. See Bertrand Taithe, *Citizenship and Wars* (Routledge, 2001), 126.
13. Hannah Arendt, *On Violence* (Harvest Books, 1970), 53.
14. Didier Fassin and Patrice Bourdelais (eds), *Les Constructions de l'Intolérable: Études d'anthropologie et d'histoire sur les frontières de l'espace moral* (La Découverte, 2005).

15. Norman Fiering 'Irresistible Compassion: An Aspect of Eighteenth Century Sympathy and Humanitarianism', *Journal of the History of Ideas* 37:2 (1976), 195–218; Roy Porter (ed.), *Rewriting the Self* (Routledge, 1997); Gregory Eiselein, *Literature and Humanitarian Reform in the Civil War Era* (Indiana University Press, 1996). On anti-slavery movements and their effectiveness see T. L. Haskell, 'Capitalism and the Origins of the Humanitarian Sensibility', Parts 1 & 2, *American Historical Review* 90:2 (April 1985), 339–61; (June 1985), 547–66; D. B. Davis, J. Ashworth, and T. L. Haskell, in the forum of the *American Historical Review* 92:4 (October 1987), 813–28.
16. See Bertrand Taithe, in Fay Bound (ed.), *Medicine and Emotion* (Palgrave, 2005); also Bertrand Taithe, 'Horror, Abjection and Compassion: From Dunant to Compassion Fatigue', *New Formations* 62:1 (2007), 123–36.
17. Thomas Laqueur, 'Bodies, Details and the Humanitarian Narrative', in Lynn Hunt (ed.), *The New Cultural History* (University Press of California, 1989), 176–204.
18. Alain Gerard, 'Action Humanitaire et Pouvoir Politique: l'Engagement des médecins Lillois au XiXe siècle', *Revue du Nord* 332 (1999), 817–36; it is in this sense that one encounters the term later on: Elizabeth Darling, 'To Induce Humanitarian Sentiments in Prurient Londoners: The Propaganda Activity in London Voluntary Housing Associations in the Inter-War Period', *London Journal* 27:1 (2002), 42–62.
19. Serge Audier, *Léon Bourgeois, fonder la solidarité* (Michalon, 2007).
20. Jean Marsil, *Réforme de la Justice militaire* (Stock, 1901), 30–1.
21. See C. de Martens, *Causes Célèbres du Droit des Gens* (Brockhaus, 1827); Robert Plumer Ward, *A Treatise of the Relative Rights and Duties of Belligerent and Neutral Powers* (J. Butterworth, 1801); *Bibliography of International Humanitarian Law, Applicable in Armed Conflict* (International Committee of the Red Cross and Henry Dunant Institute, 1980); Geoffrey Best, *War and Law since 1945* (Oxford University Press, 1994); Michael Howard (ed.), *Restraints on War: Studies in the Limitation of Armed Conflict* (Oxford University Press, 1979); G. I. Draper, 'Humanitarianism in the Modern Law of Armed Conflicts', *International Relations* 8:4 (1985), 380–96; Jacques Meurant, 'Inter Arma Caritas: Evolution and Nature of International Humanitarian Law', *Journal of Peace Research* 24:3 (1987), 237–49.
22. Conférence internationale pour étudier les moyens de pourvoir à l'insuffisance du service sanitaire dans les armées en campagne, 26–9 Oct. 1863, Geneva; Henry Dunant, *La Charité sur les champs de bataille, suites du 'Souvenir de Solferino' et résultats de la Conférence internationale de Genève* (n.p., 1864); John F. Hutchinson, *Champions of Charity*

(Westview Press, 1996); Martin Gumpert, *Dunant, the Story of the Red Cross* (Oxford University Press, 1938).

23. Article I, Hague Convention, 1899.
24. Jean Pictet, *Development and principles of International Humanitarian Law* (Henry Dunant Institute, 1985).
25. Andrew Porter, 'Roger Casement and the International Humanitarian Movement', *Journal of Imperial amd Commonwealth History*, 29:2 (2001), 59–74; Kevin Grant, *A Civilised Savagery* (Routledge, 2005).
26. H. Pensa, 'Budget du ministêre des colonies pour 1899', *Questions Diplomatiques et Coloniales* (1 Feb. 1899), 158–60.
27. Daniel Pick, *War Machine: The Rationalisation of Slaughter in the Modern Age* (Yale University Press, 1996).
28. See Jennifer Karns Alexander, *The Mantra of Efficiency: from Waterwheel to Social Control* (Johns Hopkins University Press, 2008), 144–7.
29. Michel Foucault, *Discipline and Punish* (Allan Lane, 1977); Michael Ignatieff, *A Just Measure of Pain* (Columbia University Press, 1980).
30. *Les Mémoires du sergent Bourgogne* (Arléa, 1992).
31. On My Lai there is a considerable literature: Seymour Hersh, *My Lai 4: A report on the Massacre and Its Aftermath* (Random House, 1970); Michael Belknap, *The Vietnam War on Trial: The My Lai Massacre and the Court-Martial of Lieutenant Calley* (University Press of Kansas, 2002).
32. AOM, Mission 110, 'Rapport Pallier', 15 August 1899.
33. Herbert C. Kelman and Lee Hamilton, *Cultures of Obedience: Towards a Social Psychology of Authority and Responsibility* (Yale University Press, 1989), 94.
34. Colonel Gouraud, *Zinder, Tchad, Souvenirs d'un Africain* (Plon, 1944), 219.
35. AOM, Mission 49, St Louis, 'Rapport des conclusions Laborie', GGA to Minister, 4 Oct. 1901.
36. AOM, Mission 110, Report from Kirtachi, 6 Nov. 1899.
37. AOM, Mission 110, Dubreuil to Voulet, Say 23/02/98.
38. Joalland, *Le Drame de Dankori*, 85.
39. *L'Illustration* 2511 (11 April 1891), 312–13.

BIBLIOGRAPHY

All French and English titles were published in Paris and London, respectively, unless specified otherwise. Obviously redundant publication details, such as Oxford, Oxford University Press, have been simplified to, for example, 'Oxford University Press'.

Texts written before 1945

Alis, Henry, *Nos Africains, la mission Crampel, la mission Dybowski* (Bibliothèque Nationale, 1894).

Allard, Rémi Victor, *Dissertation sur la nostalgie* (Didot Jeune, 1820).

Analoni, L. V., *De la nostalgie ou de la maladie du pays* (n.p., 1837).

Baratier, Colonel, *'Épopées africaines* (Perrin, 1913).

Barnetche, Louis Jean, *Essai sur la nostagie* (Montpellier, 1831).

Beard, George M., *A Practical Treatise on Nervous Exhaustion (Neurasthenia)*, 4th edn (E. B. Treat, 1894).

Benoist de la Grandière, Auguste, *De la Nostalgie ou mal du pays* (Adrien Delahaye, 1873).

—— *Souvenirs de Campagne: Les Ports d'Extrême Orient*, Société Française d'histoire d'Outre Mer (L'Harmattan, [1869] 1994).

Bérenger Féraud, L. J. B., *Traité clinique des maladies des européens au sénégal*, 2 vols (Delahaye, 1875–8).

Bernard, J. E., *De l'Influence du climat de la Cochinchine sur les maladies des européens*, Thèse, Montpellier, 1867.

Besse, V. M., *De la Nostalgie* (n.p., 1828).

Blache, Emmanuel Eugène, *Dissertation sur la nostalgie* (n.p., 1860).

Blain, Joseph Casimir, *Essai sur la nostalgie* (1825).

Bolis, Sgt. Ernest, *Mes Campagnes en Afrique et en Asie, 1889–1899: légion étrangere infanterie de Marine* (Claude Gassmann ed. and pub., [1905] 2001).

Bonnetain, Raymonde, *Une Française au Soudan, sur la route de Tombouctou, du Sénégal au Niger* (Paris, 1894).

Bordeaux, Henry, *L'Épopée noire: la France en Afrique Occidentale* (Denoël et Steele, 1936).

Boudet, F., *Dissertation médicale sur la nostalgie* (Montpellier, 1814).
Bourgogne, Sergent, *Les Mémoires du sergent Bourgogne* (Arléa, 1992).
Bouton, Eugène (Jean Rode) 'Un regard sur le Soudan', *La Revue Blanche* 20 (1899), 321–30.
Bouviet, Pierre Camille, *De la Nostalgie ou Mal du pays* (n.p., 1837).
Briet, Pierre Urbain, *Essai sur la Nostalgie* (n.p., 1832).
Brochet, A. R. H., *Souvenirs médicaux d'une campagne au Gabon* (n.p., 1887).
Bureau-Rabinière, J. B., *Dissertation sur la nostalgie* (n.p., 1823).
Buret, F., and M. A. Legrand, *Les Troupes coloniales: maladies du soldat aux pays chauds* (J. B. Baillière et fils, 1897).
Caine, Claudius, *Essai sur la nostalgie* (n.p., 1852).
Cassagnou, J., *Étude sur le logement des troupes européennes dans les colonies tropicales* (Firmin, 1887).
Castelnau, C., *Considérations sur la nostalgie* (n.p., 1806).
de Catilho Beneto, Jose Felicieno, *Dissertation sur la Nostalgie* (n.p., 1831).
Catrin, Dr Louis, *Aliénation mentale dans l'armée* (Rueff, 1901).
Cavasse, Marius Antoine, *Les Dégénérés dans l'armée coloniale*, Thèse de la faculté de médecine, Bordeaux, n.p., 1903.
Chanoine, Gen. Charles Sulpice Jules, *Documents pour servir à l'histoire de l'Afrique occidentale française de 1895 a 1899, correspondance du capitaine Chanoine pendant l'expédition du Mossi et du Gourounsi, correspondance de la mission Afrique centrale* (n.p., 1901).
Chanoine, Julien, 'Mission Voulet-Chanoine, itinéraire du capitaine Chanoine', *Bulletin de la Société de Géographie* 20 (1899), 221–79.
Charlopin, Ch. E., *Considération sur la dysenterie des pays chauds* (n.p., 1868).
Ciccarelli, Jacques Antoine, *Coup d'oeil sur les passions en général suivi de quelques proposition sur la nostalgie* (n.p., 1837).
Clamel, Bertrand, *Dissertation sur la nostalgie* (n.p., 1836).
Clemenceau, Georges, *Le Grand Pan* (Imprimerie Nationale, [Charpentier, 1896] 1995).
Colin, Charles, *Le Soudan occidental* (Berger Levrault, 1883).
Collin, Téophile François, *Considérations sur la nostalgie* (n.p., 1832).
Cussac, Father, *L'Apôtre de l'Ouganda, le père Lourdel* (Grands Lacs, *c.*1920).
D'Aufreville, M. L., 'La Renaissance coloniale de la France', *Revue Politique et Parlementaire* 19 (1899), 332–50.
de la Batut, Guy, *Fachoda ou le renversement des alliances* (Gallimard, 1932).
Delavignette, Robert, *Soudan, Paris, Bourgogne* (Bernard Grasset, 1935).

Devic, Oscar, *La Nostalgie ou mal du pays* (n.p., 1855).
Ducrost de Longerie, L., *Dissertation sur la Nostalgie* (n.p., 1815).
Duret, J. H. M., *Essai sur la nostalgie* (n.p., 1830).
Ferenczi, Sandor, *Le Traumatisme* (Payot, [1933] 2006).
Florence, I. N. C. A., *Dissertation sur la nostalgie* (n.p., 1814).
Fonssagrives, Jean-Baptiste, *Traité d'hygiène navale ou de l'influence des conditions physiques et morales dans lesquelles l'homme de mer est appelé à vivre* (J. B. Baillière, 1856).
Foureau, Fernand, *D'Alger au Congo par le Tchad par F. Foureau* (Masson, 1902).
Fraisse, Charles, *De la Nostalgie* (Firmin Didot, 1833).
Fritsch-Lang, Eugene, *La Nostalgie du Soldat* (Jouaust, 1876).
Fromentin, Eugène, *Un Été dans le Sahara* [1856] and *Une année dans le Sahel* [1858] (Plon, 1912).
Gaillard, E. A., *Considérations sur la nostalgie* (Paris, 1804).
Gallieni, Commandant, *Deux Campagnes au Soudan Français, 1886–1888* (Hachette, 1891).
Garnier, E., *Hygiène de l'européen à la Guyane française* (n.p., 1880).
Gatelet, Lieutenant *Histoire de la conquête du Soudan Français (1878–1899)* (Berger Levrault, 1901).
Geit, Charles François, *Quelques considérations sur la nature de la nostalgie, ses causes et son traitement* (n.p., 1874).
Girard, Henry, *Éssai de topographie médicale de Sainte-Marie de Madagascar* (Cabirou Frères, 1887).
Gochet, Alexis-Marie, *La Traite des nègres et la croisade africaine*, 2nd edn (Ch. Poussielgne, 1889).
—— *La Barbarie africaine et l'action civilisatrice des missions catholiques au Congo* (Dessain, 1889).
Gohier, Urbain, Foreword to Paul Vigné d'Octon, *La Gloire du Sabre*, 4th edn (Flammarion, 1900).
Gouraud, Colonel, *Zinder, Tchad, Souvenirs d'un Africain* (Plon, 1944).
Grant, Charles Scovell, *Petit Guide Pratique de l'Ouest Africain* (C. Doin, 1893).
Gucicard, A. A., *Quelques considérations diverses sur la basse Cochinchine* (Montpellier, 1873).
Guerbois, Denis, *Essai sur la nostalgie* (n.p., 1803).
Guillaumet, Edouard, *Tableaux Soudanais* (Flammarion, 1899).
Gumpert, Martin, *Dunant, The Story of the Red Cross* (Oxford University Press, 1938).
Hanotaux, Gabriel, *Le Partage de l'Afrique: Fachoda* (Flammarion, 1909).
Heumann, Capitaine, *Le Soudan, Gordon et le Mahdi* (Charles Lavauzelle, 1886).

Houdebine and Bounier, *Le Capitaine Joubert* (Grands Lacs, s.d.).
Huet, Bienville, and Joseph Vincent, *Dissertation sur la nostalgie* (n.p., 1821).
Hulot, Baron, 'Rapport', *Bulletin de la société de Géographie* (1900), T 1: 197–206.
Huot, Louis, and Paul Voivenel, *Le Cafard* (Grasset, 1918).
Huysp Buisson, J., *Considérations sur la nostalgie* (n.p., 1818).
Hydaspes, *The Truth about the Indian Army and Its Officers with Reference to the French Local Army of Algeria* (Simpkin, Marshall and Co., 1861).
Jacquier, François, *Dissertation sur la nostalgie* (n.p., 1821).
Jalabert, J. J. L. A., *Essai sur la Nostalgie* (Montpellier: n.p., 1827).
Joalland, Gen. Paul, *Le Drame de Dankori: Mission Voulet-Chanoine; mission Joalland-Meynier* (Argo, 1930).
Jousset, A., *Traité de l'acclimatement et de l'acclimatation* (Octave Doin, 1884).
Klobb, Arsène, *Dernier carnet de route au Soudan Français* (Flammarion, 1905).
Lachard, *Dissertation sur la nostalgie* (n.p., 1808).
Lachaume, Auguste, *Essai sur la nostalgie* (n.p., 1833).
Lacordaire, François Joseph, *Essai sur la nostalgie* (n.p., 1837).
——*L'esclavage Africain: conférence sur l'esclavage dans le haut Congo* (Siège de la société anti-esclavagiste, 1888).
Lavigerie, Charles Martial Allemand de, *L'Armée et la Mission de la France en Afrique* (A. Jourdan, 1875).
Layet, Alexandre, *La Santé des européens entre les tropiques, leçons d'hygiène et de médecine sanitaire coloniale* (Félix Alcan, 1906).
Le Bon, Gustave, *The Crowd: A Study of the Popular Mind* (Macmillan, [1895] 1996).
Lebon, André, *La Politique de la France en Afrique, 1896–98, Mission Marchand, Niger, Madagascar* (Plon, 1901).
Legrand, M. A., *L'hygiène des troupes européennes* (Charles Lavauzelle, 1893).
Leroy-Beaulieu, Paul, *Le Sahara, Le Soudan et les Chemins de Fer Transahariens* (Guillaumin, 1904).
——*De la Colonisation chez les peuples modernes* (Guillaumin, 1874).
Livret du Soldat—modèle 1897 No 30, annexe du décret du 14 janvier 1889 modifié par la note ministérielle du 9 novembre 1890 (Imprimerie Nationale, 1897).
Londres, Albert, *Terre d'ébène* (Le Serpent à Plumes, [1929] 1998).
Lourde Seilliès, P. M., *Considérations générales sur la nostalgie* (n.p., 1804).
Lyautey, Hubert, *Le Rôle social de l'officier,* (Perrin, 1892).

——*Le Rôle colonial de l'armée* (Armand Colin, 1900).
Mangin, Charles, *La Force noire* (Hachette, 1910).
Marie, Dr, 'La Folie à la légion étrangère', *Revue blanche* 26 (1902), 401–20.
Marsil, Jean, *Réforme de la Justice militaire* (Stock, 1901).
de Martens, Charles, *Causes célèbres du droit des gens* (Brockhaus, 1827).
Martin, Gustave, 'L'Influence du climat tropical sur le psychique de l'européen', in *Les Grandes Endémies Tropicales, études de pathogénie et de prophylaxie* (Vigot, 1932), 101–15.
Martin, J. J. A., *Dissertation sur la nostalgie* (1820).
Masson, J. B. H., *De la Nostalgie considérée comme cause de plusieurs maladies* (Paris, 1825).
Meynier, Octave, *A' la recherche de Voulet, sur les traces sanglantes de la mission Afrique Centrale* (Cosmopole, 2001).
——*Mission Joalland Meynier,* Collection les grandes missions coloniales (Algiers 1947).
——*Les conquérants du Tchad* (Flammarion, 1923).
Mezin, J. P., *Durantin, Essai sur la nostalgie* (n.p., 1820).
Mitre, Hippolyte, *Essai sur la Nostalgie* (n.p., 1840).
Monteil, Parfait-Louis, *Les Conventions Franco-Anglaises des 14 juin 1898 et 21 mars 1899* (Plon Nourrit, 1899).
——*De Saint Louis a Tripoli par le lac Tchad voyage au travers du Soudan et du Sahara pendant les années 1890-1-2* (Felix Alcan, 1894).
——*Vade Mecum de l'officier d'infanterie de marine* (L. Baudoin et Cie, 1884).
Monteil, Charles, *Contes Soudanais* (Ernest Leroux, 1905).
Moreaud, Pierre, *Considérations sur la nostalgie* (n.p., 1829).
Morel, Edmund, 'The French in Western and Central Africa', *Journal of the Royal African Society* 1:2 (1902), 192–207.
Mutel, Alexandre, *De la Nostalgie* (n.p., 1849).
Nachtigal, Gustav, *Sahara and Sudan*, vol iii: *The Chad Basin and Bargirmi* (Hurst, 1987).
Navarre, Juste, *Manuel d'Hygiène colonial* (Doin, 1895).
Nicolas, A., *Manuel d'hygiène coloniale* (Chaillez, 1894).
Oppenheim, Max von, *Le Domaine tchadien de Rabah* (L'Harmattan, 2003).
Parron, J. R., *Essai sur la nostalgie* (n.p., 1851).
Paulinier, J. P. L., *Sur la* Nostalgie (n.p., 1837).
Pauquet, J. L. A., *Dissertation sur la nostalgie* (n.p., 1815).
Pensa, H., 'Budget du ministêre des colonies pour 1899', *Questions Diplomatiques et Coloniales* 1.2.(1899), 158–60.

Petit, L., 'Contribution à l'étude de l'agriculture de la zoobactérie, de l'hygiène et de la pathologie vétérinaire au Soudan Français (Haut Sénégal et Haut Niger)' unpublished manuscript, book III, p. 95. AOM, Soudan, II.
Pichez, E., *De la Dysenterie endémique en Cochinchine* (n.p., 1870).
Pillement, G. L. V., *Essai sur la nostalgie* (n.p., 1831).
Poisson, Eugène, *Dissertation sur la nostalgie* (n.p., 1836).
Puel, J. A. Edmond, *De la Nostalgie* (n.p., 1822).
Quennec, A., *Guide médical à l'usage des explorateurs* (L. Murer, 1897).
Reibell, Commandant, *Le Commandant Lamy d'après sa correspondance et ses souvenirs de campagne, 1858–1900* (Hachette, 1903).
——*Cinq étoiles à notre firmament imperial: Sidi Brahim, Camerone, Fachoda, Prise de Samory, conquête du Tchad* (Raoul et Jean Brunon, 1943).
Reibell, General *Carnet de Route de la Mission Saharienne Foureau–Lamy* (Plon, 1931).
Reynal, M., *Dissertation sur la nostalgie* (n.p., 1819).
Reynaud, G., *Hygiène coloniale, II. Hygiène des colons* (J. B. Baillière, 1903).
Ringnet, Adjudant, *Épée, Fleuret, Manuel pratique du Combat suivi du code du duel*, préfaces de Paul Vigné d'Octon, E. D'Hauterive, Dr de Pradel (Henri Charles Lavauzelle, 1905).
Colonel Robin, *L'Insurrection de la Grande Kabylie en 1871* (Henri Charles Lavauzelle, 1900).
Roserot de Melin, M. I., 'Dans la région du Tchad avec la mission Tilho', *Le Tour du Monde* (1909), 421–32.
Rossel, Louis Nathaniel, *Mémoires et correspondance de Louis Rossel*, preface by Victor Margueritte with a biography by Isabella Rossel (P. V. Stock, 1908).
Routh, C. H. F., *On Overwork and Premature Mental Decay* (Baillière, Tindall and Cox, 1886).
Saint-Vel, O., *Hygiène des européens dans les climats tropicaux, des créoles et des races colorées dans les pays tempérés* (Delahaye, 1872).
Sibree, James, 'General Gallieni's "Neuf Ans a Madagascar": An Example of French Colonization', *Journal of the Royal African Society* 8:31 (1909), 259–73.
Société d'Anthropologie, Paris, *Instructions pour le Sénégal par messieurs Isidore Geoffroy St Hilaire, de Castelnau et P. Broca* (Bennyer, 1860).
Tailhade, Louis, *Quelques considérations sur la nostalgie* (Ricard, 1850).
Terrier, Auguste, 'La Mission Joalland-Meynier', *Journal des Voyages* (1901).
Thenin, A. F. A., *Essai sur la Nostalgie* (Paris: n.p., 1810).
Toussaint, Franz, *Moi, le mort . . .* (Albin Michel, 1930).
Treille, Alcide-Marie, *Principes d'Hygiène coloniale* (Carré, 1899).

——*Note sur l'hygiène au Sénégal* (Masson, 1892).

Tunnel, V. F. L., *De la Dysentrie endémique en Cochinchine et au Tonkin*, Thèse, Montpellier, 1876.

Verne, Jules, *L'Étonnante Aventure de la Mission Barsac*, 2 vols (L'Harmattan, [1913] 2005).

Vigné d'Octon, Hélia, *La Vie et l'oeuvre de Paul Vigné d'Octon* (imp de Causse, sd. *c.*1950).

——*La Vie et l'amour: les doctrines freudiennes et la psychanalyse* (Édition de l'Idée Libre, 1934).

——*La Vérité sur les origines de l'homme* (Édition de l'Idée Libre, 1931).

Vigné d'Octon, Paul, *Chair noire, préface de Léon Cladel* (Alphonse Lemerre, 1889).

Vogüé, Melchior de, Préface to Lt Col. Parfait-Louis Monteil, *De Saint Louis à Tripoli par le lac Tchad voyage au travers du Soudan et du Sahara pendant les années 1890-1-2* (Félix Alcan, 1894), p. vi.

Voulet, Lieutenant, 'La Jonction du Soudan et du Dahomey, 1896–7', *Revue Générale des Sciences Pures et Appliquées* (1898), 895–6.

Ward, Robert Plumer, *A Treatise of the Relative Rights and Duties of Belligerent and Neutral Powers* (J. Butterworth, 1801).

Yvonneau, Jules, *Considérations médico-philosophiques sur la nostalgie* (n.p., 1821).

Sources written after 1945

Abrams, L., and D. J. Miller, 'Who Were the French Colonialists? A Reassessment of the Parti Colonial, 1890–1914', *Historical Journal* 19:3 (Sep. 1976), 685–725.

Achebe, Chinua, *Hopes and Impediments* (Doubleday, 1989).

Ageron, Charles Robert, *L'Anticolonialisme en France de 1871 à 1914* (Presses Universitaires de France, 1973).

——*France coloniale ou parti colonial?* (Armand Colin, 1970).

Alata, Jean-François, *Les Colonnes de feu* (L'Harmattan, 1996).

Aldrich, Robert, 'Colonial Man', in C. Forth and B. Taithe (eds), *French Masculinities* (Palgrave, 2007), 123–40.

——*Vestiges of the Colonial Empire in France* (Palgrave, 2005).

——*Colonialism and Homosexuality* (Routledge, 2003).

Alexander, Jennifer Karns, *The Mantra of Efficiency: From Waterwheel to Social Control* (Johns Hopkins University Press, 2008).

Alloula, Malek, *The Colonial Harem* (Manchester University Press, 1986).

Amergboh, Joseph, *Rabah, conquérant des pays tchadiens* (Les Nouvelles Éditions Africaines, 1976).
Amselle, Jean-Loup, and Elikia M'Bokolo (eds), *Au Coeur de l'ethnie: Ethnies, tribalisme et Etat en Afrique* (La Découverte, 2005).
Anderson, Warwick, 'The Trespass Speaks: White Masculinity and Colonial Breakdown', *American Historical Review* 102:5 (1997), 1343–70.
——'Climates of Opinion: Acclimatization in Nineteenth-Century France and England', *Victorian Studies* 35:2 (Winter 1992), 135–57.
Andrew, Christopher M., and Sydney Kanya-Forstner, 'The French "Colonial Party": Its Composition, Aims and Influence, 1885–1914', *Historical Journal* 14:1 (Mar. 1971), 99–128.
Arendt, Hannah, *On Violence* (Harvest Books, 1970).
——*The Origins of Totalitarianism* (Harvest Books, 1950).
Arnold, David (ed.), *Warm Climates and the Emergence of Tropical Medicine* (Rodopi, 1996).
——*Colonizing the Body* (University of California Press, 1993).
——*Imperial Medicine and Indigenous Societies* (Manchester University Press, 1988).
Atkinson, William, 'Bound in "Blackwood's": The Imperialism of the "*Heart of Darkness*" in Its Immediate Context', *Twentieth Century Literature* 50:4 (Winter 2004), 368–93.
Audier, Serge, *Léon Bourgeois, fonder la solidarité* (Michalon, 2007).
Bach, André, *L'Armée de Dreyfus: Une histoire politique de l'armée française de Charles X à l'Affaire* (Tallandier, 2004).
Bacot, Jean-Pierre, *La Presse illustrée au XiXe siècle* (Presses Universitaires de Limoges, 2005).
Bado, Jean-Claude, *Médecine coloniale et grandes endémies en Afrique* (Karthala, 1996).
Baier, Stephen, *An Economic History of Central Niger* (Clarendon Press, 1980).
Bancel, Nicolas, Pascal Blanchard, and Françoise Vergès, *La République coloniale* (Pluriel, 2003).
Barker, Francis, Peter Hulme, and Margaret Ivasen (eds), *Cannibalism and the Colonial World* (Cambridge University Press, 1998).
Bass, Jeff D., 'An Efficient Humanitarianism: The British Slave Trade Debates, 1791–1792', *Quarterly Journal of Speech* 75:2 (1989), 152–65.
Bassett, Thomas J., and Philip W. Porter, 'Cartography and Empire Building in Nineteenth-Century West Africa', *Geographical Review* 84:3 (1994), 316–35.
——' "From the Best Authorities": The Mountains of Kong in the Cartography of West Africa', *Journal of African History* 32:3 (1991), 367–413.

Bba Koke, Ibrahim, and Elikia M'Bokolo, *Histoire générale de l'Afrique* (ABC, 1977).
Belknap, Michael, *The Vietnam War on Trial: The My Lai Massacre and the Court-Martial of Lieutenant Calley* (University Press of Kansas, 2002).
Bennoune, Mahfoud, *The Making of Contemporary Algeria, 1830–1987: Colonial Upheavals and Post Independence Development* (Cambridge University Press, 1988).
—— 'Origins of the Algerian Proletariat', MERIP Reports (1981).
Benoist, Joseph-Roger de, *Église et pouvoir colonial au Soudan français* (Karthala, 2000).
Bergmann, Gisèle, 'Quand la chair s'y met: approche phénomènologique de la rencontre entre civilisés et non-civilisés dans la littérature coloniale, 1870–1914', Doctoral thesis, University of Bayreuth, 2000.
Best, Geoffrey, *War and Law since 1945* (Oxford University Press, 1994).
Betts, Raymond, *Assimilation and Association in French Colonial Theory* (Columbia University Press, 1961).
Bhabha, Homi, 'Of Mimicry and Man', in Frederick Cooper and Ann Laura Stoler (eds), *Tensions of Empire, Colonial Cultures in a Bourgeois World* (University of California Press, 1997).
Biondi, Jean-Pierre, *Les Anticolonialistes (1881–1962)* (Robert Laffont, 1993).
Blanchard, Pascal, and Armelle Chatelier, *Images et colonies* (Syros, 1993).
Bloom, Peter J., *French Colonial Documentary, Mythologies of Humanitarianism* (Minnesota University Press, 2008).
Bonin, Hubert, Catherine Hodeir, and Jean-François Klein, *L'Esprit économique imperial (1830–1970)* (SFHOM, 2008).
Bouche, Denise, *Les Villages de liberté en Afrique Noire Française, 1887–1910* (Mouton, 1968).
Bourdelais, Patrice, and Didier Fassin (eds), *Les Constructions de l'Intolérable: Études d'anthropologie et d'histoire sur les frontières de l'espace moral* (La Découverte, 2005).
Bowlan, J., 'Polygamists Need Not Apply: Becoming a French Citizen in Colonial Algeria, 1918–1938', *Proceedings of the Annual Meeting of the Western Society for French History* 24 (1997), 110–19.
Brewin, Chris R., *Post-Traumatic Stress Disorder: Malady or Myth*? (Yale University Press, 2003).
Brown, Roger Glenn, *Fashoda Reconsidered: The Impact of Domestic Politics on French Policy in Africa, 1893–1898* (Johns Hopkins University Press, 1970).
Brownlie, Ian, *African Boundaries* (C. Hurst, 1979).
Brunnet, Von Klaus, *Nostalgie in der Geschichte des Medizin* (Tritsch, 1984).
Brunschwig, Henri, *Mythes et réalités de l'impérialisme francais, 1871–1914* (Armand Colin, 1960).

Brunschwig, Henri, *Noirs et Blancs dans l'Afrique Noire Française ou comment le colonisé devint colonisateur, 1870–1914* (Flammarion, 1974).
——*Brazza Explorateur* (Mouton, 1972).
——'Anglophobia and French African Policy', in P. Gifford and W. Roger Louis (eds), *France and Africa* (Yale University Press, 1971).
Bullard, Alice, *Exile to Paradise: Savagery and Civilisation in Paris and the South Pacific* (Stanford University Press, 2000).
Burns, Michael, *Rural Society and French Politics: Boulangism and the Dreyfus Affair 1886–1* (Princeton University Press, 1984).
Bynum, Bill, 'Nostalgia', *Lancet* 358:9299 (22 Dec. 2001), 2176.
Chafer, Tony, and Amanda Sackur (eds), *Promoting the Colonial Idea: Propaganda and Visions of Empire in France* (Palgrave, 2002).
Chalons, Serge, Christian Jean-Étienne, Suzy Landau and André Yébakima (eds.), *De l'esclavage aux réparations, comité devoir de mémoire* (Karthala, 2000).
Chauvaud, Frédéric, *Les Experts du crime: la médecine légale en France au xixe siècle* (Aubier, 2000).
Christelow, Allan, 'The Muslim Judge and Municipal Politics in Colonial Algeria and Senegal', *Comparative Studies in Society and History* 24:1 (Jan. 1982), 3–24.
Clancy-Smith, Julia, *Rebel and Saint: Muslim Notables, Populist Protest, Colonial Encounters* (University of California Press, 1994).
Clarence-Smith, William Gervase, *Islam and the Abolition of Slavery* (C. Hurst and Co., 2006).
Cohen, William B., *The French Encounter with Africans, White Responses to Blacks, 1530–1880* (Indiana University Press, 1980).
——*Rulers of Empire, the French Colonial Service in Africa* (Stanford, CA: Hoover Institution Press, 1971).
Cole, Joshua, *The Power of Large Numbers* (Cornell University Press, 2000).
Conklin, Alice L., 'Colonialism and Human Rights, a Contradiction in Terms? The Case of France and West Africa, 1895–1914', *American Historical Review* 103:2 (Apr. 1998), 419–42.
Conklin, Alice L., *A Mission to Civilize: The Republican Idea of Empire in France and West Africa, 1895–1930* (Stanford University Press, 1997).
Conte, Arthur, *Joffre* (Perrin, 1998).
Cooke, James Jerome, *New French Imperialism, 1880–1910: The Third Republic and Colonial Expansion* (David and Charles, 1973).
——'Anglo-French Diplomacy and the Contraband Arms Trade in Colonial Africa, 1894–1897', *African Studies Review* 17:1 (1974), 27–41.

Cooper, Frederick, 'Conflict and Connection: Rethinking Colonial African History', *American Historical Review* 99:5 (Dec. 1994), 1516–45.
Coquery-Vidrovitch, Catherine, *Brazza et la prise de possession du Congo* (Mouton, 1963).
—— 'Nationalité et citoyenneté en Afrique occidentale français: Originaires et citoyens dans le Sénégal colonial', *Journal of African History* 42:2 (2001), 285–305.
—— *L'Afrique et les Africains au XIXe Siecle* (Armand Colin, 1999).
Crocq, Louis, *Les Traumatismes psychiques de guerre* (Odile Jacob, 1999).
Crowder, Michael, *West Africa under Colonial Rule* (Hutchinson, 1968).
Crozier, Anna, 'Sensationalising Africa: British Medical Impressions of Sub-Saharan Africa, 1890–1939', *Journal of Imperial and Commonwealth History* 35:3 (2007), 393–415.
Cunningham, Andre, and Bridie Andrews (eds), *Western Medicine as Contested Knowledge* (Manchester University Press, 1997).
Curtin, Philip D., *Death by Migration: Europe's Encounter with the Tropical World in the Nineteenth Century* (Cambridge University Press, 1989).
Danziger, Raphael, *Abd Al-Qadir and the Algerian Resistance to the French* (New York: Holmes and Meier, 1977).
Daouda, Abdoul-Aziz Issa, *La Double tentation du roman nigérien* (L'Harmattan, 2006).
Darling, Elizabeth, ' "To Induce Humanitarian Sentiments in Prurient Londoners": The Propaganda Activity in London Voluntary Housing Associations in the Inter-war Period', *London Journal* 27:1 (2002), 42–62.
Daughton, J. P., *An Empire Divided: Religion, Republicanism and the Making of French Colonialism, 1880–1914* (Oxford University Press, 2006).
—— 'A Colonial Affair? Dreyfus and the French Empire', *Historical Reflections* 31:3 (2005), 469–83.
Davis, D. B., J. Ashworth, and T. L. Haskell, in the forum of the *American Historical Review* 92:4 (Oct. 1987), 813–28.
Deroo, Éric, and Antoine Champeaux, *La Force noire: Gloire et infortunes d'une légende coloniale* (Taillandier, 2006).
Digeon, Claude, *La Crise allemande de la pensée française* (Presses Universitaires de France, 1959).
Dirk Moses, A. (ed.), *Empire, Colony, Genocide: Conquest, Occupation and Subaltern Resistance in World History* (Berghahn Books, 2008).
Draper, G. I., 'Humanitarianism in the Modern Law of Armed Conflicts', *International Relations* 8:4 (1985), 380–96.
Drescher, Seymour, 'British Way, French Way: Opinion Building and Revolution in the Second French Slave Emancipation', *American Historical Review* 96:3 (June 1991), 709–34.

Ducoudray, Émile, and Ibrahima Baba Kaké, *El Hadj Umar, le prophète armé* (Les nouvelles éditions africaines, 1975).

Dulieu, Louis, *La Médecine à Montpellier*, Tom IV, vol 2 (Les Presses Universelles, 1990).

Dumoulin, Michel, *Léopold III de la Controverse à l'histoire* (Complexe, 2001).

Dunant, Henry, *La Charité sur les champs de bataille, suites du 'Souvenir de Solferino' et résultats de la Conférence internationale de Genève* (n.p., 1864).

Dunbar, Roberta Ann, 'Slavery and the Evolution of Nineteenth Century Damagaran', in Suzanne Miers and Igor Kopytoff (eds), *Slavery in Africa* (University of Wisconsin Press, 1977), 155–78.

Dunwoodie, Peter, *Writing French Algeria* (Oxford: Clarendon Press, 1998).

Echenberg, Myron J., 'Late Nineteenth-Century Military Technology in Upper Volta', *Journal of African History* 12:2 (1971), 241–54.

——*Colonial Conscripts: The Tirailleurs Sénégalais in French West Africa, 1857–1960* (Heinemann, 1991).

——'Jihad and State-Building in Late Nineteenth Century Upper Volta: The Rise and Fall of the Marka State of Al- Kari of Boussé', *Canadian Journal of African Studies/Revue Canadienne des Études Africaines* 3:3 (1969), 531–61.

Eiselein, Gregory, *Literature and Humanitarian Reform in the Civil War Era* (Indiana University Press, 1996).

Ellis, Stephen, 'The Political Elite of Imerina and the Revolt of the Menalamba. The Creation of a Colonial Myth in Madagascar, 1895–1898', *Journal of African History* 21 (1980), 219–34.

Ellis, Jack D., *The Physician-Legislators of France* (Cambridge University Press, 1990).

Fassin, Didier, and Richard Rechtman, *L'Empire du traumatisme, enquète sur la condition de victime* (Flammarion, 2007).

Ferro, Marc (ed.), *Le Livre noir du colonialisme: XVIe-XXIe siècle: de l'extermination à la repentance* (Robert Laffont, 2003).

Fiering, Norman, 'Irresistible Compassion: An Aspect of Eighteenth Century Sympathy and Humanitarianism', *Journal of the History of Ideas* 37:2 (1976), 195–218; 339–61.

Fogarty, Richard, and Michael Osborne, 'Constructions and Functions of Race in French Military Medicine, 1830–1920', in Sue Peabody and Tyler Stovall (eds), *The Color of Liberty, Histories of Race in France* (Duke University Press, 2003), 206–36.

Forth, Chistopher E., and Bertrand Taithe, *French Masculinities* (Palgrave, 2007).

—— '*La Civilisation* and its Discontents: Modernity, Manhood and the Body in the Early Third Republic', in C. Forth and B. Taithe (eds), *French Masculinities* (Palgrave, 2007).
—— and Ana Carden-Coyne, *Cultures of the Abdomen* (Palgrave, 2005).
Foucault, Michel, *Moi, Pierre Rivière* (Folio, 1994).
—— *Discipline and Punish* (Allan Lane, 1977).
Frémeaux, Jacques, 'L'Armée coloniale et la république (1830–1962)', in Olivier Forcade, Éric Duhamel, and Philippe Vial (eds), *Militaires en République, 1870–1962, les officiers, le pouvoir et la vie publique en France* (Publications de la Sorbonne, 1999).
Fuglestad, Finn, *A History of Niger, 1850–1960* (Cambridge University Press, 1983).
Gann, L. H., and Peter Duigan, *The Rules of German Africa, 1884–1914* (Stanford University Press, 1977).
Garb, Tamar, *Figures of Modernity: Figure and Flesh in Fin-de-siècle France* (Thames and Hudson, 1998).
Gentil, Pierre, *La Conquête du Tchad (1894–1916)*, 2 vols (SHAT, 1971).
Gerard, Alain, 'Action Humanitaire et Pouvoir Politique: l'Engagement des médecins Lillois au XiXe siècle', *Revue du Nord* 332 (1999), 817–36.
Girardet, Raoul, *L'Idée coloniale en France de 1871 à 1962* (La Table Ronde, 1972).
Grant, Kevin, *A Civilised Savagery: Britain and the New Slaveries in Africa, 1884–1926* (Routledge, 2005).
Grévoz, Daniel, *Les Méharistes français à la conquête du Sahara* (L'Harmattan, 1994).
Guillem, Pierre, *L'expansion, 1881–1898* (Imprimerie Nationale, 1985).
Hale, Dana S., *Races on Display, French Representations of Colonized Peoples, 1886–1940* (Indiana University Press, 2008).
Hale, Thomas A., *Scribe, Griot and Novelist: Narrative Interpreters of the Songhay Empire* (University of Florida Press, 1990).
Handane, Halima, and Isabelle Colin, *Sarranouia, La reine magicienne du Niger* (Cavis Eden, 2004).
Harding, James, *The Astonishing Adventure of General Boulanger* (W. H. Allen, 1971).
Harris, Ruth, *Murders and Madness: Medicine, Law and Society in the Fin-de-Siècle* (Clarendon Press, 1989).
Haskell, T. L., 'Capitalism and the Origins of the Humanitarian Sensibility', Parts 1 and Part 2, *American Historical Review* 90 (April 1985), 339–61; (June 1985), 547–66.
Hause, Steven C., *Hubertine Auclert: The French Suffragette* (Yale University Press, 1987).

Hawkins, Hunt, 'Conrad's Critique of Imperialism in *Heart of Darkness*', *PMLA* 94:2 (Mar. 1979), 286–99.

Herbert, Claudia, and Ann Wetmore, *Overcoming Traumatic Stress* (Robinson, 1999).

Hersh, Seymour, *My Lai: A Report on the Massacre and its Aftermath* (Random House, 1970).

Hijswijt-Hofstra, Marijke, and Roy Porter (eds), *Cultures of Neurasthenia from Beard to the First World War* (Rodopi, 2001).

Hochschild, Adam, *King Leopold's Ghosts*, 2nd edn (Pan Books, [1998], 2007).

Hogendorn, Jan, and Marion Johnson, *The Shell Money of the Slave Trade* (Cambridge University Press, 1986).

Howard, Michael (ed.), *Restraints on War: Studies in the Limitation of Armed Conflict* (Oxford University Press, 1979).

Hubbell, Andrew, 'A View of the Slave Trade from the Margin: Souroudougou in the Late Nineteenth-Century Slave Trade of the Niger Bend', *Journal of African History* 42:1 (2001), 25–47.

Hutchinson, John F., *Champions of Charity* (Westview Press, 1996).

Idowu, H. O., 'The Establishment of Elective Institutions in Senegal, 1869–1880', *Journal of African History* 9:2 (1968), 261–77.

Ignatieff, Michael, *A Just Measure of Pain* (Columbia University Press, 1980).

International Committee of the Red Cross and Henry Dunant Institute, *Bibliography of International Humanitarian Law, Applicable in Armed Conflict* (Geneva, 1980).

Irvine, William D., *The Boulanger Affair Reconsidered* (Oxford University Press, 1989).

Isaacman, Allen, and Richard Roberts (eds), *Cotton, Colonialism and Social History in Sub-Saharan Africa* (Heinemann; James Currey, 1995).

Johnson, H. A. S., *The Fulani Empire of Sokoto* (Oxford University Press, 1967).

Johnson, Marion, 'The Cowrie Currencies of West Africa', Part II, *African History* 1:12 (1970), 331–53.

Julien, Charles André, *Histoire de l'Algérie Contemporaine*, vol i (Presses Universitaires de France, 1986).

Kambou-Ferrand, Jeanne, *Peuples Voltaïques et conquête coloniale, 1885–1914* (L'Harmattan, 1993).

Kelman, Herbert C., and Lee Hamilton, *Cultures of Obedience: Towards a Social Psychology of Authority and Responsibility* (Yale University Press, 1989).

Kendrick, Oliver, 'Atrocity, Authenticity and American Exceptionalism: (Ir)rationalizing the Massacre of My Lai', *Journal of American History* 37:2 (2003), 247–68.

—— *The My Lai Massacre in American History and Memory* (Manchester University Press, 2005).

Kiernan, Ben, *Blood and Soil: A World History of Genocide and Extermination from Sparta to Darfur* (Yale University Press, 2007).

Kimba, Idrissa, *Guerres et Sociétés les populations du 'Niger Occidental' au XIXe siècle et leurs réactions face à la colonisation* (Niamey: Études Nigériennes, 1981).

Kuntiz, S. J., *Disease and Social Diversity: The European Impact on the Health of Non-Europeans* (Cambridge University Press, 1994).

Laqueur, Thomas, 'Bodies, Details and the Humanitarian Narrative', in Lynn Hunt (ed.), *The New Cultural History* (University Press of California, 1989), 176–204.

Larkin, Warren, and Anthony P. Morrison (eds), *Trauma and Psychosis: New Directions for Theory and Therapy* (Routledge, 2006).

Laumann, Denis, 'A Historiography of German Togoland, or the Rise and Fall of a "Model Colony"', *History in Africa* 30 (2003), 195–211.

Lazrey, Maurice, *The Emergence of Class in Algeria: A Study of Colonialism and Social Political Change* (Westview Special Studies, 1976).

Lehning, James R., *To Be a Citizen: The Political Culture of the Early French Third Republic* (Cornell University Press, 2001).

Lindqvist, Sven, *Exterminate all the Brutes* (Granta, 1992).

Lings, Martin, *A Sufi Saint of the Twentieth Century: Shwikh Ahmad Al'Alawî* (Cambridge University Press, 1993).

Livingstone, David N., 'Tropical Climate and Moral Hygiene: The Anatomy of a Victorian Debate', *British Journal for the History of Science* 32:1 (1999), 93–110.

Lorofi, Albert, *La Vie quotidienne des officiers de l'Infanterie de Marine pendant la conquête de la colonie du Soudan Français* (L'Harmattan, 2008).

Lund, Christian, 'Precarious Democractization and Local Dynamics in Niger: Micro-politics in Zinder', *Development and Change* 32 (2001), 845–69.

Lundy, Jean-Marie, 'Mémoire de criminologie appliqué à l'expertise médicale, Le traitement pénal dans l'armée Française sous la troisième république', Université René Descartes, Droit Médical, 1987.

Lunn, Joe, '"Les Races guerrières": Racial Preconceptions in the French Military about West African Soldiers during the First World War', *Journal of Contemporary History* 34:4 (1999), 517–36.

Lyons, Maryinez, *The Colonial Disease: A History of Sleeping Sickness in Northern Zaire, 1900–1940* (Cambridge University Press, 1992).
McClintock, Anne, *Imperial Leather, Race Gender and Sexuality in the Colonial Context* (Routledge, 1995).
McFarland, Daniel Miles, *Historical Dictionary of Upper Volta (Haute Volta)* (Scarecrow Press, 1978).
Mackenzie, John M., *Propaganda and Empire* (Manchester University Press, 1986).
Mackenzie, Kenneth, 'Some British Reactions to German Colonial Methods, 1885–1907', *Historical Journal* 17:1 (1974), 165–75.
Madiega, Yenouyaba Georges, and Oumarou Naro (eds), *Burkina Faso, cent ans d'histoire, 1895–1995* (Kathala, 2003).
Maestri, Robert, *Commandant Lamy, un officier francais aux colonies* (Maisonneuve et Larose, 2000).
Mamani, A., *Sarranouia, le drame de la reine magicienne* (L'Harmattan, 1980).
Mangin, L. E., *Le Général Mangin* (Lanore, 1986).
Mann, Gregory, *Native Sons: West African Veterans and France in the Twentieth Century* (Duke University Press, 2006).
Mark, Peter, 'The Future of African Art in Parisian Public Museums', *African Arts* 33:3 (Autumn 2000), 1–93.
Masquelier, Adeline, 'Road Mythographies: Space, Mobility and the Historical Imagination in Postcolonial Niger', *American Ethnologist* 29:4 (2002), 829–56.
Massa, Gabriel, and Yves Madiéga (eds), *La Haute Volta coloniale* (Karthala, 1995).
Mathieu, Muriel, *La Mission Afrique Centrale* (L'Harmattan, 1995).
M'Bokolo, Elikia, *Resistances et Messianismes, histoire générale de l'Afrique* (Agence de Coopération, 1990).
Meurant, Jacques, 'Inter Arma Caritas: Evolution and Nature of International Humanitarian Law', *Journal of Peace Research* 24:3 (1987), 237–49.
Micale, Mark, *Approaching Hysteria, Disease and its Interpretation* (Princeton University Press, 1995).
—— (ed.), *Traumatic Past* (Cambridge University Press, 2001).
Michel, Marc, *La Mission Marchand, 1895–1899* (Mouton, 1972).
—— *Gallieni* (Fayard, 1989).
Migozzi, Jacques, and Philippe Le Guern (eds), *Production(s) du Populaire* (Presses Universitaires de Limoges, 2004).
Morton, Patricia A., *Colonial Modernities: Architecture and Representation at the 1931 Colonial Exposition, Paris* (MIT University Press, 2000).
—— 'National and Colonial: The Musée des Colonies at the Colonial Exposition, Paris, 1931', *Art Bulletin* 80 (1998), 357–77.

Mouralis, Bernard, and Anne Piriou (dir.) with the collaboration of Romuald Fonkoua, 'Robert Delavignette, savant et politique (1897–1976)' (Karthala, 2003).

Narducci, Henry Mark, 'The French Officer Corps and the Social Role of the Army, 1890–1908', Wayne State University, 1981.

Nourrisson, Didier, *Le Buveur du XIXe siècle* (Albin Michel, 1990).

Nye, Robert, *Crime, Madness and Politics in Modern France: The Medical Concept of National Decline* (Princeton University Press, 1984).

—— *The Origins of Crowd Psychology: Gustave Le Bon and the Crisis of Mass Democracy* (Sage Publications, 1975).

Osborne, Emily Lynn, 'Circle of Iron: African Colonial Employees and the Interpretation of Colonial Rule in French West Africa', *Journal of African History* 44 (2003), 29–50.

O'Sullivan, Lisa, 'Dying for Home', Doctoral Dissertation, University of London, 2006.

Painter, Thomas M., 'From Warriors to Migrants: Critical Perspectives on Early Migrations among the Zarma of Niger', *Africa: Journal of the International African Institute* 58:1 (1988), 87–100.

Patton, Adell, *Physicians, Colonial Racism and Diaspora in West Africa* (University Press of Florida, 1996).

Paulson, Ronald, *Sin and Evil: Moral Values in Literature* (Yale University Press, 2007).

Pedersen, Susan, 'National Bodies, Unspeakable Acts: The Sexual Politics of Colonial Policy-Making', *Journal of Modern History* 63:4 (Dec., 1991), 647–80.

Perkins, Kenneth J., *Qaids, Captains and Colons: French Military Administration in the Colonial Maghrib, 1844–1934* (New York: Africana Publishing Co., 1981).

Persell, Michael, *The French Colonial Lobby (1885–1938)* (Stanford University Press, 1983).

Person, Yves, *Samori: la renaissance de l'empire Mandingue* (ABC, 1976).

Phillips, Anne, *The Enigma of Colonialism: British Policy in West Africa* (James Currey; Indiana University Press, 1989).

Pick, Daniel, *War Machine: The Rationalisation of Slaughter in the Modern Age* (Yale University Press, 1996).

Pictet, Jean, *Development and Principles of International Humanitarian Law* (Henry Dunant Institute, 1985).

Porter, Andrew, 'Roger Casement and the International Humanitarian Movement', *Journal of Imperial amd Commonwealth History* 29:2 (2001), 59–74.

Porter, Roy (ed.), *Rewriting the Self* (Routledge, 1997).

Power, Thomas Francis, *Jules Ferry and the Renaissance of French Imperialism* (Octagon Books, 1944).

Prestwich, Patricia E., *Drink and the Politics of Social Reform: Antialcoholism in France since 1870*, (Society for the Promotion of Science and Scholarship, 1988).

Prochaska, David, *Making Algeria French: Colonialism in Bône, 1870–1920* (Cambridge University Press, 1990).

Raskin, Jonah, '*Heart of Darkness*: The Manuscript Revisions', *Review of English Studies* NS, 18:69 (Feb. 1967), 30–9.

Renault, François, and Serge Daget, *Les Traites négrières en Afrique* (Karthala, 1985).

—— *Tippo-Tip: un potentat arabe en Afrique centrale* (L'Harmattan, 1987).

—— *Libérations d'esclaves et nouvelles servitudes* (Nouvelles éditions africaines, 1976).

Rivet, Daniel, 'Le Fait colonial et nous. Histoire d'un éloignement', *Vingtième Siècle. Revue d'histoire* 33 (Jan.–Mar. 1992), 127–38.

Roberts, Richard, and Martin Klein, 'The Bambare Slave Exodus of 1905 and the Decline of Slavery in the Western Soudan', *Journal of African History* 21 (1980), 375–94.

—— *Warriors, Merchants and Slaves: The State and the Economy in the Middle Niger Valley, 1700–1914* (Stanford University Press, 1987).

Robinson, David, *The Holy War of Umar Tal* (Oxford University Press, 1985).

Rosen, George, 'Nostalgia a forgotten psychological disorder', *Clio Medica* 10 (1975), 29–52.

Roth, Michael S., 'Dying of the Past: Medical Studies of Nostalgia in Nineteenth Century France', *History and Memory* 3 (1991), 5–29.

Rouch, Jean, *La Religion et la magie Songhay* (Anthropologie Sociale, Université de Bruxelles, 1989).

—— *Les Hommes et les dieux du fleuve, essai ethnographique sur les populations songhay du moyen Niger, 1941–1983* (Artcom, 1997).

Roynette, Odylle, *Bon pour le service: l'expérience de la caserne en France á la fin du XiXe siècle* (Belin, 2000).

Salo, Samuel, 'Le Moog-Naaba Wogbo de Ouagadougou (1850–1904)', in Madiega, Yenouyaba Georges, and Oumarou Naro (eds), *Burkina Faso, cent ans d'histoire, 1895–1995* (Kathala, 2003), 631–57.

Sardan, Jean-Pierre Olivier de, *Concepts et conceptions Songhay-Zarma* (Nubia, 1982).

—— *Les Sociétés Songhay-Zarma (Niger-Mali): Chefs, guerriers, esclaves, paysans* (Khartala, 1984).

Şaul, Mahir, and Patrick Royer, *West African Challenge to Empire: Culture and History in the Volta-Bani Anticolonial War* (Ohio University Press, 2001).

Şaul, Mahir, and Patrick Royer, 'Money in Colonial Transition: Cowries and Francs in West Africa', *American Ethnologist* 106 (2004), 71–84.

Sernam, William, *Les officiers français dans la nation, 1848–1914* (Aubier, 1982).

Shapiro, Ann-Louise, *Breaking the Codes: Female Criminality in Fin-de-siècle Paris* (Palo Alto, CA: Stanford University Press, 1996).

Sheriff, Abdul, *Slaves, Spices and Ivory in Zanzibar* (James Currey, 1987).

Sibeud, Emmanuelle, *Une Science impériale pour l'Afrique? La construction des savoirs africanistes en France, 1878–1930* (EHESS, 2002).

Simoen, Jean-Claude, *Les fils de rois: le crépuscule sanglant de l'aventure africaine* (Lattès, 1996).

Slavin, David, *Colonial Cinema and Imperial France* (Johns Hopkins University Press, 2001).

Spiers, Edward M., *The Victorian Soldier in Africa* (Manchester University Press, 2004), 159–79.

Spurr, David, *The Rhetoric of Empire: Colonial Discourse in Journalism* (Duke University Press, 1993).

Stoler, Ann Laura, *Carnal Knowledge and Imperial Power* (University of California Press, 2002).

Stoller, Paul, *Embodying Colonial Memories: Spirit Possession, Power and the Hauka in West Africa* (Routledge, 1995).

Taithe, Bertrand, *Citizenships and Wars* (Routledge, 2001).

—— *Defeated Flesh* (Manchester University Press, 1999).

Tessier, Arnaud, *Lyautey, le ciel et les sables sont grands* (Perrin, 2006).

Thomas, Édith, *Rossel 1844–1871* (Gallimard, 1967).

Thompson, J. Malcolm, 'Colonial Policy and the Family Life of Black Troops in French West Africa, 1817–1904', *International Journal of African Historical Studies* 23:3 (1990), 423–53.

Tidjani Alou, Antoinette, 'Sarraounia et ses intertextes: Identité, intertextualité et émergence littéraire', *Sudlang* 5 (2005), 44–70.

Tilley, Helen, and Robert J. Gordon, *Ordering Africa, Anthropology, European Imperialism and the Politics of Knowledge* (Manchester University Press, 2007).

Tombs, Robert, *The War against Paris* (Cambridge University Press, 1981).

—— *The Commune of Paris* (Longman, 1999).

Triaud, Jean-Louis, *Tchad 1900–1902, une guerre franco-lybienne oubliée?* (L'Harmattan, 1988).

Tshitongu Kongolo, Antoine, 'L'étonnante aventure de Blackland', in Jules Verne, *L'étonnante Aventure de la Mission Barsac*, 2 vols (L'Harmattan, [1913] 2005).

Turin, Yvonne, *Affrontements culturels dans l'Algérie coloniale, écoles, médecine, religion, 1830–1880* (François Maspéro, 1971).

Tymowski, Michal, *L'Armée et la formation des états en Afrique occidentale au XIXe siècle – essai de comparaison, l'état de Samori et le Kenedougou* (Warsaw: Wydawnicta Uniwersytetu Warszawkiego, 1987).

—— 'Les Esclaves du commandant Quiquandon', *Cahiers d'Études Africaines* 158 (2000), 351–62.

Venier, Pascal, *Lyautey avant Lyautey* (L'Harmattan, 2000).

Warshaw, Dan, *Paul Leroy-Beaulieu and Established Liberalism in France* (North Illinois University Press, 1991).

Webster, Paul, *Fachoda: la bataille pour le Nil* (Edition du Felin, 2001).

Werner, Wolfgang, '"Playing Soldiers": The Truppenspieler Movement among the Herero of Namibia, 1915 to ca. 1945', *Journal of Southern African Studies* 16:3 (Sept. 1990), 476–502.

White, Owen, *Children of the French Empire: Miscegenation and Colonial Society in French West Africa, 1895–1960* (Oxford University Press, 1999).

Wolf, Eric R., *Peasant Wars of the Twentieth Century* (Faber and Faber, 1973).

Yee, Jennifer, 'Malaria and the Femme Fatale: Sex and Death in French Colonial Africa', *Literature and Medicine* 21:1 (2002), 201–15.

Young, A., *The Harmony of Illusion: Inventing PTSD* (Princeton University Press, 1995).

Zarabell, John H., 'Framing French Algeria: Colonialism, Travel and the Representation of Landscape', Ph.D., University of California, 2000.

Zehfuss, Nicole M., 'From Stereotype to Individual: World War I Experience with Tirailleurs Sénégalais', *French Colonial History* 6 (2005), 137–58.

INDEX